Crop Circles

Signs of Contact

by Colin Andrews
with Stephen Spignesi

New Page Books
A Division of The Career Press, Inc.
Franklin Lakes, N.J.

CROP CIRCLES
EDITED AND TYPESET BY JOHN J. O'SULLIVAN
COVER DESIGN BY LU ROSSMAN/DIGI DOG DESIGN
PRINTED IN THE U.S.A. BY BOOK-MART PRESS

The article published in Chapter 12, "The Diatonic Ratios in Crop Circles," is ©1996 Gerald Hawkins, which is used with permission.

To order this title, please call toll-free 1-800-CAREER-1 (NJ and Canada: 201-848-0310) to order using VISA or MasterCard, or for further information on books from Career Press.

The Career Press, Inc., 3 Tice Road, PO Box 687,
Franklin Lakes, NJ 07417
www.careerpress.com
www.newpagebooks.com

Library of Congress Cataloging-in-Publication Data

Andrews, Colin.
    Crop circles : signs of contact / by Colin Andrews with Stephen J. Spignesi.
        p. cm.
    Includes index.
    ISBN 1-56414-674-X
        1. Crop circles—Miscellanea. 2. Curiosities and wonders—Miscellanea.
3. Science—Miscellanea. I. Spignesi, Stephen J. II. Title.

AG243.A54 2003
001.94—dc21
                                        2002045245

*To **Synthia**, my wife,*
who has been a tremendous pillar of support,
and a friend I love and respect so much.

—COLIN ANDREWS

*To my brother, **David Spignesi,***
a stalwart paladin of self-awareness and self-improvement.

—STEPHEN SPIGNESI

Acknowledgments

Colin Andrews

In the past 20 years, many people have contributed to my research in various important ways, and I thank them all from the bottom of my heart. To name but a few:

Gordon and Elsie Andrews (Mom and Dad), David Andrews, Peter and Jean Andrews, Helen and Hayley Andrews, the late Richard Andrews, Mary and Jean Noel Aubrun, John Barrell, Mandy and Peter Butcher, Terry Butcher, Ian Chistopher, Iris Demauro, Pat Delgado, David Duhig, Marie Galbraith, Yeva Gladwin, Dave Haith, Gerald Hawkins, Simeon Hein, Victoria Jack, Pam Jones, the late Count Carli Kanitz, Countess Irene Kanitz, Shelly Keel, Toby King, Franz and Mona Lutz, Chris McMillan, Sue Paruch, Reg Presley, Suzie Ramsby, Quinn Ramsby, Laurence Rockefeller, Jane Ross, Ron Russell, Valerie and Evan Scurlock, Freddy Silva, Peter Sorensen, Steve Spignesi, Busty Taylor, Ruben Uriarte, Valenya, Chuck Walker, John White, Matthew Williams, and the tolerant farmers.

Stephen Spignesi

As usual, I received more help and support with this book than I could have ever hoped or prayed for. The gratitude I feel for all of my caring angels knows no bounds.

Pam Spignesi, Lee Mandato, Dolores Fantarella, John White, Barbara White, Colin Andrews, Synthia Andrews, Jim Cole, Bill Savo, Gayze DiRienzo, Mike Lewis, Ron Fry, Stacey Farkas, John J. O'Sullivan, Anne Brooks, Georgio Simeon, Production Transcripts Inc., Mick Garris, Jay Holben, Steve and Marge Rapuano, Busty Taylor, Laura Lattrell, Carter Spignesi, Kim McDonald, Paul Vigay, Lucy Pringle, William Gazecki, Kevin Quigley, Publishers Marketplace, Stan Wiater, Jodi Branson, Dr. Michael Luchini, the University of New Haven, Dean James Gustav Speth and the Yale University School of Forestry and the Environment, Utrecht Inc., Manischewitz and Streit Matzos.

*The nature of God is a circle
of which the centre is everywhere
and the circumference is nowhere.*

—Empedocles, c. 500 B.C.

Contents

Appendices

Introduction

The Telling
by Stephen Spignesi

Credible people telling of incredible things.

This is the center, the goal, even the "mission statement" of this book. And Colin Andrews is in a unique place as the premier authority on the crop circle phenomenon.

When one reads Colin's findings, it is self-evident that he is such an expert. But this is not all: He is also an intelligent, kind, spiritual gentleman with whom it has been a pleasure to work. Sometimes, a book can act as a catalyst for change. I think Colin would agree with me that if *Crop Circles: Signs of Contact* inspires even one reader to be more environmentally conscious, then we will have done our job. There is probably no greater mission for us all.

It has been an honor to work with Colin Andrews on this book, this "report to the world" that has been two decades in the making. Crop circles have meaning, and that, in as succinct a way as this sometimes prolix writer can state, is the essence of this book's mission statement.

There are real crop formations all over the world, and science does not know how or why they are formed. There is hard sci-entific evidence that some circles are un-deniably *not* manmade. Changes in the plants that cannot be duplicated in hoaxed circles; odd sounds that have been re-corded in authentic crop circles; and, per-haps most astounding, the sudden appearance of enormous formations in mere minutes—creations that would take many men many hours to produce appear in minutes. Skeptics have their work cut out for them—I ask them to read the chap-ter in this book about the 900-foot Julia Set near Stonehenge that appeared in a span of 45 minutes before leaping to manmade conclusions.

This book is Colin Andrews's story, and I am grateful to have been sitting around the particular campfire where and when he decided to tell it.

My Circle

There are several stories in this book of people who have "requested" a crop for-mation, and one has subsequently appeared for them.

The words "wished for," "prayed for," and "asked for" are used to describe these petitions to the "circlemakers."

In early November 2002, I, too, joined the ranks of those who have had such an experience and, at Colin's request, I relate the story here.

During the weekend of November 2, 2002, I tried a crop circle experiment. I had been working closely for weeks with Colin Andrews on this book, and he had told me many intriguing stories about crop circle manifestations appearing "upon request." I decided to give it a try.

Outside my office window is the "backyard" of our condominium development. It is all pristine green grass and, during that autumn weekend, I asked for a pattern to appear in the grass, but I also requested that it be in a precise spot: the spot where my eye fell when I turn my head to the right and look out my window.

A few days went by, but I saw nothing in the grass. I began to wonder if I had not worded my request properly, or if I was simply not attuned to the circlemakers in the manner in which the others whose wish had been granted had been.

But then, on Wednesday morning, November 6, 2002, I saw something. Tuesday had been a stormy day in Connecticut, with a great deal of rain and wind. On Wednesday morning, I looked out my window, and there I saw a design in the grass—and it was in the exact spot where I had asked that it appear. I saw a perfect circle of grass in the middle, surrounded by a wide ring of soil, with a spur of soil extending out of the northwest corner of the circle. I grabbed my copy of the Andrews Catalogue and began flipping through the pages, quickly stopping on page five. There it was: T107. The exact grass design, turned clockwise, and with two small satellites that I did not see in my grass.

The grass was pressed down from the rain and wind, creating a perfect T107. I estimated it as approximately 3 to 4 feet long, and 2 to 3 feet wide. I later realized that not only was this pattern one of the recorded designs, it was also very similar to an ice circle that had appeared in Churchill, Maryland, in February 2001—and which I had been writing about around the time I made my request.

I did not take a picture of the design, and the following morning, it was gone. The grass dried in the sun and wind and filled back in, and the soil ring was covered. I could still glimpse a shadow of the center grass circle, but overall, it was now nothing but a normal expanse of suburban grass.

I know what I saw, and I know that the design was most assuredly *not* there when I initially requested it.

What has this experience taught me?

It has confirmed for me that Colin Andrews is truly on to something with his belief that human thought plays a role in the crop circle phenomenon. What I found most intriguing about this experience is that the design appeared in the only possible way I would be able to see it: by flattening ordinary backyard grass. Grass is not a cereal crop, and yet nature spoke up (stepped in?) with her rain and wind, and then there was a perfect circle of grass surrounded by a ring.

In the introduction to my book *The Weird 100*, I wrote that I remain open to all the wonders of reality, consciousness, and the unknown because I do not believe that I know everything. I experienced a UFO sighting one time in my life. And now I have experienced a crop circle.

There are wonders to be discovered. They may make themselves known to us in the sky, or in the fields, and I truly believe that the 90 percent of our brains that we do *not* currently use must have been given to us for a reason. Perhaps it is what we will use to understand all that we do not now know.

—SJS
December 30, 2002

Introduction

My Mission Statement

by Colin Andrews

With *Crop Circles: Signs of Contact*, I hope to inform the general public about the crop circle phenomenon in an accurate and truthful fashion.

I also hope to remove the "weird" stigma attached to crop circles.

We have deliberately tried to write a book for the mainstream reader, the world citizen who knows about crop circles, may have seen the movie *Signs*, is curious about what is actually going on, but is not interested in complicated discourses on plant biology, mythology, mathematical theory, or paleoclimatology.

People do want to know what is going on in their world, on their planet, and are interested in what the crop circle enigma means for their future. People know the earth's environment is in trouble. Parents today know that their grandchildren, and possibly even their children, may enter adulthood worrying about water shortages and breathing problems caused by pollution. Our problems are not of the future; they are here now. It is our belief that crop manifestations may somehow be tied into this.

I have researched this mystery longer than anyone else, and in this book, I share my data, views, and findings with my readers. I also hope to stimulate discussion, and foster an atmosphere of open-minded inquiry and curiosity.

The publication of this book is my opportunity to communicate to my readers the importance of the crop circle phenomenon, and to provide the evidence of its significance in an open and honest forum.

About the Photo on the Cover

Mystery creates wonder and wonder is the basis of man's desire to understand.

—Astronaut Neil Armstrong

The photo on the cover of this book—a proven authentic crop formation—represents our Solar System, minus the planet Earth, as it will be aligned on September 1, 2033, and on May 6, 2101.

The design depicts the Sun, the planet Mercury, the planet Venus, Earth's orbit minus the Earth, the planet Mars, Jupiter's orbit without Jupiter used as the outer ring of the solar system element of the formation, an expanse of empty space, and then an asteroid belt.

This crop formation was discovered on the morning of June 22, 1995, by a farmer on his land at Longwood Warren, near Winchester, Hampshire, England.

It was determined to be a "genuine" formation (that is, not manmade) by the renowned biophysicist William Levengood, who found distinct and measurable cellular changes in plants taken from the formation.

Other evidence pointing to its authenticity included no damage to the plants or soil compression; no tracks to vital construction points; and *very* complex braiding of plants in the outer ring where numerous circles were positioned, and which was determined to be extremely difficult, if not impossible for humans to achieve *without leaving evidence of their presence.*

Also, two eminent scientists, Gerald Hawkins and Robert Hadley, both confirmed that the scaling and placement of the "planets" within the crop formation were extraordinarily accurate and that it was a very precise replica of our solar system.

Also, I personally had extensive discussions with members of the only organized group of counterfeit circlemakers working at that time (to my knowledge) and none of them claimed responsibility for the formation, nor knowledge of who else could have made it.

Frozen in time is our solar system, with the Earth missing from its orbit.

This formation has a history, and a profound meaning.

The first thing this crop pattern does is call attention to Earth's empty orbit. When we also consider that this celestial configuration is what the solar system will look like in approximately 30 years, and again in 100 years, the question arises: Are we being sent a message? Is the universe telling us of our possible fate? Are we being warned that if we continue on the reckless, damaging path we are on, then the future of mankind is at risk?

When Marcus Thompson, the writer and director of the crop circle–themed movie *A Place to Stay*, came to me to discuss his project, I suggested that he should include this solar system design in the film. I felt that the formation, and its possible message was important enough to replicate precisely, and include within the storyline of the movie. Marcus was including a powerful environmental message in the film, and I felt that this design would contribute to his mission. He agreed, and I supplied aerial photographs (including the one on the cover of this book) to his production team to assist them in their construction work. I asked Matthew Williams and his team to create the solar system formation in the fields.

The formation was ultimately made (and is seen in the movie), and all agreed that it was a very close duplicate of the original. But that's where the similarities ended. The created formation had extreme plant damage, widespread soil compression, major errors in the geometry of the design, and it took so long to make that many of the public were able to see the half-finished pattern in broad daylight. Even though we provided the measurements, ratios, and scaling data to the construction team, they were still unable to complete it in one night and, when it was finished, it was so obviously manmade, that it reminded us even more so of the truly amazing nature of the spontaneous, authentic formation.

All our research convinced us that the original formation was authentic. Its possible message struck a chord with all of us, and thus, my recommendation that it appear in the movie, and my decision to highlight it on the cover of *Crop Circles: Signs of Contact*.

The Madison Square Garden Speech

Scattered throughout the book are a handful of excerpts—greatly abridged and heavily edited for clarity and space—from a two-hour speech I gave at Madison Square Garden in the fall of 1996. Some of the subjects discussed in this speech are covered in greater depth elsewhere in this book. Please look to the Contents or the Index for further information on any of the topics in this speech about which you would like to know more. The complete speech I gave is available on videotape, and includes the slides and graphics I showed at the presentation.

Introduction

My Friend Colin
by Reg Presley

Reg Presley is the lead singer and songwriter for the legendary band The Troggs. He sang the song "Wild Thing," and wrote the classic "Love Is All Around" and countless others, and his first book, *Wild Things They Don't Tell Us*, was recently published. Reg and I were neighbors in England for many years and I count him as one of my cherished friends. I am grateful and honored that he agreed to write something for this book.

•••

After 12 years investigating crop formations, it seems to me that we still have a long way to go before we can truly button down the answer to the question: Who are the circle makers?

If we put aside manmade formations for the moment, and concentrate on what some investigators claim are the real phenomenon, there are still too many theories one can choose from, and each, in their own way, is believable. It really does depend on your own point of view and how your understanding sits with what you have experienced along the way.

Too many profess to know the answer, and if their view is challenged, then they will usually throw a fit and ostracize anyone who doesn't quite see it their way. That, I'm sure, is not the way to the truth.

I see my friend Colin as a mentor to all would-be-followers of this circle mystery. He has thrown his life into it, trying to get at the truth. Although others have come and gone in a flurry of publicity, he has stuck it out, determined to get to the end of what has become a very long road. I take my hat off to him for his perseverance.

At this point in time, I have an overwhelming feeling that a higher intelligence is not only helping mankind, but is trying to save us from ourselves.

Perhaps it is Mother Earth herself? Or our new neighbors that as yet we haven't met?

We may see the outcome; we may not.

Whatever or whomever that higher intelligence ultimately belongs to may not have unlimited patience, especially if they were around when the dinosaurs inhabited our planet.

History dictates that we very rarely listen when new ideas are first put forward. When some said the world was a sphere, we took no notice and still believed it was flat. When someone put forward the theory that the Earth went round the Sun and not the other way round, we did not believe it. If we had at least listened to minority thinking, it could have sped up all our learning processes over the last 2,000 years or more. Instead we usually ignore them.

When minorities are ignored, the fanatics rear their ugly heads and all hell breaks loose. We humans should learn to listen and listen to learn. The way the majority think and live is always evolving but only with the help of new ideas—we are living in the status quo while those new ideas are being born by the minority.

Colin is willing to share all his findings with anyone who is willing to listen, and you don't even have to get out of your armchair.

This book is a must for any thinking person.

Reg Presley, singer/songwriter with The Troggs, and now, also an author and paranormal researcher. Reg's book, Wild Things They Don't Tell Us, *was published in 2002.*

Introduction

Circular Evidence
The Story Behind the "Crop Circle Bible"

When Pat Delgado and I co-wrote *Circular Evidence*, the first book ever to look at the crop circle phenomenon, we never imagined that such a small pebble dropped into such a big pond could create such enormous, ever-expanding rings of influence. The book ultimately sold over a half million copies, and was translated into several languages, including Spanish, Italian, Japanese, and German.

The book was originally Pat's idea. At the time, he had been studying crop circles for eight years, and I had been at it for six.

One day, as we were going over the voluminous data and great number of aerial photographs we had amassed over the years, he suggested we should write a book about our findings. We then talked at length about the effect such a book might have on our privileged access to the circles. Many of the farmers had long been supportive and helpful in our research, and we were often allowed access to fields to investigate virgin formations before anyone else was even aware something had occurred. We knew that this situation might change if we went public about the subject. We also wondered about the possibility of damage to crop formations and to farmers' lands if people began traipsing through the fields looking for crop circles after reading our book.

We ultimately decided that it was more important for the public to know about the phenomenon, and so we decided to move forward with the book.

Most of the photographs in the book were taken by Pat and I, with a half dozen images contributed by Busty Taylor. I did most of the writing, and the book was published within six months of Pat's initial idea. We both had a great deal to say about the phenomenon and the information and photos in the book were new and exciting to readers who were just becoming aware of the crop circle mystery.

The book ultimately became an international best-seller, and we followed it in 1990 with a sequel, *Crop Circles: The Latest Evidence*, which likewise became a worldwide best-seller.

The book generated an enormous media response and it wasn't long before Pat and I were in all the newspapers, on TV and radio, and the book was being talked about in as varied settings as the street corners and the pubs, and all the way up to Buckingham Palace.

The royalties from *Circular Evidence* allowed me to resign my government job and devote myself to researching crop circles full-time.

The book caused two things to happen: Hoaxed crop circles began to proliferate like wildfire, and scientists and researchers began to take the subject seriously. The book touched the imagination of people all around the world and it soon became known as the "Crop Circle Bible." Interestingly, in these early days of the phenomenon, the book was taken quite seriously by both the scientific community and by the media. Today, after decades of counterfeits, and bizarre theories, crop circles have a stigma attached to them and are often lumped into the same category as UFOs and Bigfoot sightings. This is a pity, and hoaxing had a great deal to do with this change in perception.

Colin Andrews and his co-author for Circular Evidence, *Pat Delgado.*

Part I

A Holy Curiosity

Madison Square Garden:
The Beginning

My name is Colin Andrews, and I have been in a unique position since 1983, a position, my friends, that I did not ask for.

I was an electrical engineer and a local government officer in England and, one day, as I was simply driving between my offices, a chance glance out of my car window pulled me into this phenomena.

This is a unique situation. I have seen the growth of a mystery which was, at that time, new to the world. I've seen the "people problems" grow with it; and I've witnessed the media response in all its manic intensity.

I have also seen how intelligence agencies on either side of the water have infiltrated the research organizations and I have seen firsthand how they pull you aboard, offer you money to write books on the subject, and all of it is simply to write you off and remove you from the scene.

This has been one hell of an opportunity, and I have learned by it.

As I said, I am an electrical engineer by profession. I went into government during the reorganization of local municipalities in Great Britain back in 1974, and I rose through a number of posts fairly quickly. I was fortunate to be given a promotion about every six months or so.

My position looked pretty good. Things were looking rosy and then I saw five circles in a field. As soon as I saw my first crop circles, something threw a switch.

I was not aware at the time that I walked into that field that, within hours, I was to become one of only three people in the world researching these phenomena.

Within days of that July afternoon in 1983, I joined forces with Dr. Terence Meaden, who was, and still is, the head of the Tornado and Storm Research Organization in Great Britain. I also teamed up with Pat Delgado ,who had just retired from his job at NASA tracking the Mariner Project at the Woomera Tracking Ranges in Australia and Busty Taylor, a driving instructor and light aircraft pilot who lived in my home town.

I became known in the area very quickly by tapping on lots of doors: farmer's doors, military doors, police doors—just about everybody I could get to—asking them what they knew about these things, how long had they been there, and anything else they could tell me.

The first thing the farmers told me was that these five circles were not the only ones they had ever had.

Almost every farmer whose door I knocked on in that area of southern England told me that their forefathers had had these things on

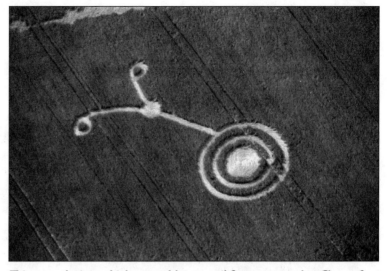

This crop design which resembles a snail first appeared at Cheesefoot Head, Hampshire, England in 1991. (This was found in the same field that I saw my first Celtic Cross formation in 1983.)

their land, and they had all heard them spoken of when they were children. This was concrete evidence that crop circles had been around for at least 30 years.

I was then formally approached by a military person who asked me to supply technical and scientific reports—the first reports about the crop circles—to the secretary of state for the Margaret Thatcher government. The reports were for a senior man in the cabinet, one of the top five people in Great Britain.

The outcome of my three reports was that, in the mid-1980s, an announcement was made in the British House of Commons that they accepted that there was a real phenomenon. Their official position was that crop circles were an unusual phenomenon, but it was not any type of paranormal mystery.

A common theory was that they were being caused by a new kind of whirlwind, a new meteorological phenomena, one commonly referred to now as a plasma vortex— a rotating field of electrified air, which during the night, would account for the golden balls of light people claimed to have seen above

the fields in which crop circles appear.

I spoke to many of the leading meteorologists with whom we were working in Europe, and most of them found it hard to imagine that that kind of phenomena could cause even a single crop circle because of the well-defined cut-off edges, and the lack of damage in crop circles. There was no evidence that that kind of plasma vortex could cause an effect of that kind.

Remember that Pat and I and our colleagues were all investigating crop circles before hoaxing became a part of the scene.

In 1989, Pat and I decided to write a book, *Circular Evidence*. Frankly, the decision to write the book took an awful lot of debate and we had many discussions as to whether or not we should, indeed, do this, because we would be "showing our cards," so to speak, and putting the phenomenon of crop circles right into the public domain.

But at the same time, we thought it was very important that this should be shared with the public and so we published our book. The result was an extraordinary level of hoaxing.

Chapter 1

The Path

The important thing is not to stop questioning. Curiosity has its own reason for existing. One cannot help but be in awe when he contemplates the mysteries of eternity, of life, of the marvelous structure of reality. It is enough if one tries merely to comprehend a little of this mystery every day. Never lose a holy curiosity.

—**Albert Einstein**

An opening thought: Would mankind have a collective nervous breakdown if it was revealed that UFOs were real and that crop circles were messages from extraterrestrials? The odds of that being true are unlikely, but even if it were the case, I give humanity more credit: I do not think that we as a species would automatically reject a new neighbor who has sent us a greeting, do you? This is something we should keep in mind as we explore the crop circle mystery.

1.1 In the Beginning

"This is the beginning of something important."

The year was 1993, and I spoke those words at the Omega Communications *UFO Experience* conference in North Haven, Connecticut during my presentation on crop circles. During that talk, I described the crop circle formations that had been appearing around the world as "signs." The Mel Gibson movie was a decade away and yet I sensed something was happening, something of a global, and possibly cosmic scale, something I interpreted even then as a sign. Without fully understanding the scope of my journey, I had taken the first steps down a long, and tumultuous path.

1.2 Life Changes

After seeing my first crop circle in July of 1983, my life changed in every imaginable way.

At that time, I was an electrical engineer employed by regional government in Great Britain. My work was based upon traditional science, and I had devoted my career to investigating, studying, and chronicling things you can see, count, measure, weigh, and record. I solved problems in a structured, logical manner.

And then, in July of 1983, I saw something very unusual, and instantly compelling; something that seemed to exist outside the boundaries of the mechanical sciences in which I had been working my entire professional life. I was intrigued, and my curiosity—both personal and scientific—was immediately piqued.

Over the years, I have applied as much hard scientific research practices and protocols to the study of crop circles as possible. I have turned to the disciplines of engineering, chemistry, radiography, physics, and geometry in an attempt to understand this phenomenon. I have come to realize that when trying to understand something that may be of paranormal genesis, there is as much—if not more—to be learned by the intuitive instincts and abilities that we possess, and that many of us ignore and often fail to utilize.

I have had some unusual experiences. Many I would classify as paranormal. I don't know how else to explain them. However, throughout my years of study of crop circles, I have always tried to maintain an open-minded approach, and to listen and respond to the intuitive part of my psyche.

Over time, I have become more intuitive. Some might say I've become more psychic and there have certainly been experiences that suggest that I am a different person in many ways.

My life has changed in more practical ways as well. I was doing a regular day-to-day job, which I eventually left as a result of what I saw in the fields in July 1983. I resigned my position to participate full-time in researching crop circles and trying to unravel this mystery.

That admittedly somewhat drastic change in my lifestyle was not well received by members of my family. In fact, my marriage broke down because of my new interest and focus, and because of the time and energy I was putting into studying the crop circle phenomenon. My whole world changed literally almost overnight. I had a new group of friends; I was traveling constantly and my financial situation went from secure to drastically insecure, again, almost overnight. My first wife and I ultimately divorced and, in addition to this personal trauma, I came to realize that

many of my friends and professional colleagues were embarrassed by me and my work. I was very visible on television in Great Britain in the 1980s, and the unusual nature of my research mortified my former co-workers, many of whom made it quite clear to me that they wanted nothing further to do with me, as long as I was committed to pursuing this odd line of inquiry.

And so, every aspect of my life changed following my first glimpse of the enigma in the fields.

Eventually, all of these elements conspired to have a much larger effect than simply turning one man's life upside down, My work, and the continued appearance of authentic crop circle formations, changed Great Britain itself. I realized that the subject of crop circles was a fuse that I had lit, and I needed to make some decisions about how to continue my work.

I came to the United States in 1991 to speak about crop circles at a UFO Conference and it was there that I met my wife Synthia. We ultimately married, and we mutually decided that we would live in Branford, Connecticut. I relocated permanently to the United States and I now maintain the home office of Circles Phenomenon Research International out of Branford.

I am still pursuing this mystery, but now under a very different set of circumstances.

1.3 Mistakes and Regrets

Very early on in my research, one of the biggest mistakes I made was mentioning publicly the possibility of crop circles being formed by extraterrestrial intelligences. In the early days of my investigation, I began to feel that there could well be some external factor creating the formations, and that perhaps it could be some form of intelligence. I was not stating with certainty that this possible intelligence was extraterrestrial: It could just have easily been terrestrial in nature. But the media in

Great Britain (and later around the world), interpreted my speculations cynically, exploitatively, and in a very sensationalistic manner.

They painted a picture of me as an eccentric proclaiming that crop circles were being created by little green men, and I was, as might be expected, ridiculed and attacked. This caused me tremendous anguish and embarrassment. Looking back with absolutely flawless hindsight (as hindsight is always wont to be), I think I would have handled that quite differently. My thinking now is that the media, and by extension, the public, were not adequately prepared for what I was suggesting. The world needed to be educated about the mysteries of cereology, and that knowledge base had not been disseminated widely enough for my more "unusual" theories to be accepted, or at least considered, with reason and open-mindedness.

I should have been somewhat more circumspect when presenting the odder theories. We would have come to these theories eventually: They are all part of the equation. But I now know that I offered cutting-edge ideas too soon. I was looking at something new, and was engaged and motivated, and my entire being was focused on uncovering the truth and on understanding what was happening. I was naive in my assumption that others would be as enthusiastic as I was about the more radical ideas relative to the crop circles phenomenon.

I became a target. And today, it is worse, because of the widespread crop circle counterfeiting problem. (And as I state repeatedly throughout this book, hoaxers could not create counterfeit crop circles if they did not have real ones to copy.)

I have modified and refined my position on the possible genesis of crop circles, and yet the resistance by certain factions remains. It is an understandable paradigm: Crop circles and their de facto "oddness," combined with a team of "artists" laying claim to actually being the ones responsible for them, combine to make the serious researchers of the phenomenon objects of ridicule, who are too often dismissed without being taken seriously.

I've tended to be something of a "one-man band" when it comes to making statements about crop circles and as to how the "movement" to study the formations has developed and acted over the years. I deliberately, and with great forethought, have worn and continue to wear, this mantle of responsibility. This is because I am the one putting myself out there in a very visible position, and I expect to be the one torn to shreds by critics and skeptics. I have worked with a great many people over the years—good, sober-minded, smart people who have contributed greatly to the study of crop circles. These people have helped me at *my* request: they should not have to deal with being lambasted for *my* conclusions.

If I could do anything differently, I would involve more people in the decision-making process regarding the furthering of the discipline and the directions of the study. I would invite input as to the specific avenues of research we should embark upon, and I would consult on what should be stated publicly.

1.4 Sharing the Mystery

It is better to understand little than to misunderstand a lot.

—Anatole France

My instincts and my intuition tell me that an important purpose of the crop circle message is to call attention to what we are doing to our world. We need to wake up and recognize what we have been doing—for far too long—to the earth. Our environment—

the plants, the animals, the waters, the sky— all are integral parts of the earth's ecosystem, and we are mistreating every element of this complex and fragile biological totality. The element of respect is missing from our behavior: We do not act out of respect for the *other* living entities on this planet. We are not alone. And yet, we act as if the earth and everything on it exists solely to serve man.

The crop circle phenomenon may be, in essence, a wake-up call. Or it could be a cry for help. The day must come when we understand this, and act for positive change.

I do not think it is a coincidence that crop patterns have been appearing regularly at places that for millennia have been centers of spiritual focus—places where people have gathered for hundreds and thousands of years for prayer, meditation, worship, and to seek enlightenment. The human quest for peace and higher consciousness has often been expressed in outdoor places such as Stonehenge, and in cathedrals and temples. Crop circles often appear in or near these places, and in my opinion, this is a critical part of the overall meaning of the phenomenon.

These places manifest an energy that speaks to our inner selves, and crop circles could, in effect, be serving as living signs identifying and calling our attention to these sacred places.

Emotions have consequences. Positive emotions that have love as their source, result in positive energies. The exact opposite occurs with negative emotions.

I think that crop circles are giving us all a spiritual nudge, and that they are part of the process of understanding ourselves. Humankind is inching along, with *innumerable* setbacks, of course, towards enlightenment, and a God-centered consciousness. Perhaps by focusing on a common mystery, we are creating a unified energy that will ultimately be our salvation.

I have met an extraordinary range of individuals in crop circles. They have run the gamut from priests to politicians and everyone in between and the only thing they—*we*—all have in common, aside from our innate humanity, of course, is the sharing of a mystery.

The crop circle mystery brings us all together, and a new bond is created. The process is painfully slow, but it is occurring.

My thinking is that this interaction and this common interest—the sharing of the mystery—will ultimately show us that we have so much more in common than we have differences. We all share a living planet, and there is only one race—the human one.

We must keep an open mind, and we must eliminate animosity from the equation.

We must act with a sincerity of endeavor to seek knowledge and truth, and to reach a higher place of consciousness and understanding. And most importantly, we must all have faith.

I am not speaking solely theologically here. I personally believe that God is different for everyone, and that each religion is essentially a different road to the same place. I am speaking about faith that something greater than us exists, and that we have the power and ability to strive for this elevated state of being. We must have faith that there is something beyond us and this planet. Our goal should always be to reach higher.

The answers are coming, and they will not come solely from science.

We do need to keep scientific inquiry at the forefront of our investigation into the mystery, but we must also allow room for information to come to us through different doors and open windows.

We need to continue to evaluate the crop circle phenomena rationally, scientifically, and logically. We need to continue to measure, and record, and test, and study. But we also need to open our hearts and allow our intuitive side to speak to us.

We are moving forward, albeit slowly, but the journey will be well worth the wait. Incredible times await us.

1.5 My Quest for the Truth

Only the curious will learn and only the resolute overcome the obstacles to learning. The quest quotient has always excited me more than the intelligence quotient.

—Eugene S. Wilson

I have long referred to my crop circle research as a quest. The genesis of this feeling was the very moment back in 1983, when I saw the first set of five circles forming a traditional Celtic Cross in a field. I have often said that it felt like a switch was thrown in my stomach. There was an overwhelming emotional and spiritual effect on me, but there was also a palpable physical effect as well. This was quite special and a feeling I have experienced many times throughout my decades of research. I was quite conscious of a sense of mystery, of awe, of something beyond our mortal ken.

I can recall being overwhelmed upon first seeing the formation, and I also remember how this feeling grew inside me as I walked closer to the circles. The awe and wonder embraced me like a white light permeating every cell of my body.

This powerful sense of mystery triggered a resolve in me to learn as much as I could about this phenomenon. It did, indeed, become a quest. It became a quest for understanding and for truth.

A part of this process has been the realization and the acceptance that my work with the crop circle phenomenon may be part of a larger plan for me.

I say this because of something that happened when I was around 12 years old. This did not happen to me, however, but to my parents and younger brother.

The time was the late 1950s. I lived with my parents and my younger brother in England near Salisbury Plain, not very far from Stonehenge. On Sunday afternoons, we would often pile into my dad's old jet-black motorcar and go for a drive. The fields and landscapes of that part of central southern England are absolutely glorious, and we all found a leisurely drive to be quite a respite from the bustle of the previous week.

One particular Sunday afternoon, for some inexplicable reason, I chose not to go with my family for our weekly drive. I remained home while my parents and my younger brother headed out in dad's motorcar.

Off they went, and from what I was told, the drive started out as quite normal and very pleasant.

Then something extraordinary happened and, to this day, I regret that I was not with my family at the time.

As my dad was driving in the countryside, just northeast of Stonehenge in a very remote area near an ancient English manor, they came upon a narrow country lane, which was no more than the width of one vehicle. As my dad drove carefully down this lane, a disk-shaped object suddenly appeared over the top of some conifer trees along the side of the road.

The object was swaying from side to side in the air, and it was perfectly visible to them all. The road was next to an open field and there was a clear line of sight to the stand of trees over which this object hovered.

My father stopped the car and he and my brother got out and walked to the side of the road. They were less than 100 yards from this object and both had a very clear view of it. It was a silvery craft and, as they watched, it began to rise up. My mother, who had remained in the car, became very frightened at this and began calling to my father and brother, pleading with them to get back in the car. She later told me that she was afraid that the craft was going to fly right at them, and she desperately wanted to flee the scene.

As she shouted at my father and brother—"Get back!" she cried—suddenly a narrow beam of white light shot out of the bottom of the craft, and then the UFO took off. It shot away incredibly fast over the top of the trees and my parents recalled that it veered slightly to the right as it flew away. It did not just vanish, or "pop out." It flew away at an extraordinary rate of speed. In fact, my parents later told me that it moved so quickly that they were unable to follow it with their eyes. They were adamant about what they saw: a solid object was there one minute, and then it was gone.

My father and brother hurried back to the car and they sped off home. As soon as they entered the house, they told me what had happened and, even at the age of 12, I was strangely affected by what they had experienced. As they told me of their UFO encounter, I felt somewhere deep inside that I should have been there with them. Never for a moment did I doubt their story. Aside from the unconditional trust I had in my parents, I also knew, even then, that these were credible people telling of an incredible event.

Now, fast forward to 25-years later. A mere 15 miles from where my family had seen the UFO, I had my first crop circle sighting. All of what had happened to my parents and my brother came flooding back to me. At that time, I actually reexperienced the emotions of that day back in the 1950s—not only those of myself, but also what my parents were feeling as well. Here I was, seeing markings in a field, and I couldn't help but

wonder if, somehow, that it was related to that UFO sighting from so long ago.

This time, however, the event was not transitory, and it was not elusive. It did not "fly away." This time, I was being presented with something physical, something that could be measured, and photographed, and tested. Something that remained in the fields until it was plowed under, patient and quiet, allowing me to take all the time I needed to study it.

I knew then that I was being given an assignment: a mission. It was, and still is, a mission of understanding. It has become my quest.

1.6 Answered Prayers

I have long believed that our minds are part of the crop circle phenomenon. Human consciousness is a force unto itself, and I believe that it is possible, perhaps even necessary, that humans as a species work towards positive use of the power of enlightened minds and higher consciousness.

One of the most important events in my life was the manifestation of a crop formation after I consciously wished for it to appear. Could this even be possible? That is the question I asked myself following this experience. And yet, the facts are the facts.

Shortly after my introduction to the crop circle mystery, I began to ponder deeply, thinking about what they meant, and asking myself why I seemed to be drawn to them.

One night in the mid-1980s, in the early years of my research, I asked for a crop formation. Some may call such a request hubris; some may call it folly. At the time, I was (and still am, for that matter) ardently seeking understanding and knowledge about these unusual manifestations in the fields and, thus, I boldly requested that a crop circle appear for me.

I asked for a Celtic Cross formation—four circles surrounding a center circle with a concentric ring through the center of the four satellite circles—and I asked that it appear as close to my home in central southern England as possible. A Celtic Cross had, to the best of my knowledge, never appeared before. I visualized the cross in my mind, and I sent out a request for one to appear in the fields near my home.

The exact formation that I had visualized in my mind did appear in a field near my home—the only field in the area that had not yet been harvested. The field was approximately four or five miles away from where I lived, and the farmer who owned the land called me the morning after I had made my "request." A few days after visiting the site, I realized that the field in which the cross had appeared was the closest field to my home in which it *could* have appeared. Because all the fields in the area had already been harvested, the Celtic Cross appeared in the closest field possible.

I was stunned by the response from whatever intelligence is creating these designs. And yet, I feel that this is much too special for me to claim as my own. However, it did appear at my behest and the odds of it *not* being associated with my psychic request are quite slim, indeed.

This experience—combined with others that have followed—convinced me wholeheartedly that our minds are part of the phenomenon.

And I believe that we are getting closer to the truth as each year goes by.

1.7 An Evolving Puzzle

Facts do not cease to exist because they are ignored.

—Aldous Huxley

More than a decade ago, I used the term "evolving" to describe the increasing complexity of crop circle formations. I was seeing changes in crop formations that clearly indicated an evolution in design and intricacy.

In the early days, at the start of our research, the patterns in the fields were quite simple: single circles of varying sizes.

But then a single circle was joined by a smaller circle nearby; and then we saw three in a straight line; and then five forming a cross. And then, in 1986, we saw the first rings around circles. On May Day 1990, for the first time, we suddenly saw two circles connected by a straight line.

It cannot be denied that these patterns have been evolving before our eyes, and they have also been expanding in their geographic distribution. Their reach has now extended to almost every country on earth, and the density of reports within individual countries has also been on the rise over the past several years.

The unavoidable conclusion is that the phenomenon is evolving, and this has convinced many people around the world—many of whom were long-time skeptics—that the crop circle mystery is real, and that it has meaning.

The simple has now become complex; few has become many; random has become commonplace. Logically, this kind of measurable evolvement—this gracious unfolding of spectacular beauty—must have a purpose, and I believe that purpose to be the transmittal of some kind of information. The phenomenon is moving towards something; perhaps towards many things, and its increasing complexity and its insistence on making itself known through bolder and more widespread formations, may have great import for mankind and the future of this planet.

It is my belief that the meaning of the crop circle mystery has evolved into something that needs to be understood by man, and that this message is important and should not be ignored.

We began by not knowing anything beyond the fact that we were looking at flattened plants in a circle. We now know that hundreds of plants flattened into a series of forms creating an overall geometry—the Julia Set (Chapter 6) comes immediately to mind—arises from the science of fractal mathematics. We know that all of nature is comprised of fractals and that we can see their geometric patterns in everything: from the Nautilus mollusk shell, to the spiraling arms of the galaxies. The science of fractal mathematics describes a geometric pattern that is repeated endlessly at ever small scales to produce irregular shapes and surfaces that cannot be represented by classical geometry.

Fractals are paradoxes. Using nothing but squares and straight lines, a curve can be created. As the squares decrease in size, a graceful spiral curve is created by connecting specific points of the smaller and smaller boxes. This spiraling "infinite curve' can be found in flowers and other natural forms, and its proportions have been used in art and architectures since man first scratched symbols onto cold cave walls. We do not know how or where this will end.

I have long believed that the most important "door opener"—the "Eureka moment"—will be when we are able to fully understand not only the meanings of the individual patterns, but also the meaning of the designs within the context of *all* the authentic worldwide formations. Placement will become a key factor in tying everything together, and *where* designs appear will become as significant to the overall meaning and understanding of the mystery as to *what* particular patterns appear in any given year.

For instance, seemingly random occurrences will become meaningful. Circle A will appear around the time of Event B, which will take place near ancient archaeological site C, and all of these clues will come together and give us the answers we are seeking.

At some point in the future, the crop circle phenomena will have done its job and we will all fully understand its true purpose. That moment has not yet arrived however, and so we must continue our work, and continue to open our hearts and minds to the enigma in the fields.

1.8 Spirituality and Crop Circles

The first act of awe, when man was struck with the beauty or wonder of Nature, was the first spiritual experience.

—Henryk Skolimowski

I have often used the term "spiritual nudge" to describe what I consider to be one of the fundamental purposes of crop circles.

Throughout recorded history, man has responded to symbols in a spiritual way. The symbol of yin and yång, the mandala, the cross, the symbol for infinity, and other stylized, geometric designs have long been used as aids to meditation, prayer, study, insight, and personal growth. Meditating on these symbols expands consciousness and opens the door to spiritual growth. Religious symbols create a certain state of mind in people, often described as feelings of well-being, serenity, and a sense of the mysterious. These are aspirations towards higher consciousness, towards enlightenment. Crop circles often appear near ancient archaeological sites that were once used for prayer and meditation. People visit these sites and almost always come away feeling rested and at peace. Is there a connection? There seems to be.

The crop circle mystery may very well be part of a broader spiritual plan, conceived by authors who, so far, prefer to remain anonymous.

Why would mankind need to be given a spiritual nudge?

The world is a tinderbox.

On any given day, a war is raging somewhere on our planet. There are hate crimes, kidnappings, political torture, terrorism, pollution, poverty, starvation, genocide, assassination, embezzling, drug addiction, domestic violence, illiteracy, rape, murder, homelessness....

The list goes on and on and on, and it all adds up to one undeniable fact: The world needs a spiritual nudge; a push towards the higher aspirations of peace and enlightenment.

An important fact to keep in mind when attempting to fully understand the crop circle mystery is that the phenomenon not only manifests itself in beautiful geometries that speak to the human yearning for harmony and brotherhood, but also that these magnificent pictograms are formed with an obvious respect for the plants involved; they embody a non-destructive modus operandi that does not kill. This "regard for life" is unquestionably subliminally communicated to those who experience crop circles, and all report being fully aware that they were in the presence of something mysterious and special.

Simply seeing these formations elicits this identical feeling of well-being. People in aircraft flying above the fields have reported a sense of serenity when looking at crop formations from above. There seems to be absolutely no difference between the effect of the crop circles on people from the ground or from the air.

We are living in difficult times. Everyone knows this. And we are all searching for answers. Right after September 11, 2001, attendance at churches around the world rose dramatically for a spell. The yearning for answers, and the longing for peace is everywhere.

Perhaps the crop circle mystery's purpose is to move mankind into a mindset in which the most positive elements of human nature will be brought to the forefront, and acted upon with passion.

1.9 Intelligent Design?

Let us permit nature to have her way; she understands her business better than we do.

—Michel de Montaigne

I believe that there is an intelligence behind the creation of crop circles. It is apparent to me that intelligent design is visible in the authentic formations; the "hand of an author," if you will.

The placement of these designs seem purposeful to me: it is clear that they were intended to be seen, and that their beauty and fascinating geometric patterns were intended to intrigue us, and to stimulate us. This again speaks to intelligent design and deliberate purpose.

Bolstering this view is the fact that there is consistent, ongoing interaction between the phenomenon and the researchers; some might say the phenomenon *responds* to the researchers.

There have been cases involving the design and placement of formations that argue against simple coincidence. For instance, there are reports in the literature in which an identical pattern has appeared a few days after the *original* pattern was plowed under. Why? And what can this mean? This has only happened when a formation was destroyed before researchers had a chance to study it. Again, it is as if the intelligence behind the mystery wants to be sure that those who are paying attention receive *all* the information they are attempting to communicate to them.

We do not know the nature of this intelligence. I have been lambasted in the past for using the word "intelligence" somewhat imprecisely. I was excoriated because many people interpreted my use of the word "intelligence" to mean aliens. Extraterrestrials.

This formation appeared close to the town of Devizes, Wiltshire, England in the year 2000. The pattern was joined within days by other significant formations in nearby fields.

Thus, I use the word cautiously now, and when I do, I am careful to explain that "intelligence" can mean many things, and that I am not specifically referring to E.T. coming down and making crop circles.

For instance, there is an intelligence to the human immune system. This complex biological system continually evaluates threats to the human body and, in a sense, "decides" when to respond to danger and attack the intruder. This type of automatic, non-human "thinking" goes on in varying degrees of complexity and sophistication throughout the entire spectrum of life forms.

I am using this analogy vis-a-vis crop circles to illustrate that it is possible that the manifestations that we all can see— the authentic patterns and designs—could be an autonomic response from the earth, similar to the innate, and undeniably intelligent responses of the human immune system. This does not demand a conscious entity "wielding the controls," so to speak. It simply reacts as a highly functioning biosystem, much like the human body, or the global ecosphere.

The concept of intelligence does not always have to include use of tools and the development of language.

Nature is intelligent. It reasons, it thinks, it responds. Astronaut Edgar Mitchell, the 12th man to walk on the moon, believes that the universe itself is an intelligent, self-correcting entity.[1]

Intelligence does not always require consciousness. Sometimes, intelligent action is simply part and parcel of the matrix of all reality.

Notes

[1] Stephen Spignesi, *The UFO Book of Lists.*

Chapter 2

What Are Crop Circles?

They contain information which is as much about our past as our future. They are subtle nudges, tweaks you might say, to our consciousness. The information gives us vital building blocks, which will help with changing our attitudes and actions towards life on our planet. You could say we are looking at our future and as long as we are open to that idea, it will take us to a new place,

—**Colin Andrews** on *The Sally Jesse Raphael Show*

2.1 Crop Circles: a Definition of Terms

Crop circles are circular shapes usually found in cereal crops in which the vegetation is bent over at right angles and spiraled into an often complex pattern. Authentic crop circles show no damage to the plants, unlike hoaxed circles in which the stalks are broken and crushed. In authentic crop circles, the plants are gently bent over, yet continue to grow. The plants in faked circles are often killed by the "circlemakers."

Initially, in the early years of the 20th century manifestations of this phenomenon, the shapes were nothing more than simple circles. In later years, the patterns actually became much more complex, and have consisted of combinations of complex geometric designs, including straight lines, spirals, angles, and other clearly discernible and recognizable patterns.

2.2 Numbers

There have been 3,000 fully documented crop circles that have occurred in the last two decades. In my master database of crop circle formations, there are over 10,000 documented formations. There were over 700 crop circles during 1991. This was the highest number of occurrences during the last 20 years, but on average, approximately 200 crop designs appear worldwide each year.

2.3 Obvious Intelligence

It is clear to me that the evidence is growing exponentially that whatever or whomever is involved in the creation of the genuine crop circles around the world has a collective "mind." There seems to be a consciousness at the very source of the formations, and it is obvious that there is thought involved. Where or what that source is at this moment in our history, and in the history of the phenomenon, is very difficult to ascertain. However, I believe that we are all involved in a process, the final goal of which is a complete understanding of precisely what is going on. An integral part of this process is the continuing interaction between the events in the fields and the researchers. In some cases, this interaction includes a few of the people that are making some of the formations (that is, the hoaxers). I suspect that we are all players in an enormous cosmic play, and that we all have our part. I do not think that many of us—researchers, farmers, witnesses, and hoaxers—fully understand what our ultimate role will actually be.

2.4 Magic

My fascination with crop circles is, in essence and at its core, a deep-rooted bewilderment. I continually marvel at the lack of human presence, and I revel in the magical atmosphere that exists when I visit these formations. The feeling is palpable. There is something elusive and thrilling at the sites of the authentic formations. I really cannot define it; nor can I measure it, but it is there: a tangible sense of...well, *magic* might be the right word. What is remarkable about this feeling for me is that, outside of crop circles, I have only experienced this sense of awe in churches and cathedrals—special places where there is clearly an undercurrent of revelation.

Sometimes, some of us seem to be capable of receiving "transmissions" from other places, other states of being, other dimensions. Many of us often talk about intuition, hunches, the feeling that someone is watching us, or the knowledge that someone is talking about us. We seem to have a kind of sensory radar that sometimes allows us to pick up messages that speak to us without words. There is usually no rational explanation for these kinds of experiences, but I have personally felt this

sense of awareness when visiting authentic crop formations, and it continues to fascinate me. I am constantly trying to learn more about it.

2.5 Crop Circles of the Past

There are many historical accounts of crop circle formations before the 20th century, some going back many hundreds of years.

The first recorded account of an event that has many of the characteristics common to the formation of a crop circle dates from August 8, 1590, and was detailed in a book published in 1686 called *The Natural History of Stafford-Shire* by Robert Plott.

A peasant named Nicolae Lang-Bernhand was walking to his home around midday that day when he noticed some peculiar activity going on in a field by the side of the road. Upon closer investigation, he saw a group of people dancing in a circle in the field. Upon even *closer* investigation (close enough to see their legs and feet) he saw that some of them had cloven feet. As Lang-Bernhand observed them, the dancers all suddenly rose into the air and disappeared. In the field where they had been cavorting appeared a circular indentation, which remained on the ground until the farmer who owned the field plowed it under the following harvest time. According to Plott, many people from the surrounding area visited the crop circle while it existed. No mention is made of what happened to the cloven-foot dancers. Plott also states that powerful whirlwinds rose up during this event, and that one of them was strong enough to pick up the farmer and carry him to a field some distance away.

A measure of skepticism is called for when evaluating this account since it was, after all, recounted almost 100 years after it supposedly took place. But even if we strip away some of the more fanciful elements

A 1678 depiction of what many believe to be the formation of a crop circle.

of the story (such as the cloven-foot dancers and the daylight vanishing), the essence of the tale is that a crop circle appeared in a field, and many people witnessed it.

In John Aubrey's *Natural History*, the story is told of a school teacher who, in 1633, saw fairies and elves dancing in a field and then spoke of "the green circles made by those spirits on the grass."

And later still, recorded in English folklore dating back to 1678, there was reference to an event that many of us today might describe as an account of the formation of a crop circle. There are differences in some of the specifics of the case, but there are too many similarities to a classic report of a crop circle to dismiss it out of hand.

The event occurred in Hertfordshire, England. In writings of the time, the local people speak of a fiery devil coming out of the sky and cutting a circle in a field of oats—again, cereal crops—in a village in Hertfordshire. A woodcut exists of what has come to be known as a "mowing devil," a horned and tailed creature cutting through a field of oats with a scythe.

The story is told of a farmer who asked a local laborer what he would charge to cut his field of oats. Apparently the farmer was not too pleased with the laborer's estimate, and so they argued, reportedly with great choler and exchanging of curses.

The farmer had the final say, though, when he declared boldly and with seemingly little Christian fear, that he would rather pay the devil himself to mow his field than fork over the exorbitant amount demanded by the worker. "May the Devil reap it!" he is reputed to have shouted. The laborer stormed off, the farmer stormed off, and the fields remained uncut, until later that evening. Supposedly, the farmer's oat field was bathed in a fiery light. The following morning, his entire crop was neatly cut, arrayed in "round circles."

There are many other similar references dating from the 15th century in England. Many can be dismissed as pure fiction, although one could see the medieval mind interpreting natural phenomena as paranormal occurrences.

Moving into the 19th century, one of the most compelling accounts of this phenomena comes from 1880. In a letter published in the July 29, 1880 issue of *Nature*,

John Rand Capron reports on an anomalous event he witnessed in a field near Guildford in Surrey, England:

The storms about this part of Surrey have been lately local and violent, and the effects produced in some instances curious. Visiting a neighbour's farm on Wednesday evening [July 21, 1880], we found a field of standing wheat considerably knocked about, not as an entirety, but in patches forming, as viewed from a distance, circular spots.

Examined more closely, these all presented much the same character, viz., a few standing stalks as a center, some prostrate stalks with their heads arranged pretty evenly in a direction forming a circle round the center, and outside these a circular wall of stalks which had not suffered.

I sent a sketch made on the spot, giving an idea of the most perfect of these patches. The soil is a sandy loam upon the greensand, and the crop is vigorous, with strong stems, and I could not trace locally any circumstances accounting for the peculiar forms of the patches in the field, nor indicating whether it was wind or rain, or both combined, which had caused them, beyond the general evidence everywhere of heavy rainfall. They were suggestive to me of some cyclonic wind action, and may perhaps have been noticed elsewhere by some of your readers.

There are also accounts of crop circles from the early years of the 20th century.

After the broadcast of a BBC program on which I appeared and talked about the field in which I saw my first crop circle in 1983, I was contacted by a farmer named Chapel. Mr. Chapel told me that from 1923 to 1925, his farm had been on the parcel of land I showed on the program, and that in that same field, he had witnessed four crop circles form a square. Also, farmers in Whiteparish, Wiltshire saw simple circles in 1946 and 1947.

In 1966 in Tully Queensland Australia, farmers witnessed aerial phenomena after which crop circles appeared. Vegetation was seen to spiral and collapse in circular forms.

In the mid-1960s at the Stonehenge site, a farmer witnessed simple circles but did not report it until just recently. In that field today, there are complex geometric shapes, a seeming evolution from the simple circles the farmer saw in the mid-1960s.

From 1975 on, crop formations have evolved and increased in complexity and geographic distribution.

2.6 Crop Circles and Sacred Sites

In 1985, my colleagues and I noticed something remarkable about the geographical location of some crop circles. For years we had been gathering information about the location of circles and their dimensions, and eventually it became clear to us that there were large clusterings of crop circles around what have come to be known as "sacred sites."

As we continued to gather the data regarding the location of the crop circles, it became evident that there were large clusterings of formations around sacred sites in southern central England, particularly at Stonehenge, Avebury, Silbury Hill, and other ancient tumuli. My fellow researcher Freddy Silva now describes this area as "the heart of crop circle country."

In later years, when we began to receive reports from the United States about the appearance of crop circles there, we were not surprised to learn that many of them were very close to Indian burial grounds.

This spurred us to look much more closely at this element of the phenomena. Since the beginning of our involvement with the mystery, we have had computers continuously looking for correlation in the massive amounts of data collected about crop circles.

That research has resulted in two connections that stand out dramatically: we learned that many of the crop formations appear close to circular archaeological sites and/or underground water reservoirs. Those are the two major correlations, but with the archaeological connection—the appearance of formations near ancient sites—there is more to it than simply proximity.

The dimensions of crop formations that are near specific circular sacred sites are very similar proportionally.

2.7 Stonehenge

I recall a day back in 1985 when my friend and fellow researcher, pilot Busty Taylor, casually told me something that had occurred to him one day as he was flying over Stonehenge. During his flight, he suddenly realized that he was looking at approximately the same proportions in Stonehenge as in the crop circles that he had just recently begun to see from the air. This was something of a revelatory moment for all of us, but we needed some kind of confirmation for Busty's "hunch." For the next six months, we looked again at all the data we had compiled, and we concluded that his intuition had been correct.

Astonishingly, we discovered that the dimensions of the earliest simple circles, the first circles with rings around them, and the first double circles, were all within centimeters of the dimensions of the horseshoe semicircle of the Stonehenge monument. We were looking at the same geometry, the same proportions, the same scale.

This has continued, and sacred sites in other countries also reflect this relationship.

In Malta, for example, there are churches and temples built with the same "sacred geometry" scale and proportions.

Throughout history, man has found that certain geometric configurations—many of which are mirrored in nature—are meaningful to us as a species.

We don't know the reason for this attraction—this intuitive appeal or "pull" that certain shapes and proportions have—but it is real, and it is common.

Certain geometric patterns involving arcs, angles, circles, squares, and other shapes and dimensions are manifested in nature. The perfect spiral of the Nautilus shell is a dramatic example.

The Golden Mean is a ratio of angles and squares that create this perfect spiral. And it is an element that is found in many natural formations and living beings. It is our suspicion that the seemingly intentional (or at the least, repetitive) use of the Golden Mean design in many crop circles may be a tool that is being used by some higher power to communicate with us.

Are the circular swirls present in many crop circles somehow related to the dimensions and location of the pyramids?

Is there a connection between the mathematical properties of the Golden Mean and the earth's natural magnetic lines of energy?

These questions are still being asked now, decades after the first simple circle appeared, and we are getting closer to a definitive answer. That answer may ultimately prove that there is an undeniable connection between a simple nautical shell, the complex spirals of crop circles, and the eternal, evolving universe.

Stonehenge, for instance, is believed by many to be a stone monument built on the site of an early crop circle. This theory contends that the ancients discovered a complex crop formation, probably believed it was a divine message, prayed over it and in it, and then spent years, perhaps decades or longer, putting up giant stone markers exactly duplicating the layout of the original formation, assuring that this message from the gods, would be visible and remembered in perpetuity.

This theory cannot be proven, of course, but even a cursory examination of Stonehenge's triptychs leads the viewer reflexively to mentally "fill in the blanks" where stones are broken or missing. It does not take a great deal of imagination to picture what the original Stonehenge monument might have looked like, and to recognize its similarity to countless crop circle patterns.

2.8 Sacred Geometry

"Sacred" geometry comprises shapes, equations, dimensions, and ratios that have been applied to designs, art, and architecture over millennia, especially hallowed buildings such as churches, cathedrals, and temples; and prayer and meditation designs such as mandalas.

The Romans, the Greeks, the Celts, and other early peoples used these sacred ratios in the construction of their buildings and in their artwork, providing evidence of their knowledge of these dimensions, all of which mirror nature—from the spiral of the Nautilus shell, to the spiral galaxies of the cosmos.

2.9 The Triangle

There is a geographical triangle in southern central England in which many crop formations have appeared. The existence and identification of this phantasmal triangle is very important to me because I did not recognize its parameters at first. To this day, I believe I was deliberately given a message, which I will explain in detail, to steer me in the direction of understanding its significance.

In the early years of my research, I studied crop formations one by one. At that time, I was focused on understanding each new crop circle, and documenting its specific characteristics and details. I knew intuitively that there had to be some kind of connection, some kind of yet uncovered nexus that would link them all and perhaps explain what was going on, but my attention was mostly focused on each single manifestation as it appeared.

What I did do, however, was mount a large map of England on my office wall and, when a new crop circle appeared, I would place a colored push pin on the map at its location. Each year was represented by a different color pin, and thus I went about my business, placing a pin whenever a new formation appeared.

As the months passed, more pins went into the map. But there did not seem to be a pattern or an alignment—at least to my eyes. I was careful to record each new formation, but the placement of the pins seemed random and unconnected. There were the occasional clusters of appearances, near Stonehenge and Silbury Hill, but I failed to see a particular overall pattern to their arrangement.

As I continued my research, I would often collect plants and soil from inside crop circles. Usually, these went to labs for analysis; occasionally, they remained with me for a time. During one field trip to a crop circle in Wantage, England on September 4, 1986, I took a soil sample from inside the formation, and then left the area precisely at 4:15 p.m. I returned to my home office, placed the soil sample on my desk, and then put it out of my mind as I collated my notes, and tended to household duties and dinner.

That night—actually the morning of September 5—something exceedingly strange happened.

Colin Andrews in the office where he discovered the Wessex Triangle crop circle alignment.

Intruder alarm activations began to occur at my home at precisely 4:15 in the morning. My wife and I, as well as our daughter, were always sound asleep, and the alarms would wake us, and, of course, terribly frighten us. Bright lights would blaze on; buzzers would blare. Everyone in my house would awaken, as well as several of my neighbors, none of whom, as might be expected, were very pleased about what was happening. This went on for 14 nights in a row. I am an Electrical Engineer and have designed home alarm systems, so I checked everything out, and the equipment was functioning perfectly.

One night after the alarm went off yet again, I walked, mystified and groggy, into my computer room where I had several computer systems working to record and evaluate all the crop circle data I had been compiling. I kept asking myself why was this sophisticated alarm system repeatedly going off at 4:15 every morning?

I sat down at my desk, and my gaze automatically rose to the map on the wall. I had stared at this map countless times, and yet this time, something struck me about the placement of the color-coded push pins. "What was I seeing?" I asked myself. What *was* I seeing?

Then it hit me. In a moment of insight that struck me like a cold wind in the face while standing in the middle of a desert, I realized that the locations of the crop formations I had recorded in southern central England formed a perfect equilateral triangle. The three points of the triangle were Wantage in Oxfordshire, Winchester in Hampshire, and Warminster in Wiltshire, known as England's "UFO capital" for its plethora of UFO sightings.

The sides of the triangle were corridors several miles wide rather than perfectly straight lines, but the configuration of the triangle was undeniable.

I was flabbergasted.

Instead of seeing this obvious design, I had been looking *through* it for years, and all the while it had been hiding in plain sight.

I instinctively knew that this was an exceedingly important development, and so I grabbed my ruler and compass. Placing a point at the center of each of the three towns of the equilateral triangle, I measured the sides of the triangle.

The length of each of the three sides of the triangle was 41.5 miles.

This triangle has come to be known as the Wessex Triangle and it is still where the vast majority of total worldwide crop circle activity occurs.

All the hair on my neck and arms stood up when I realized what this meant. I had been sent a message; a message that had taken me time to comprehend.

The 4:15 alarm activations ceased that very day. Experiencing this revelation reached deep inside me, and moved me almost beyond words.

I had been sent a message. I believed it then, I believe it now.

This acceptance has been difficult for me, and an ongoing struggle. The engineer side of me is always doing battle with my intuitive side. I have repeatedly asked myself why I did not recognize this myself on my own, without "help" from whatever intelligence or force is behind this phenomena. This was clearly something I needed to know, and yet I was not able to make the breakthrough myself. It had been dropped right into my lap, and yet I missed it. I have accepted this as a part of the learning curve, but I now try to pay more attention to that intuitive voice when I hear it speak to me. I realize now that not all the answers I am seeking will come from intellectual reasoning.

This experience convinced me that I was involved in something very unusual, and it was, ultimately, the incident that put an end to my first marriage.

At some point during my last day in the house, I stood at the top of the stairs, and I sensed a presence. The feeling was quite vivid and very real to me, but I did not see anything and I did not know what it meant.

I carried on with my business, and that was that. I did not sense this presence again for quite some time. However, two years later, something quite unusual happened, and I suspect it may have been the being or spirit from that day when I discovered the 415 link.

I was sitting at my desk when suddenly, out of nowhere, a male voice said, quite clearly and distinctly, "What *are* you doing?" The emphasis was on the word "are" and I immediately interpreted it to mean, *I am disappointed—you're not getting it.*

I have replayed that moment over and over in my mind many times since that day, and I still do not know where that voice came from, or if my interpretation of the question asked of me was correct. Again, the engineer in me began to think technically: I began to muse about how such a voice could be projected in free space, but I knew that this was the wrong approach. The realm of known physics was not the place I needed to visit to understand what had happened.

The questioner had imparted information to me. Yes, a question had been asked, but by the inflection in his voice, I knew that the answer could actually be found within the question itself.

I sensed disappointment, and I knew that I was being told that I was erring in my approach to the mystery.

I had overlooked the 41.5 miles information and I viscerally knew that I was not paying attention to what was truly important.

I was spending days at the computer, typing in ratios and dimensions and locations and measurements—mountains of boring, and perhaps meaningless, information—all the while ignoring the intuitive knowledge being offered to me; the wisdom being presented to me in the fields themselves, each time I visited a new crop circle.

Pay attention, I was being told.

This I knew at my very core.

Pay attention.

Heed your senses. See with your third eye. Listen to your inner voices.

And thus I silenced the engineer, and began to seek the truth. A verse from the Upanishads tells us "He who has found Truth, seeks no more; the riddle is solved...he is at peace." And the Chinese philosopher Lao Tzu tells us "the spiritual and the material, though we call them by different names, in their origin are one and the same. This sameness is a mystery—the mystery of mysteries. It is the gate of all wonders."

Since my experience of being awakened to the power of *knowing* without thinking, I have been trying to truly understand the mystery.

2.10 A New Language?

A friend of mine who is a well-known authority in higher consciousness and the paranormal recently told me that he was convinced that authentic crop formations were a form of friendly communication because the circles were public, gentle, and benign. He told me he believed that a higher intelligence would choose just such a form of communication because it was not threatening or damaging, and it was also a method that did not require advanced education or scientific training to understand. He suggested the possibility that the sum total of the genuine crop circles amounted to a new, unknown language that we would ultimately need to translate to understand.

I was extremely interested in my friend's thoughts and it occurred to me upon reflection that *our own* attempt at communicating with alien life forms (the March, 1972, Pioneer 10 plaque sent into space, currently 7.5 billion miles away from Earth) likewise used symbols and drawings to communicate a message.

I do believe that the authentic crop formations are an attempt to communicate, but I am not convinced that "language" is the right word to describe the means of communication.

Rather, it is a new, symbolic, terralinguistic geography that is intended to arouse emotion, and I wholeheartedly agree with my friend that these symbols are intended to be seen.

They have been deliberately placed in fields of cereal crops—life-giving vegetation that has been planted by man—and because of their placement, they were guaranteed to be seen. The natural growth cycle assures that the farmer and his family and crew will return to the fields to harvest their crops; plus, the open fields guarantee that passersby will also see the huge, beautiful agriglyphs etched into the acreage.

Pictograms are not found in lifeless desert sands, or scratched into cold, inhospitable rocks. They are found in crops that will feed people. And, as we discussed earlier, the plants found in crop circles do not die. They continue to grow, often with increased vitality.

The glyphmakers want to engage us, and now they have. It took us over four centuries to catch on, but now many of us realize we are being "spoken" to. We recognize the crop formations as being the means of communication. And we are working enthusiastically to understand the authors' message.

It has been suggested to me that the designs of all the authentic crop circles in the world constitute pieces of a massive puzzle, and that man has been given the "assignment," so to speak, of collecting the individual pieces, dismissing the hoaxes, assembling the puzzle, and figuring out its meaning.

What I have learned is that there are different crop designs found in different countries around the world, and I suspect that they all may be part of a huge message to all peoples, being parceled out to us in individual sections. The notion of one overall communication may have some validity. No matter how varied the actual formations found in countries other than England (where the majority are still found), we may ultimately learn that the totality of the information is the same everywhere. In less-developed countries, we find that the designs are less complex than in the more industrialized regions of the world.

And what is that information? First and foremost would seem to be the environmental message that the planet is ailing. In all countries, the authentic patterns have arrived as simple geometries that mirror ancient markings. All are identical in design throughout the world.

I contend that this is a deliberate ploy to secure our attention. There is a paradigm in the appearance, presence, and eventual decay or destruction of the crop designs, which I believe illustrates a state of chaos in our natural vegetation, on a global scale.

When one attempts to find meaning in this model, the deterioration of our environment comes immediately to mind. One of the most convincing elements of this archetype is that the exponential rate of deterioration of the individual crops in which patterns appear is mirrored by the rate of degradation of the world's crops—as measured especially by the expanding aggregate of toxic chemicals in our food.

Remember: Many of the designs appear in our world's vegetation that is at greatest risk of damage from environmental impact.

There seems to be a deliberate attempt to make the message understandable, no matter where the crop circles appear.

I have been working for years to gather all the data I can from all over the world, and make this information available to scientists, engineers, researchers, politicians, and other interested parties. I believe it is important to collect all the pieces and make the sum total of the information readily available to anyone who wants to see it.

I do believe that the overall message will only make sense when we see all the pieces of the puzzle.

2.11 To Every Season, Turn, Turn, Turn...

I am frequently asked about what happens to crop circles. Because there is often an emotional component involved for people who have seen, or who have been inside crop circles, there is great interest in their fate when the seasons change. I am asked, "Do farmers simply plow them under?" Is there ever an effort made to permanently preserve crop formations—and is that even possible?

The sequence of events that plays out with the crop circle mystery is all part of nature's way, and, personally, I consider it quite a wonderful cycle.

As we have seen, crop circles and pictograms appear in cereal crops, which means that they are, in a sense, in our food. Life-giving grains are the paints and the earth is the canvas the authors use to form these incredible designs. Nature's way is for seed to be planted, crops to be grown and harvested, and then food to be made with the harvested grain. One cannot help but wonder if this is all part of the plan.

The force creating the authentic crop formations must be cognizant of the cycle of planting, growing, and harvesting; it must be aware of the change of seasons and the cold slumber of the earth in the winter.

Crop formations appear in grown crops where they will be most visible, but where they will soon disappear.

I have always sensed an inherent respect in the crop circle mystery—a respect for this cyclical pattern that results in life-sustaining nourishment.

It is also quite revealing to me—and quite important, I suspect—that some crop designs *re-appear* if the first formation is ignored. We have evidence showing that if someone did not acknowledge a particular formation and photograph it, measure it, and study it, an almost identical design will appear the following growing season.

It is almost as if we are being told silently to look carefully, think clearly, and try to understand. If the genuine formations are, indeed, a symbolic geographic language, then perhaps we are being told we should not skip a page—or a chapter.

Crop formations are erased from the landscape. What is special one day, is removed the next. I think this also signifies that it is not crucial that we understand everything *immediately*. The energy I have personally felt in crop circles is patient. It is positive and respectful of all life. There is nothing aggressive, nothing threatening, nothing frightening. I believe this is intentional, and that the use of the growth cycle as the means of communication is an important part of the message, as well as being the vehicle by which we are being spoken to.

2.12 The Farmers

I am often asked about the farmers on whose fields crop formations appear. How do the farmers respond when a crop circle appears in their crops? Are they angry?

Do they avoid that area of their field, so as to leave it pristine? Do they ever prosecute trespassers when a known hoax formation appears? Do they welcome visitors? Are they resentful of the attention? Or are the majority of them embracing of the phenomenon, if not the trespassing hoaxers?

There are many answers to these questions, and I will discuss them from two perspectives: the early years of the phenomenon, and the way things are today.

In the beginning, the farmers were elated when a crop circle appeared on their land. Farmers felt privileged to have been "chosen," so to speak, and they were genuinely pleased at the sudden manifestation of a crop circle—whether it was a simple circle, or one of the more complex designs. In the early years, farmers considered it an honor.

Farmers would gather their families at the site, and they would call their friends to come and visit the wondrous and beautiful creation that appeared in their fields. I have arrived at the scene of a crop circle to find the farmer ushering friends and family members through the formation, acting almost as a tour guide.

That is still the case today with some farmers, but they are fewer in number as the phenomenon continues, and as it continues to be bastardized by the hoaxers, many of whom are well-organized and persistent.

The crop circle phenomenon has been going on for decades now, with the majority of the formations occurring in the farmlands of central southern England, and the patience of many of the farmers in that area is growing thin.

We live in a world where we expect experts to give us immediate answers. If something happens, we expect round-the-clock TV coverage, constant media attention, and an army of authorities and experts telling us everything we could possibly need or want to know, along with a great deal of information for which we have absolutely no use. A new ailment? Give us the medicine that will cure it. A new disaster? Send in the rescue efforts and then tell us exactly how the tragedy happened.

A mysterious phenomenon? *Explain it.*

And that is where the rules change. Crop circles are real, and while we have many theories to explain them, the experts—including myself—are somewhat baffled by this Earth anomaly, this planetary mystery. We have not been able to provide all the answers to all the questions about this extraordinary enigma.

The crop circles have not gone away. Farmers have improved their security, locked their gates, and put barbed wire around their fields, and yet they still keep appearing. And the farmers' resolve is being tested.

The hoaxers have compounded the problem by treating farmers' private property as public land. And so we have entered phase two of the phenomenon, which is marked by frustration and, in some cases, anger.

The anger comes when people do not respect the land. Here are hard-working men and women trying to make a living off the land, and they have to contend with people tramping through their fields.

Much of the visitors' behavior shows a horrid lack of respect. Crop circle tourists have left gates open and there have been instances where cattle have walked out onto the highways and been killed. There have been cases where tourists have trod over healthy crops with such carelessness that they have damaged or killed the plants.

In addition to the circus in the fields, there is also the question of liability.

Farmers are, in the end, the ones responsible for the safety of the people on their land. When cereal crops are very dry, they are very combustible, and one single dropped cigarette could turn acres of crops into an inferno. One lit cigarette could wipe out 100 acres of ripened wheat in minutes. Fires in the field happen regularly when harvesters overheat, but the difference is that the farmer can usually put it out quickly, and there aren't dozens, or in many cases, hundreds of people milling about at the site of the blaze.

In central southern England, there are patterns that have hundreds of people in them at any one time. People come from all over the world to see them, and it is not too difficult to imagine what goes through a farmer's mind when he sees all these strangers walking through his fields. Many crop tourists are quite a distance away from the road when they are visiting and photographing crop formations. If a fire started, and a wall of flames fed by the ripened wheat began racing across the fields, would the visitors be able to outrun it?

How many would die?

How many would be seriously burned?

How much damage would be done to the crops?

What would be the farmer's personal liability?

Would he lose his farm?

These are the questions that run through farmers' minds these days.

Added to all these liability worries is the added stress of the questions and taunts from friends, relatives, and the public. When a formation appears on a farmer's land, he is often questioned about its authenticity. The media has convinced many people that all crop formations are manmade, and farmers have to deal with those kinds of questions, in addition to the accusations that they are the ones responsible for the formation.

Many of the questions asked of them by friends and the media are outside their realm of expertise. Some farmers are extremely cooperative with researchers and I have been granted very generous accommodations for my work. Sometimes, farmers will harvest around a formation and then allow us in to take our notes and photographs before finishing the field. If they are asked with respect, and we agree to work around their schedule and needs, then many are very helpful.

2.13 Anything for a Price?

As a response to the problem of masses of people wanting to visit crop formations, farmers, of late, have been agreeing to allow visitors on their land, but for a fee.

Many farmers came to the unavoidable conclusion that they needed to have some means of recompense for the damage done to their fields, as well as for the time they had to spend babysitting camera-laden croppies in their fields. They needed to figure out how to manage the large numbers of people and researchers coming onto their land, and many decided to charge people an admittance fee.

As often happens in human endeavors that involve money, the profit motive sometimes takes over. This has happened with some farmers who turned their crop formations into a money-making business.

This has caused problems, finger-pointing, and accusations of profiteering, because most of the farmers who initially began to charge an admission fee said they did so only to recoup their losses. A farmer in Alton Barnes, for instance, sustained damage to his crops worth approximately $650. The formation on his land was one of the first multiple pictograms and he ultimately collected almost $9,000 from members of the public who wanted to see the formation.

Money was made, and it is not an enormous leap to imagine a farmer willingly allowing a hoax formation to be made and then charging people to see it.

I personally know of farmers who have charged crop hoaxers a fee and then allowed them to create a formation on their land. The standard fee has been hovering between $150 and $350. During a recent trip to England, I spoke to one farmer who had allowed crop circle artists to make five formations on his land, and he charged them a little over $300 for each one. The artists needed a place to make them, and they and the farmer worked out a deal. This was all done out in the open and, frankly, I think this is a much better arrangement than crop artists trespassing onto a farmer's land in the middle of the night. In those cases, formations would "mysteriously" appear and then researchers such as myself would need to commit resources—money and people—to researching something which appeared unbeknownst to the farmer.

When a fee is charged and everyone knows what's going on, it allows serious attention—and the commitment of very limited resources—to the genuine crop formations. The artists can do their thing, and we can then devote our efforts to the *real* thing.

Regarding these "art for a price" cases, though, to the best of my knowledge, I have not heard of profit being made from charging people to see it, and in the majority of cases, the work is made solely for the purpose of creating experiential art. This is quite different from deliberately having a formation made, passing it off as real, and charging people to see it.

I do not know of one single case where a farmer has actually encouraged people to come onto his land and make a crop circle for financial gain.

Personally, I fully support farmers charging an access fee to their land. The exchange of money for a service is noble and just, and it allows me and my fellow

This design was discovered during the filming of the movie, A Place To Stay. *This photograph was also chosen by Disney to promote the movie,* Signs.

researchers (as well as the interested public, of course) admittance onto private property without the fear of having a gun pointed at our backside. Money grants permission, and I am grateful for the opportunity to visit important sites, and I am more than happy to compensate the farmer.

2.14 Lighting the Way?

There have been many reports of golden lights seen above fields in which crop circles later appear. Sometimes, the lights are reported above existing crop circles.

What are these lights, and do they have anything to do with the making of crop circles?

These lights, which are known as the Avebury Lights because of their prevalence in the Avebury area of central southern England, are self-luminous and can be seen during the day. They have an amber, or golden color at night, and are approximately 14 inches in diameter. A great deal of film footage exists of these lights and I myself

have five "movies" of them, showing them moving around seemingly purposefully. They have also been captured in still photographs on 35 millimeter film.

They do not simply float; they flit about above the fields and there have been times when I felt like they were reading my mind and responding with specific movements. Sometimes, they appear as silver balls, and I have gotten the impression that they were made of aluminum or stainless steel, or some other flatly reflective white metal.

These lights are so ubiquitous that accounts of them exist in English folklore and there is actually a hill near Alton Barnes, near the East Field in Wiltshire known as "Golden Ball Hill."

We do not have any evidence that these golden lights are involved in creating crop circles. And yet, they seem to be around quite often in areas where crop circles appear. Thus, the evidence is circumstantial and anecdotal, but there certainly does seem to be some kind of association.

Chapter 3

The Undeniable Evidence
Facts in Search of a Theory

3.1 Biology

The plants inside crop circles are changed in a way that is beyond human ability.

—**Joseph E. Mason**

There are definite biological changes to crops taken from crop circle formations believed to be authentic.

William C. Levengood, an eminent biophysicist at the Pinelandia Laboratories in Michigan, has looked at the plants from crop circles from many countries for a number of years. What he has discovered is that the internal structure of the plants is changed at the cellular level, and that the cell pit walls within the structure of the plants are fractured and have expanded. What is important about these findings is that this effect has most assuredly *not* been replicated by human beings tramping on plants.

Along the length of cereal crops are "knuckles" known as nodes. These nodes allow the plant to return to the vertical position if they are somehow placed in the horizontal position during their growth period. These nodes normally expand slightly during growth, and this expansion is a common effect known to farmers all over the world.

The nodal expansion in crops taken from within crop circles is extremely unusual when compared to normal nodal expansion: the ratio of expansion is greatly increased and this effect is specific to crops found in what are believed to be genuine crop formations. This greatly amplified nodal expansion, again, can not be duplicated by counterfeit circlemakers stomping around a field with boards and twine.

According to Levengood, the largest expansion occurs in the center, and to a lesser degree, around the periphery of the circles.

There is a profile of enlargement that is proportional to the profile of the real crop circle from which it was taken. This appears

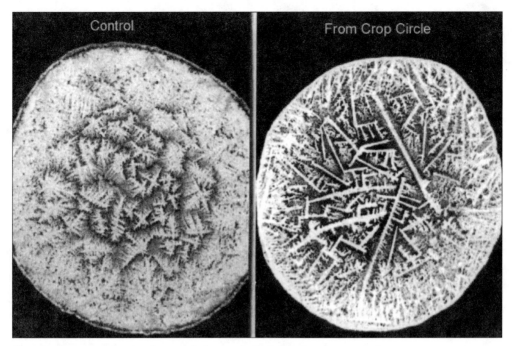

Control | From Crop Circle

The changes seen in starch crystals from plants taken from crop circles.

to be an explicit connection between the geometries of the master circle and the dimensions of the nodal expansion.

And once again, this is not found in hoaxed circles.

Interestingly, Levengood has also determined that there is magnetic material impregnated in some of the plants from authentic crop circles, as well as in the soil taken from around those plants

This magnetic material, to date, has only also been found in a small number of meteorites. This would suggest that the construction of crop circles involves energies from outside our planet and that some high-energy event may have been responsible for impregnating magnetic meteoritic material inside the plants from crop formations.

Levengood has posited that microwave radiation could cause many of the expulsion cavities and nodal changes found in crop circle plant stalks. In fact, as part of his research at the Pinelandia Labs,

Levengood was able to duplicate the specific nodal changes by exposing normal plants to microwaves. However, one element of the changed plants he could *not* duplicate through microwave exposure was the genetic changes to the nodes found in crop circle plants. Further work needs to be done, but the early results seem to indicate that some type of microwave radiation, perhaps a form of energy still not fully understood, may be responsible for the changes in crop circle plants.

Levengood's research has been criticized by skeptics, mostly for the allegation that he has not conducted much of his work in a double-blind manner. Thus, because the very core of his research practices are challenged, any results he obtains are cavalierly dismissed as unreliable.

Closer study of his work is revealing, however, and regardless of the skeptics' immediate rejection of even the possibility of a crop formation being "non-hoaxed," there are distinct and quantifiable results in

Levengood's findings that are *not* found in known hoaxed formations.

There is a great deal in Levengood's work that should be taken seriously. He has written over 50 peer-reviewed papers, and I know for a fact that he does not embark on a research protocol recklessly, or with less than the highest standards of control, monitoring, and recording.

Seed heads collected from plants inside crop circles suspected of being authentic were malformed, and yet often manifested speeded-up germination. Rapid, widespread heating of the nodes is present in crop formations that show no evidence of a human hand.

The negativity of ardent skeptics, in my opinion, does more harm than good. Skeptics proceed from an agenda that states unequivocally that paranormal events are impossible, that they do not happen, and that anyone who believes they do or takes them seriously is at the least, deluded, and at the worst, crazy.

From my experience, I have determined that there are two types of skeptics: Type A and Type B. The Type A's are malfeasant in intent and deliberately interfere with research and progress within any field of endeavor. Their mindset is one of malice, and they work diligently to stifle progress. The Type B's, on the other hand, are open-minded (albeit ardently skeptical), and their input is essential for rational debate.

Why would a scientist of the caliber of William Levengood, the holder of five patents—obviously, a serious man—commit time, resources, and his reputation to studying something that is nothing but a fantasy? Levengood is one of those credible people, and I, for one, am not so ready to dismiss his work and his findings as nothing but a silly waste of time.

Perhaps he does not have all the answers. Perhaps his research could be more

extensive. Perhaps some of his findings are controversial.

But who does have all the answers? The skeptics? I doubt it. And what researcher couldn't use more time and money to expand their work? And if some research results are perplexing and eyebrow-raising, well, isn't that what the quest for truth is all about?

All that said, however, I am doubtful that the truth about the crop circle phenomenon will ever be fully understood using just science. As I state repeatedly throughout this volume, the answers may lie within us, and require looking through the lens of the soul, as well as the lens of the microscope.

3.2 Radiation

Some years ago, the Center for Crop Circle Studies (C.C.C.S.) commissioned a research project in which radiation was measured in crop circles that were believed to be authentic. Some unusual radioactive isotopes were found in a number of these crop circles.

The analysis of the results was done in a U.S. Government laboratory and, after the findings were made public, the prevailing opinion was that they were very unusual and further research was recommended.

And then something odd happened.

Within a few days of the announcement of the findings, the government laboratory that had performed the analysis suddenly backpedaled and announced that a contamination within the laboratory had been discovered, and that they now believed that the results on the isotopic readings were a result of lingering contamination from an earlier experiment.

The tests were not repeated, and I now believe that this clearly is something that needs to be looked at again. Currently, as it stands, the report was nullified by the claim that contamination had resulted in incorrect conclusions.

Personally, I have been carrying a Geiger counter into crop circles for many years, and have yet to discover anything truly unusual.

3.3 Robust uh, Growth?

I would like to discuss briefly one of the more unusual "benefits" attributed to spending time inside crop formations: robust erections.

This has come to be known as the crop circle "Viagra Effect," and there have been men who have reported becoming aroused and achieving an erection while walking through certain crop formations.

These claims have also been made about certain sacred sites in England such as Silbury Hill, which is in the center of "crop circle country." There is speculation among the believers that there is a strong connection to the archetype of the Goddess at Silbury Hill, and that a powerful female energy—reported by both men and women—is present there. I myself have felt this energy while visiting the site.

As for erections, however, I believe that they are purely psychosomatic; that is, they are created by the believer's mind. When someone is told that something *might* be possible, in many cases, this becomes *unquestionably* possible in their mind. And, thus, if someone walks into a crop formation believing that they may get an erection, in many cases they do, indeed, get an erection.

Does this mean that it was caused by the energies in the crop formation? Personally, I tend to doubt it, and I myself have never had that type of physical reaction during any of my visits to the almost 3,000 sites I have been in around the world.

I do know men who have claimed they have gotten erections while standing inside a crop circle, and who completely believe it was caused by the formation, but I think it was due more to their mind than the circle.

3.4 Full Circle

I know of breweries in Connecticut and California in the United States that brew beer from grain harvested from fields in which a crop circle has appeared.

Also, cereal crops in which formations appear are commonly harvested and then used to make bread.

I am often asked if I think there is any potential risk to humans from consuming food and drink made from "crop circle" crops.

Not only do I doubt that these foods can hurt us, I suspect the exact opposite is actually the case. The plants from authentic crop circles are certainly healthier and more vibrant than ordinary plants, and they are larger and have better color and formation. Levengood has conducted research that has shown that crop circle plants can grow up to 40 percent larger than ordinary plants, that their root structure is 40 percent stronger, and their grain is markedly healthier.

So, all that considered, it would seem to me that, if anything, crop circle food and drink might be better for humans than ordinary foods, although, as far as I know, there has not been any scientific testing to support this belief.

I myself have not eaten bread from crop circles, but I drank crop circle beer. The two breweries currently making crop circle beer both use barley plants from East Field crop circles in Wiltshire, England.

Regarding crop circle bread, I recall one particularly unfortunate incident from my career, during which I got into quite a bit of trouble with the British farmers and England's National Farmer's Union.

Back in the late 1980s, I was doing a great many television interviews in England. During one of these interviews, I innocently suggested that perhaps it was not wise to harvest the actual plants from crop circles until we knew more about what was causing the formations and what changes were occurring in the plants. I expressed concern about the possible unknown effects on humans from eating food made with crop circle plants, and I opined that perhaps the farmers should set aside these crops and not sell them for consumption. I took quite a verbal thrashing for that one, and I was accused of scaring the public needlessly, and also of threatening the livelihood of the farmers. Since then, I have been very careful about such statements, and, as I have stated, I have drunk crop circle beer and am no worse for the partaking.

Beer made from grain harvested from a crop circle.

Part II

The Making of a Crop Circle

Madison Square Garden:
Geography

From the year 1678, we have a wood cutting called "The Mowing Devil." The writing that accompanies this carving tells us that a farmer and some local people in a hamlet of Hertfordshire witnessed the devil appearing in a chariot of fire, in a *ball of light*—remember that—from the sky and cutting the farmer's oats into a crop circle. We also have two other references from the late 1600s that are extremely similar.

Around 1923 or 1924, a farmer farming Cheesefoot Head in Southern England, saw four crop circles in the very same field as I saw my first five circles in 1983.

The farmer had seen me on a BBC television program talking about this particular field, and he wrote me a letter teling me that he had had circles in the same field back in 1923.

He was not the first to step forward.

We have had many farmers tell us that crop circles have been appearing on their land for many, many years.

These firsthand, eyewitness accounts validate our data.

This is not random.

There seems to be something important about certain locations.

The same fields are revisited time and time again and, in three specific cases in my files, they appeared on the same identical spot.

Clearly, location is important, but we have not yet discovered why.

Crop circles frequently appear very close to water. I have found a 90 percent correlation between the appearance of crop circles and the existence of underwater aquifers. Also, the vast majority of patterns appearing worldwide are within 40 miles of Stonehenge.

Many, many crop circle formations are conglomerated in that area, a place notable as having the highest level of ancient circular archaeological sites in the world. The design of Stonehenge mirrors many of the basic patterns of crop circles.

Stonehenge itself has, as a design, a crop circle pattern.

Chapter 4

The Theories

Let mystery have its place in you; do not be always turning up your whole soil with the ploughshare of self-examination, but leave a little fallow corner in your heart ready for any seed the winds may bring...

—Henri Frederic Amiel

The Making of a Crop Circle: The Many Theories

There are many theories as to how and why crop circles are appearing on our planet. In this chapter, I will discuss separately the principal and most compelling hypotheses for these enigmatic, unearthly "terran beauty marks."

In no particular order, I will look at the prevailing theories. It is a fact that crop circle manifestations are real and that there is scientific evidence to prove that there are differences between the plants in hoaxed formations and the plants in authentic manifestations. But because crop circles don't really *do anything*—other than appear in the fields and stun the senses with their beauty—science has been loath to commit time and resources toward explaining and understanding them.

Perhaps we are not meant to delve too deeply into the "mechanics" of their formation. Perhaps their purpose is to speak to our souls...

That said, however, here are the most-often cited explanations for the mystery.

- The Gaia theory: plight, warnings, and pleas.
- Magnetism.
- Life-force energies.
- Underground water.
- Microwaves.
- Plasma vortexes and whirlwinds.
- Aliens make them: ETs and UFO landing sites.
- Messages from the dead? Oliver Lodge.
- Government satellites.
- Snow circles and ice rings.
- Crop circles and cattle mutilations: Is there a connection?

4.1 The Gaia Theory: Plight, Warnings, and Pleas

We begin with the theory that Mother Earth herself is actually involved in some way in the construction of crop circles. This theory suggests that the living Earth is communicating through natural energies that can be glimpsed in the complex grid of alignments of sacred sights and areas of paranormal influence around the world known as ley lines.

This theory is based on the Gaia Theory, which was first hypothesized in 1970 by the scientist Timothy Zell, and expanded and refined by the British chemist James Lovelock and U.S. microbiologist Lynn Margulis in 1972. In 1979, Lovelock wrote the seminal book, *Gaia: A New Look at Life on Earth*, which profoundly changed the way scientists, as well as ordinary people, looked at life on earth, and the life *of* the earth.

Is the earth "alive?" Is the planet a functioning life-form that breathes, reproduces, and responds to threats by complex biochemical self-defense mechanisms? And if the answers to these questions are "yes," can crop circles be a conscious— or, at the least, autonomic—response to atrocities committed against the planet by man and all our endeavors? And again, if the answer to the question of whether or not the earth is a living entity is yes, is it possible for the earth to die? What would be the fate of mankind and all the other lifeforms inhabiting this blue planet if that should happen?

The Gaia Theory proposes that our planet is not simply a mass of lifeless rock flying through space; not simply a "lucky accident" in the cosmic scheme of things. In 1929, Russian scientist V. I. Vernadsky foreshadowed the development of the Gaia Theory[1]:

Life appears as a great, permanent and continuous infringer on the chemical "dead-hardness" of our planet's surface....Life therefore is not an external and accidental development on the terrestrial surface. Rather, it is intimately related to the constitution of the Earth's crust, forms part of its mechanism, and performs in this mechanism functions of paramount importance, without which it would not be able to exist.

Is the living planet earth having problems with the support mechanisms that sustain her? From David Orrell's essay, "Gaia Theory: Science of the Living Earth"[2]:

Three billion years ago, bacteria and photosynthetic algae started to remove carbon dioxide from the atmosphere, producing oxygen as a waste product. Over enormous time periods, this process changed the chemical content of the atmosphere— to the point where organisms began to suffer from oxygen poisoning! The situation was only relieved with the advent of organisms powered by aerobic consumption.

Orrell also reminds us that the heat of the sun has increased by almost 25 percent since life began on Earth, and yet the atmospheric temperature has remained approximately the same. How has the earth compensated for such a significant increase in heat, and kept the temperature within the ideal range for all lifeforms on the planet?

Lovelock and Margulis discovered a number of regulatory processes that they described as feedback loops which, in effect, served to cool the planet. One example is the cycle in which soil bacteria removes carbon dioxide from the atmosphere. Soil bacteria is more active in hotter temperatures, so as the sun's heat increased over the eons, soil bacteria increased their activity, the net result of which was a continuous cooling of the planet. Life responded to a threat by adapting its own biochemical processes as a defense mechanism.

If the earth is a living organism, crop circles may be a response to injury. Much the way the human body responds to a wound by exhibiting a welt, or a bruise, or by bleeding (and later, scarring), can the earth be responding to industrial and automotive pollution and other environmental insults and assaults by exhibiting welts or bruises in the form of crop formations? The Gaia Theory is one explanation for the phenomenon.

I find great merit in the Gaia Theory and believe that even if it does not ultimately explain the crop circle phenomenon, it makes an important contribution towards educating the public and making us all more environmentally conscious.

One of my colleagues recently suggested to me that the crop circle hoaxers, along with those who fixate on what percentage of crop formations are fakes and what percentage are real, are completely missing my point. He believes that my environmental concerns are often overlooked in lieu of an obsession with the numbers. I understand his point, and I agree that oftentimes my environmental message takes a back seat to the paranormal aura persistently attached to the crop circle phenomenon.

I think that our attention should be on our wounded planet, and I think that the crop circles may be a way for nature, or some unknown intelligence, to redirect our focus back to the environment—where it used to be by all peoples in the pretechnology eras. In those days, there was a direct link between the environment and life; people knew it, and they respected this. The weather, the land, the animals, the crops, the trees, the waters—all were integral components of survival. Technology has moved modern man several degrees of separation away from this way of life. When there are always loaves of bread on the grocery store shelves—loaves that have been baked, sliced, packaged, and dated for freshness— it is very easy to forget that before the final product of the loaf of bread reached you, cereal crops had to be grown, harvested, ground, baked, and shipped to the baker.

Crop circles appear in plants that will be used for food. This is quite blatant: *Look at these beautiful designs; they are in fields of crops; you will one day eat these crops. Pay attention to that which sustains life.*

Are we learning to respect the planet? Have we learned to use wisely the plants and the animals given to us? I do think that as a species we are thinking more about our actions and their effect on other lifeforms, but I don't think we are doing anywhere near enough.

Today, there are pockets of environmentally-aware communities, both in the United States and around the world, where people recycle, have more respect for trees, and take into account the impact on the foliage and the water when planning buildings and roads. But it is not widespread enough and we need to do more. There is an increased awareness, especially in the Western world, of environmental matters, and this is something we need to cultivate (pun intended) and expand.

My own feelings about the planet go very deep.

I am privileged and honored to be in regular contact with a great many scientists, engineers, politicians, writers, professors, and native peoples in different parts of the world, and from many different walks of life. I hear over and over from these diverse people that the earth is suffering from extraordinary damage. James Gustave Speth is Dean of the Yale School of Forestry & Environmental Studies, and he provided me with the following alarming facts about our planet and the species that inhabit it:

- The rate of extinction of birds and mammals today is estimated to be

100 to 1,000 times the rate that species naturally disappear.

- For 20 years, tropical forests have been cleared at the rate of one acre per second.
- One-quarter of all species of birds are now extinct.
- Half of the available freshwater on earth is being consumed and most people will soon live in water-stressed areas.
- For more than 20 years, 15 million acres of agricultural land has been lost *every year* to desertification and soil degradation.
- An estimated half of the world's wetlands have been destroyed.
- Forty years ago, 5 percent of the marine fisheries were overfished. Today, that figure has risen to 70 percent.
- Industrial processes that fix nitrogen at rates that exceed nature's has resulted in 50 oxygen-starved ocean dead zones, including one in the Gulf of Mexico the size of New Jersey.
- Professor Jane Lubchenco, newly elected president of the International Council of Scientific Unions recently stated, "The trajectory we are on is not sustainable. We are definitely destroying the life systems of the planet."

And speaking of native peoples, approximately 15 years ago, the Kogi people came down from their mountain in South America where they had lived for centuries, to meet with a journalist from the BBC. This was the first time in 300 years that they had spoken to their "Younger Brother," which was their term for the white man.

They came down to report that snow had stopped falling on their mountaintops. They desperately need this snow for water, irrigation, and other life support purposes. Because of this, the tribe had to relocate, and one of the members spoke to a reporter to express their deep concerns for the health of the planet. The Kogi believe that all the terrible changes occurring on the planet are from the actions of Younger Brother. These people have never taken up arms and are a very quiet, spiritual people. For them to take such a drastic step as leaving their mountain and speaking to those in civilization, their fears and concerns had to have been profound indeed.

I share their view.

We now see that it is not just those mountains in South America. Climatic changes are accelerating at an extraordinary rate. We are damaging our home.

I feel very deeply about this. Ten years ago, I was optimistic that a new thinking was taking hold; a new environmental awareness that would spur critical changes—and hopefully before it was too late.

Today, I am sorry to say that I have an intuitive sense that it might now *be* too late.

Around the world, temperature and precipitation records are being broken every day. Have we upset the fragile ecological balance necessary to sustain life for the long term?

Our planet is under attack. And I reject the placations of those who tell us we are simply in a turbulent period of a natural cycle and that the earth has been through this before, and it will adapt as it has in the past. We have the data. The earth has never been through what it is going through now—the pollution, the toxic emissions, the excessive extinctions. This is something different, and to fix it is going to require a major change in our thinking as a species—

what is known as a paradigm shift. A new generation of politicians must take the reins and assure the survival of mankind and all our allied species.

The British movie *A Place to Stay*, (which is reviewed in this volume), makes the point that the earth is the place where we must stay—there is nowhere else to go right now and, so, if we destroy this home of ours, where will we live? The day may come where we colonize other planets and have several more "places to stay," but right now, this is it.

There is a theory of late that posits that we quite simply *cannot* harm our planet beyond repair. Why? Because the oil we burn is from dinosaurs who died and became part of the ecology. Thus, this theory goes, we are doing nothing more than *extremely* long-term recycling. Anything we pump into the ecosphere, no matter how it has been changed, is still part of the biological aggregate and, therefore, cannot hurt the planet, or anything living on it. It is a closed loop, according to this theory.

Much of this makes perfect sense. But this closed loop theory requires a self-contained, closed atmosphere within which cycles repeat over and over. And that is where this theory comes undone. Manmade chemical compounds—combinations of elements not found in nature—are thinning the ozone layer that protects us from ultraviolet rays. This adds an unknown variable to the equation and opens the closed loop.

The fully analyzed 2001 data shows the most serious situation to date over the Arctic. There was a minor positive deviation in 2000, but the mean curve is negative overall. This speaks powerfully to the serious degradation of the ozone layer, and the potential—and still not-fully-known consequences—of such deterioration.

Almost the entire continent of Australia is, today, almost completely exposed to ultraviolet radiation because of the hole in the ozone layer above it. I think this is an extremely serious situation and one that is often either minimized or ignored by both scientists and politicians. And the average person couldn't care less about the hole in the ozone layer. It does not affect his or her daily life. And that is true.

But what happens when this exposure to UV rays takes its toll, and we start to see the worst droughts in history, devastating floods that seemingly come out of nowhere, and extreme storm periods unlike any we have seen before, not to mention the real possibility of serious birth defects?

And we are not talking about a century from now. We are talking about major ecological and environmental problems for our grandchildren, and their children.

Whether or not the Gaia Theory is the true explanation, or, in fact, the *only* explanation for crop circles has yet to be determined. But there is great merit, and long-term benefit, in opening the door to the notion that Mother Earth might be trying to tell us something. I do think it is in our best interest to listen.

4.2 Magnetism

Another theory that attempts to explain crop circles involves the earth's magnetic fields.

Over a period of five years, and continuing today, I have been conducting magnetometer surveys in the proximity of crop circles and inside the circles themselves.

I have been measuring the earth's magnetic field in circles in central southern England and, in a small number of circles, we have recorded increases in the earth's magnetic field by approximately 120 percent.

Incredibly, that increase, when mapped out by computers, shows the same magnetic fingerprint—the identical profile—as the crop design over which it has been measured.

This is very significant.

These findings have allowed us to calculate that the dipoles—the pair of electric charges of equal magnitude but opposite polarity that would produce that level of magnetism—are buried at 20 feet below ground or, surprisingly, suspended 20 feet above the ground.

The level of magnetism we recorded was maintained for a period of several days. This was not a momentary event. It occurred over a period of time. We could see nothing in the sky, and the British Ministry of Defense did not permit us to excavate that particular parcel of land, so we were unable to determine with certainty the source of the magnetism.

Localized fluctuations in the earth's magnetic field are thought to be a major element in the creation of crop circles. This theory presumes that there is also some kind of unknown energy field—perhaps a "brother" to magnetism—that is also at work and is the actual force that flattens the plants.

As we have seen, unusually high levels of magnetism have been measured inside some crop circles which, when mapped out into a distribution profile, resembles the actual crop circle design in which it was measured.

There is speculation that a high rate of rotational acceleration of this magnetic anomaly creates a force that creates crop circles.

There is concrete evidence to support this theory. It is a known fact that plants thrive and that their growth rates increase inside elevated magnetic fields. Also, many human beings can detect magnetic fields. It is thought that these "human magnetometers" have this ability due to the iron content within their human hemoglobin, which is constantly provided to every cell in the human body through the blood. They detect and interpret magnetism as feelings of well-being and, in some cases, they manifest improved health, or even healings. Even the glowing "globes" described by some crop circle witnesses, and which many believe to be UFOs, could be accounted for by this process.

One of the common arguments against the magnetism theory is that, if it were true, then we would have had manifestations and accounts of crop circles throughout all of recorded history, not just in the past few hundred years.

At first glance, this does have some semblance of sense and logic, but on deeper analysis, we find that there are flaws with this argument.

My challenge hinges on the fact that the earth today is not the same as it was hundreds and thousands of years ago. We do not have *all* the facts regarding ancient geology, the state of the primeval ecosphere, and exactly what the climate was like before recorded history, but we have certainly acquired a great deal of information from the ice cores, the fossil record, and from scientific models.

One conclusion we can state with certainty is that thousands of years ago, the planet earth was not in the state it is today.

There is something new going on.

The climate is mutating; the environment is changing at an accelerated rate, and this change can be seen in the composition of the ice cores, located around the world at both poles, and in Greenland, China, Russia, and South America.

The United States Geological Survey describes the mountain of information recorded in ice cores:

> *Ice cores contain an abundance of climate information—more so than any other natural recorder of climate such as tree rings or sediment layers. Although their record is short (in geologic terms), it can be highly detailed. An ice core from*

the right site can contain an uninterrupted, detailed climate record extending back hundreds of thousands of years. This record can include temperature, precipitation, chemistry and gas composition of the lower atmosphere, volcanic eruptions, solar variability, sea-surface productivity and a variety of other climate indicators.

It is the simultaneity of these properties recorded in the ice that makes ice cores such a powerful tool in paleoclimate research....Over the past decade, research on the climate record frozen in ice cores from the polar regions has changed our basic understanding of how the climate system works. Changes in temperature and precipitation which previously we believed would require many thousands of years to happen were revealed, through the study of ice cores, to have happened in fewer than 20 years.

These discoveries have challenged our beliefs about how the climate system works. We have been required to search for new, faster mechanisms for climate change and we have begun to consider the interaction between industrial man and climate in light of these newly revealed mechanisms.[3]

One of the valuable pieces of information we have acquired from our study of the ice cores is that carbon dioxide (CO) levels in the atmosphere are higher in the past 30 years than they have been in the past 500,000 years. The topmost centimeters of the ice cores show this and, while we do not know precisely what the long-term effect of this increase in CO_2 will be on the biosphere and on human survivability on earth, the fact that such a monumental change in the environment has happened within an infinitesimally small (in geologic terms) period of time cannot, in this researcher's opinion, bode well.

And this also bolsters my argument that it is impossible to make judgements about the possible existence of crop circles in the distant past, based on the state of the planet today.

It has long been my contention that the recent crop manifestations are a sign, and perhaps a symptom of a major, and perhaps tragic, change in the earth's biological health.

I myself am an electrical engineer, and I have consulted with physicists, paleobiologists, and other scientists, and we are all in agreement that the earth's magnetic field alone cannot be causing the plants in crop circles to collapse to the ground in swirled, sometimes complex patterns. There is obviously some other element to the equation, again, perhaps that unknown brother to magnetism, or some type of byproduct of magnetism that combines with other earth forces to provide the lateral force necessary to create these designs. This is one theory, and we may ultimately learn that it goes hand in hand with the Gaia Theory and that the final, persistent message is that the earth—and every living creature on it—is in danger.

A moving magnetic field will induce a current and if that current has some other type of energy applied to it, it can achieve lateral movement that could cause plants to collapse in an organized manner.

But what is this unknown "other type of energy?" Intelligence, perhaps?

And as I mentioned earlier, I was stunned to discover that in one case, a magnetometer reading I took within a specific crop circle was a mirror image of the design of the crop pattern itself. This was astonishing and baffling at the same time.

So there is some kind of as yet unidentified distortion going on, in which the earth's magnetic field is manipulated, perhaps deliberately, to cause rapid lateral movement of the energy waves and cause plant collapse within seconds.

4.3 Life Force Energies

Another theory, and yet another corollary to the Gaia hypothesis, is that esoteric, indefinable forces commonly described as "life force energies" are creating the patterns. This theory states that anything and everything that is alive—human beings, animals, insects, plants, and indeed the planet itself—in some way sustain life on earth by working with an interconnected life force energy, and that when any one component of this complex paradigm is in significant danger of not being able to adequately sustain itself, there is a reaction, part of which could be the appearance of crop circles.

Austrian physician Wilhelm Reich (1897–1957) identified this vital life force as orgone energy, and he believed it was the force that explained all processes in the biosphere—from gravity to nuclear energy.

The life force theory suggests that the human race as a species, being the dominant life form on the planet, and having the most complex and sophisticated morphology, somehow recognizes, at a subconscious level, that the earth is in danger, and that all life on the planet is threatened. We somehow sense this in our primal forebrain, in our primeval limbic system where there is sense memory of our earliest genetic existence. Crop circles are, in this way, constructs created by our subconscious and with interplay from other lifeforms, in response to perceived threats to our aggregate existence. Orgone is the energy permeating everything and perhaps the collective unconscious is manipulating this energy to create crop patterns for a multitude of urgent reasons.

4.4 Underground Water

Another theory is that the large reservoirs of underground water in the earth's geo-structure, all of which expand and contract depending on the amount of rain that falls, create a static charge that builds up and ultimately discharges at surface level, and that the configuration of these specific electrical charges create the crop circle patterns.

In recent history, this expansion and contraction rate has been greater due to global warming and changes in the weather systems, and this increased volatility of water levels may be responsible for anomalous electrical discharges. Crop circles could be an effect of these discharges, much the way desert winds create patterns in sand dunes.

There is supporting evidence for this theory, specifically the fact that an overwhelming majority of the authentic crop formations around the world manifest in very close proximity to underground aquifers.

4.5 Microwaves

One of the most intriguing theories regarding the formation of crop circles is the theory that microwave radiation is responsible for the changes found in the nodes of plants in crop formations. Microwave radiation is suspected as causing the explosion or swelling of the nodes of individual stalks of crop circle plants and vegetation.

Microwaves—which are between infrared and shortwave radio waves—are high-frequency electromagnetic waves, one millimeter to one meter in wavelength.

Low levels of microwaves are emitted from almost everything on earth. It has been demonstrated, for instance, that if two tin cans are placed next to each other, they will connect to each other with straight lines of microwave radiation. Likewise, trees can link to other trees using microwaves, and people can sometimes subliminally communicate with each other without speaking through the unconscious, yet quite real, exchange of low levels of microwaves. Have you ever felt like someone was looking at you and when you turned, someone was? Some researchers believe that in instances such as these, the "watcher" is emitting trace amounts of microwave radiation that is being received by the person being watched. Something autonomic is triggered and a message is sent to the brain telling us we are being observed, and that we need to evaluate this monitoring as either being a threat, or as being harmless.

At these levels, however, it is unlikely that there would be enough microwave energy in nature to cause plants to collapse. Also, microwaves do not move laterally with force, and lateral movement and patterning is commonly seen in crop circle formations.

Microwaves could be responsible for the swollen, or exploded nodes of plants from crop formations. The microwaves could rapidly heat the moisture locked inside a plant node and cause it to boil and blow out the node.

But is there an identified process in nature that could generate enough microwave radiation to create a crop circle? No.

Therefore, it is my opinion that even if microwaves are involved in some manner—its presence suggested by the exploded nodes—microwaves in and of themselves are not strong enough to bend crops and create a pattern.

Some interesting experiments have been conducted with plants and microwave ovens. Plants have been placed in a microwave and, when the oven was turned on and the plate rotated (thereby creating lateral movement), the plants did bend themselves into a spiral pattern. But the plants died, and there is also nothing in nature that can create the concentrated levels of microwave radiation emitted by a microwave oven. In the fields, the plants do not die.

4.6 Plasma Vortices and Whirlwinds

Another theory is that meteorological atmospheric vortices—some previously unknown, weird new whirlwinds—are responsible for the formations. This theory likewise ties into the Gaia Theory since it is generally assumed that these pattern-forming vortices are a manifestation and response of a changing global environment; a damaged, struggling environment. The vortices most commonly credited with the creation of formations are water and plasma.

Water vortices are air and water in a rapidly spinning whirlwind carried across the land, leaving behind circles and other patterns in the cereal crops.

Plasma vortices are spiraling columns of electrified air which, on impact with the vegetation, likewise create patterns. The analogy for this process would be electrocution. The plasma vortex electrocutes the plants into a circular form, the source of the final design ultimately being a natural meteorological phenomenon.

But, realistically, can such an unfocused, intermittent meteorological event be responsible for any crop patterns beyond the simplest of circles? Probably not, and yet there is enough evidence, most of which has come from Dr. Terence Meaden, to credit these vortices with some of the plain, unadorned circles.

4.7 Aliens Make Them: ETs and UFO Landing Sites

There has long been a great deal of speculation that crop circles are formed when alien spacecraft—be they visible or invisible—land in fields. In fact, the earliest appearance of crop circles in Australia were originally called "saucer's nests" because of this belief.

I myself have not seen or interviewed anyone that can provide evidence that UFOs are actually responsible for the creation of crop circles. However, that said, there are many reports and a number of very impressive films showing spheres approximately 14 inches in diameter moving in the fields where crop circles have already formed. I don't believe this is at all coincidental. These particular spheres are rarely seen outside of crop circle fields. There is one case, which will be discussed later in this volume, where a man claims to have seen these spheres actually making crop circles.

I do not think we yet have the evidence that UFOs are making crop circles, but there is definite evidence—both on film and by eyewitnesses—that they are in the proximity and appear to be "showing an interest" in what's occurring.

There are approximately 50 eyewitness accounts by people who claim to have seen crop circles forming. I have interviewed many of them, and none claim to have seen UFOs in the sky when the crop circles form. A CIA remote viewing project in which the participants all had documented remote viewing abilities, concluded that the crop patterns are intended to serve as "sign posts," informational postings by one extraterrestrial species to another and that human beings actually have no part in the phenomenon whatsoever. That particular experiment concluded that crop formations are not intended for we Terrans. Of course, that conclusion has been challenged by other theories.

I would rule out the notion of complex crop circles being formed as a physical impression in a field created by the landing of a UFO, although we cannot conclusively rule out the possibility that some simple, single circles could have been created by the landing of a craft.

Another theory is that extraterrestrial beings are making crop circles.

The authentic crop formations boast of intelligent design. There is no denying that. The earth's *real* crop circles, the ones that appear in astonishingly brief periods, and which show no evidence of crop destruction, appear to be well thought out and deliberately designed. There are some who contend that aliens are the architects and authors of these formations, and that they have somehow always been involved with the phenomena. The belief is that the crop circles are some form of communication from an extraterrestrial species. If this is the case, the extraterrestrials' message is still being erratically communicated and is undeniably ambiguous.

4.8 Messages From the Dead?

Another theory, which is a relatively new line of thought and actually quite bizarre in my opinion, is that crop formations are communications from the dead. The emergence of this theory may simply be a response to the ongoing popularization of talking to the dead, commonly seen in books by self-described psychics and channels such as James Prager and John Edward. Prager writes books in which he reports on his conversations with the deceased, and John Edward hosts a very popular television show on which he delivers messages to audience members from their departed loved ones.

Is there any validity to this theory as it relates to crop formations? Mathematicians assert that the dead are creating crop circles in specific geometric ratios to get our attention. Eventually, the theory goes, a code will emerge from the various authentic formations that will reveal something of great import to mankind. Thus, the dead are acting as couriers of some important message for the living. Obviously, this theory needs continuing investigation, as well as some hard evidence for it to be considered a viable hypothesis.

Oliver Lodge

There is some evidence, however, in the story of Oliver Lodge and his possible posthumous communication using crop circles, that bolsters the credibility of this theory. Lodge was a scientist and spiritualist who demonstrated the possibility of transmitting radio waves, work which led to Marconi's development of true wireless communication. Lodge believed in the survival of the self after death.

In the article in this volume, "Diatonic Ratios in Crop Circles" by Gerald Hawkins, we learn of the relationship between the dimensions of crop circles and the Western musical scale. Professor Hawkins also expanded his research into the diatonics found in crop circles by taking the musical notes he had decoded in the circles depicted in my book *Circular Evidence*, and applying letters to the notes, using a method known as the Boethian Method, named for the fifth century Roman philosopher, Boethius.

This system of encoding—applying letters to musical notes and concealing them within a composition—has been used by musical composers for centuries. In fact, in Johann Sebastian Bach's final fugue, he hid the letters B-A-C-H repeatedly. When Hawkins applied the Boethian to crop circles, he came up with a set of initials over and over. The initials were "O.L." Later, he also learned that other sets of initials that he had "translated" belonged to colleagues of Lodges, including several board members of the spiritualist organization he founded.

Was this Oliver Lodge attempting to speak to us from the beyond using crop circles as the "instrument" of communication? Lodge had stated emphatically throughout his life that he would communicate with the world after his death. Are the "O.L." initials his? And if so, what is Lodge trying to tell us?

4.9 Government Satellites

Another theory that has been mentioned lately, and which has not been conclusively disproved, is that government satellites—high-tech satellites in orbit all around the world, launched by many governments—are projecting an energy that constructs crop patterns.

Personally, I do not believe that governments are involved with the phenomena for one very simple reason: the crop circles phenomenon pre-dates airborne technology by centuries. Crop formations were here long before man invented the satellite.

Let's put aside the anachronistic problems with this theory for a moment, though. The notion of governments deliberately beaming some kind of energy ray into cereal crop fields to create complex geometric patterns begs the question, "Why?" What could a government gain from such an exercise?

- Would it provide a strategic edge in global politics? No.
- Would it provide some type of military advantage? No.
- Would there be economic benefits to be gained? No.

Would crop circles and the resulting discussions and investigations further some long-range plan of one or more governments that warranted the time and expense to create them? Possibly, but if this is the case, there haven't been any stunning revelations that would support this theory. If "government-made" crop circles ultimately convinced a population that money should be spent to defend it from some unknown extraterrestrial threat, then conceivably such a plan could be underway, but thus far, my conclusion is that this theory is nothing but conspiracy-tinged speculation with no evidence whatsoever to support it.

4.10 Snow Circles and Ice Rings

Snow circles and ice rings, both of which are quite rare, have been discovered in the mountains of Turkey and Afghanistan, in Canada and Germany, and in the United States on the frozen Charles River outside the Massachusetts Institute of Technology (MIT).

Snow circles manifest visual similarities to crop circles, except that instead of plants bending over and forming a geometry, snow or ice is displaced to form a recognizable geometric pattern.

One of the most complex ice rings to date is the aforementioned design on the Charles River. The river froze, and a thin layer of snow covered the ice.

MIT Professor John C. Marshall, quoted in the February 24, 1993, issue of the MIT publication *Tech Talk*, stated, "One of us ventured onto the ice and...in the bitter cold we started speculating about what was happening. These speculations included: frozen-in eddies spawned by the sluggish flow of the Charles over the bottom, point sources of effluence issuing from submerged pipes, wind driven patterns akin to the 'crop-circle' phenomenon common in the summer in Wiltshire, England..."

These theories notwithstanding, many of us believe that the ice rings on the Charles River were part of the same phenomenon as the crop circles. Other than the "wind-driven" component of his speculation, two of Dr. Marshall's theories involve the movement of the river. In February 2001, a perfect ice ring formed on a small pond near Churchill, Maryland. The formation measured approximately 30 feet across and consisted of a ring with a spur extending from its outer edge. Apparently, this design was very similar to a pictogram which appeared in a barley field in Hampshire, England in 1987.

In 1998, several ice rings and snow circles appeared and were photographed in Germany, and the photos show quite clearly that the circles are in an expanse of virgin snow, in that a footprint would be quite visible.

4.11 Crop Circles and Cattle Mutilations: Is There a Connection?

Some of the more speculative (and, truth be told, imaginative) members of the UFO and crop circle communities have suggested that there may be a connection between the appearance of crop circles and the mysterious cattle mutilations that occur on some farmers' land.

I would like to state unequivocally for the record that I do not believe there is even the remotest link between the two phenomena. In fact, I think they are diametrically opposed to each other, in both purpose and in energies utilized.

In all my years of research, I have come across only one incident in which the mutilated carcass of a cow was found on a farmer's land in proximity to a crop circle. I myself have personally investigated firsthand over 2,500 crop formations and have never come across a cattle mutilation.

In the case I am referring to, a farmer in the United States reported that one of his cows had been eviscerated in the manner most often associated with the phenomena (and most often credited to UFOs): its blood had been removed, there were well-defined, surgical incisions that were done with high heat, believed to be a laser, and the cow's internal organs had been removed all the

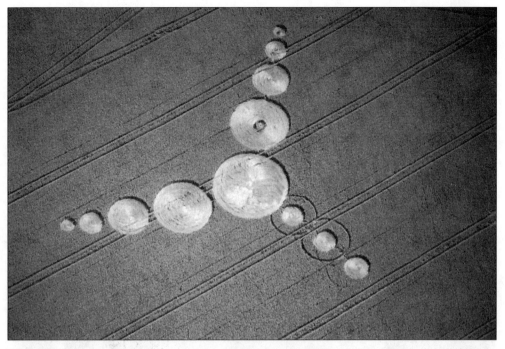

This unusual and impressive crop geometry was found by a farmer near Collingbourne Ducis, Wiltshire during the summer of 2000. It was in an area new to crop circles.

way down to their nerve attachments. There was a single crop circle nearby, within a hundred feet or so, but the carcass was not in the circle itself.

I consider this single event—out of a reported 10,000 crop formations around the world—to be nothing but a coincidence and totally unrelated to the crop circle phenomenon. As I said earlier, the energies are quite at odds with each other. The forces behind cattle mutilations are dangerous, harmful, and callous towards life. The crop circles are pastoral, benign, and beautiful.

I refuse to consider that the two could in anyway be linked.

Notes

[1] V. I. Vernadsky. *La Biosphere.*
[2] *www.gaianet.fsbusiness.co.uk/ gaiatheory.html*
[3] United States Geological Survey

Chapter 5

Location, Location, Location:
A Crop Circle Gazetteer

*Until we accept the fact that life itself is founded in mystery,
we shall learn nothing.*

—**Henry Miller**

5.1 Crop Rotation

A great many countries on Earth report the appearance of crop circles. There is one exception, however: the countries of South Africa. There are no reports of crop formations from that country. It is not known if this is because of governmental and media censorship, or the actual dearth of crop manifestations.

Crop circles are reported in just about every other country, including Russia, the whole of Europe, North and South America, Canada, Australia, New Zealand, and elsewhere.

In many cases, though, the reports come to us too late for any meaningful research to be done. Often, by the time we hear of a crop formation in a distant country, it has already been plowed under. This is unfortunate, but I am encouraged by the improvements in the reporting system that have been occurring of late. The Internet has been a huge influence in rapid dissemination of new information, and television continues to be a valuable tool. It has been, overall, a slow process, but I am optimistic for the future of the "reporting" network.

A new and growing awareness of the phenomenon is reaching even distant places these days thanks, in part, to American television shows such as *Unsolved Mysteries*, which are syndicated all over the world.

This geographic distribution speaks volumes regarding the claims of hoaxers.

No less a luminary than the United Kingdom's scientific adviser to the Queen commented that in order for all the crop formations found around the world to have been hoaxed, there would need to be a highly organized, well-funded, worldwide conspiracy, and there are, quite frankly, very few in either camp—believers or skeptics—who would accept such a far-fetched notion.

Let us play devil's advocate, however, and stipulate that a worldwide plot to create crop circles does exist. This suggests one simple question: What's the point? What would be the point of such an effort? Until the global hoaxers step forth and provide a rational answer to that question, logic tells us that such a theory is balderdash.

•••

This gazetteer provides details on dozens of countries around the world where crop circles have appeared in the past several decades. There are over 3,200 crop circles accounted for here and this total comprises the documented formations in the Circles Phenomenon Research International (CPRI) database. The actual worldwide total of crop formations is believed to be approximately triple this number.

Sometimes I feel that the earth is a canvas on which the crop circle authors are painting their signs of warning. The regular appearance of crop circles all over the world would seem to substantiate this notion.

(**NOTE**: The countries are listed in descending order of appearances.)

5.2 England
1,784 recorded crop formations

The vast majority of reports in England come from a circular area extending 40 miles out from its center point at Stonehenge. Every year, from late April until early September, circles are reported, and as many as 15 in a single day have been discovered. During the early 1960s through around 1978, only single circles

appeared. In 1978, the first quintuplet set was found, and during 1986, the first circles with rings were discovered.

From May 1990 through today, complex patterns are routinely found. As might be expected, a high level of hoaxing is also commonplace in England, although it is unlikely that crop circle counterfeiters could account for the vast array of formations.

5.3 United States of America
228 recorded crop formations

The first reports of crop circles in the United States that made the official database came from farmers who watched a 1989 broadcast of *Unsolved Mysteries*, the first in-depth television coverage of the mystery in United States.

Subsequent research has uncovered single circles and single rings across the United States from 1952 through 1989. The first complex design appeared in 1990, the same year as such a pattern appeared in the United Kingdom. Most of the complex patterns in America tend to be sloppy and irregular, and are likely manmade.

That said, however, a genuine crop formation appeared in Lyle Spiesschaert's wheat field in Forest Grove, Oregon during the summer of 2002. The formation consisted of three connected circles topped by a crescent with an attached key-shape appendage. Biophysicist William Levengood investigated the formation and concluded that it was genuine. In an interview with Lisa Waggoner in the *Hillsboro Argus*, Levengood ticked off the evidence for authenticity:

• Magnetic particle deposits higher than the average of the controls (control areas). Soil within the circle had over 90 times the upper limit found in normal soil.

Close-up of an insect "melted" onto a stalk from a crop circle plant.

- (Wheat) node expansions greater than average of control sets. Of 44 formation sets of wheat stalks, 36 had greater node expansions.

- A strong resemblance between its F-shaped downed area and wave guides, constructed metal tubes used to efficiently direct microwaves or ultra-high frequency energy.

- Linear lay patterns in the F-shaped area, rather than circular lay patterns as within the circular formation.

- Significantly suppressed seed germination from plants taken from within the crop circle, compared to plants outside it.

Some media skeptics in the area suspected the formation had been made in conjunction with the release of the movie *Signs*, but Levengood's findings put the suspicions and hoaxer's claims to rest.

5.4 Canada

135 recorded crop formations

Crop circles in Canada have generally evolved similarly to those in the United Kingdom, with simple circles and rings appearing back in the 1950s, and the first complex design appearing in 1989.

Several dead porcupines have been discovered in Canadian crop circles. Manitoba, Saskatchewan, and Alberta are the hot spots and, in most years, there are reports from these provinces.

5.5 Germany

105 recorded crop formations

There are very few reports from Germany of simple circles, and that is unusual. Most of the reports are of complex designs. The very first report of a crop circle in Germany did not come until 1990, and that *was* a simple circle. In 1998, Germany's peak year for crop circles, more than 25 formations appeared over a period of several months.

The most famous—and the strangest—crop circle report coming out of Germany told of three metallic plates found by a man with a metal detector under a large complex crop pattern near the small town of Grasdorf. The gold, silver, and bronze plates were approximately 12 inches in diameter and one inch thick and on the top of each plate, the design of the crop pattern beneath which they were found was molded into the metal. The pictogram included symbols that came from German antiquity. Was it all an elaborate hoax? Or were the plates somehow connected to the appearance of the crop formation? I myself held two of the plates in my hand and they were unquestionably authentic. The gold plate was melted down before further research into the engraving on their surfaces could be undertaken.

5.6 Australia

71 recorded crop formations

Some of the earliest reports of crop circles in Australia came during 1966, and most were associated with official UFO eyewitness reports. In fact, many of the crop circles reported during this period were described as "saucer nests," since many in Australia believed they were evidence of UFO landing sites.

Since those first reports, many simple circles have been found, but not one complex pattern has ever appeared in the country, and that is unusual.

In contrast, the largest manmade crop design ever constructed is in an Australian desert. It is called the *Marree Man* (See pattern No. T691 in the *Andrews Catalogue* in this volume); it is two and a half miles wide; and it is visible from outer space. (This design joined the short list of manmade structures visible from orbit. The Great Wall of China is on this list.)

In 1971, a former Member of the Australian Parliament discovered the body of

These small crop circles were just a handful of hundreds filmed across the English countryside in 1989.

his missing son next to a crop ring at Tellebang, Queensland.

There is a very high level of UFO reports associated with crop circles in Australia.

5.7 The Netherlands

62 recorded crop formations

In 1997, two intricate crop patterns appeared in the Netherlands, followed within weeks by another 22 reports of formations. There have been fewer reports in recent years. A very active location is Hoeven, Noord-Brabant.

5.8 Hungary

23 recorded crop formations

Single circles have been reported almost exclusively in Hungary, except for the report of a crop triangle in 1992. The peak year for Hungary was 1992, which was approximately one year after a flurry of activity in the United Kingdom.

5.9 Japan

19 recorded crop formations

The first report of a crop circle in Japan occurred in 1977 near Nakanom, and this formation appeared in a rice paddy.

It was not until 1991, when a formation was discovered in a wheat field, that a circle appeared in cereal crop.

Several simple circles have been discovered in long grass, but most of the crop formations in Japan are found in rice paddy fields.

On one occasion during 1990, two designs appeared adjacent to each other, making it the most complex formation to date. The designs consisted of a single circle and a circle with a concentric ring around it. Japan's crop formations are generally very simple in comparison to those appearing in many other countries.

The numbers of reported formations has been falling since 1991, which was Japan's peak year. Interest in the subject is very big in Japan. Numerous in-depth television programs air regularly and cover developments around the world.

5.10 Wales

15 recorded crop formations

Wales is a principality of the United Kingdom on the western peninsula of the island of Great Britain. Even though it is part of the British mainland, Wales reports far fewer crop circles than in England.

The terrain in Wales is not conducive to crop circles. The country's landscape is strewn with large hills and mountains that cover much of its geography.

During 1989, an American visitor took a photograph of a field with two circles in

it from the top of Goodrich Castle. When the film was developed, there was a strange blood-red ball on the print very close to the circles. The ball had not been visible to the photographer when he snapped the picture. Interestingly, similar "invisible" objects have been seen on photographs taken in crop circles elsewhere over the years.

5.11 France

13 recorded crop formations

Mostly simple circles have ever been recorded in France, and the number of reports have been minimal, with the first stretching back to 1954. A complex pattern, believed to be the first one in the country, was reported in 2002.

Aside from the dearth of formations, though, there have been some odd crop circle-related occurrences in France. One day in 1964, sometime during the early morning hours, two neighbors witnessed a single circle forming at St. Souplet. The circle formed in a back garden and the two neighbors were awakened by a strange, very loud sound as a bright light moved into the garden. Their bedroom windows were shattered into small pieces of glass and pulverized powder during this event. The circle that appeared after the sound and light was reported to be in a plot of spinach.

5.12 Scotland

12 recorded crop formations

Most of the crop patterns in Scotland are believed to be manmade. One particular formation was reported by a man who claimed to have witnessed it form, and who later infiltrated the crop circle research groups and made himself known to me as a CIA operative. This man's "eyewitness" claim is thought to be a cover for his clandestine intelligence activities. The full account of this incident appears on the DVD

Ultimate Crop Circles: Signs from Space (Central Park Media).

5.13 Switzerland

12 recorded crop formations

Since 1972, there have been sporadic reports of simple circles and designs from different regions in Switzerland. There were three reports of formations in 2002, which was the most reports from Switzerland in a single year. No complex designs have been reported.

5.14 Czech Republic

11 recorded crop formations

It was not until August 1994 that the first crop formation in the Czech Republic was reported. Over the next two years, there were another half a dozen reports with increasing regularity, until the number of reported formations peaked at 16 separate patterns and simple circles during 1999. There has been a steady decline since that year. The largest formation to be reported was 315 feet long (96 meters), at Nemilkov on July 28, 1996.

5.15 Austria

8 recorded crop formations

There have been very few discoveries of crop formation in Austria, but the ones that have been reported were very similar to the designs found in England. Several simple patterns have actually been identical to British formations, with a similar quality of precision.

5.16 Italy

8 recorded crop formations

Only simple circles and single rings have been discovered in Italy. Most of these were reported during the 1980s and there has been no trend towards evolving complexity, and no reported hoaxing.

5.17 New Zealand

7 recorded crop formations

All of the New Zealand formations are almost certainly manmade. A very complex fractal design was made by English artists for an NBC television documentary during 1998. Also, Japan's Nippon Television flew Englishman Matthew Williams to New Zealand with a small team in February 2002 to make two patterns.

The reason manmade patterns are so popular in New Zealand is because of their growing season: cereal crops are available in the country during the northern hemisphere's winter.

Shortly after I appeared on Australian television talking about crop circles, a farmer reported two new crop rings in his wheat field.

Only a handful of simple circles remain unexplained and unattributed.

5.18 Russia

6 recorded crop formations

There has been a suspiciously small number of reports for such a vast country, but most are thought to be real. Again, it is difficult to know if this is due to censorship or actual dearth of formations.

Luminous spheres, similar to the ones witnessed in the United Kingdom, have been reported associated with some of the crop circles in Russia.

Interestingly, the Russian Army investigated the reported formations and deployed agricultural experts who discovered that the soil under the flattened plants in circles had been baked.

Other circles found in the country have shown no evidence of damage or tampering.

5.19 Finland

6 recorded crop formations

All discoveries of crop formations in Finland were made during the period 1996 through 1998, and they were all intricate and impressive geometries. There have been no reports in recent years.

5.20 Israel

6 recorded crop formations

For three years, from 1997 through 1999, simple circles and geometric shapes appeared in the Jezreel Valley in southern Galilee [near Nazareth].

The first report of a crop circle in Israel came in 1997, and it was accompanied by a UFO sighting. Biophysicist William Levengood analyzed plants from the Israel circle and concluded that the changes he found could not have been the result of a hoax.

5.21 Poland

5 recorded crop formations

The only reports of crop circles in Poland have come in the last few years. The formations reported are mostly simple, well-formed circles, with no damage of any kind.

A complex pattern that looked like a flower was found in wheat at Wylatowo Village near Mogilno during July 2002.

All of Poland's crop circles have appeared in cereal crops.

5.22 Brazil

5 recorded crop formations

All Brazilian crop formations are simple designs and appeared in grass and corn.

The most complex pattern seen was a quintuplet set—a traditional Celtic Cross— which was found in long grass during the summer of 1996 near the capital city of Brasilia.

There have been no reports coming out of Brazil since 1997.

5.23 Mexico

5 recorded crop formations

The first report of a crop circle in Mexico dates from 1954, and was of a single circle.

During 1993, two intricate designs appeared in long grass, a few miles apart, in the state of Hidalgo. One of these patterns was accompanied by a strange sound heard by witnesses on the night it formed.

5.24 India

4 recorded crop formations; 800 possible unreported formations

There have been only four reports of crop circles from India that have detailed sketches accompanying them.

These circles were reported to me by a scientist with the Indian government, who said that "huge designs" had been photographed on the prime minister's land and in other parts of India. This gentleman also claimed that approximately 800 other patterns of which he had direct knowledge had appeared across the country.

This "800 patterns" quote was cited recently by M. Night Shyamalan during interviews in which he talked about writing the script of his blockbuster movie, *Signs*.

This scientist also told me that the same patterns that had appeared in wheat fields had also appeared in black soot on ceilings in some residences in the area, always following a religious ceremony.

5.25 Sweden

4 recorded crop formations

In 1946, there were several reports in Sweden of single crop circles. The first report was of a 40-foot diameter circle that came from Angelholm, Sweden during May, 1946.

One circle was discovered during 2002.

5.26 Ireland
4 recorded crop formations

There have been only four reports of crop circles from the Emerald Isle.

Following one of my radio interviews in Ireland, an Irish farmer rang me up to report that during 1989, he found four circles forming a square in a remote wheat field on his land.

The rivalry between the English and the Irish—often marked by humorous insults flung by both sides—caused much to be made by the English observers who crowed that only in Ireland could crop "circles" make a square!

5.27 Yugoslavia
3 recorded crop formations

Crop circles have been reported in Yugoslavia only during the last two years, and each pattern has been intricate. One of them was the familiar "Celtic Cross" design.

5.28 China
2 recorded crop formations; possibly several hundred unreported formations

One of the two reported crop circles in China was witnessed during the decade of the country's failed "cultural revolution"— 1966 through 1967—when reporting or discussing such superstitious and possibly paranormal things as crop circles was not only discouraged, it was illegal.

According to Zhang Hui, research fellow of the Xinjiang Museum in Urumqi, an eyewitness saw the second circle form in a very short period of time. This eyewitness was in the company of China's Red Guard in Northeast China when it took place.

Hui believes that many of the ancient stone circles in China are permanent markings of old crop circles. This theory is also held by many regarding Stonehenge and other circular archaeological sites in England.

5.29 Other Countries
The following countries have reported crop circles:

COUNTRY	NUMBER OF REPORTED CIRCLES
Argentina	2
Croatia	2
Denmark	2
Peru	2
Romania	2
Siberia	2
Slovakia	2
Spain	2
Turkey	2
Afghanistan	1
Bulgaria	1
Chile	1
Egypt	1
Isle-Of-Man	1
Lithuania	1
Luxembourg	1
Malaysia	1
Nigeria	1
Norway	1
Sardinia	1
Tasmania	1
Ukraine	1
Uruguay	1

Part III

Stonehenge

Madison Square Garden:
Insecurity

Hundreds of crop circles had been appearing in the English landscape when the matter was finally taken to the British government. Crop circles were appearing not only in the public areas, they were appearing in the secret military areas as well. They were appearing on Salisbury Plain, which is an exclusion zone. No one is permitted to fly over it, let alone drive through it. The area is surveyed from the air with satellites and constantly monitored at ground level for intruders. It's a very secure area, yet crop circles are appearing inside these secure areas.

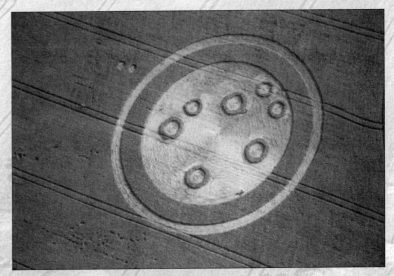

This unique cluster of rings within a ringed circle appeared near Hungerford, Berkshire, England in 1994.

Chapter 6

The Stonehenge Julia Set
Out of Nowhere?

The realities of nature surpass our most ambitious dreams

—**Francois Rodin**

One of the most compelling and important moments in crop circle history was the sudden appearance of an incredible formation—a "Julia Set"—in a field across the road from Stonehenge in a span of less than one hour.

There has been controversy about the Julia Set since the moment it appeared in 1996. Naysayers have come forward and claimed to know the hoaxers who made this extraordinary formation. However, they do not name names or provide evidence, thus destroying their credibility. Also, many of their claims have been repudiated by the facts.

One of the most convincing arguments for the Julia Set's authenticity is that honest, respectable people have attested to its almost instantaneous appearance. These are credible people telling of incredible things. Nowhere is this more evident than in the accounts provided by people who would have nothing to gain, and a great deal to lose, by making up such a story.

A "Julia Set" is, by definition, a pattern created using fractal geometry. Fractal geometry is a component of the relatively recent field of chaos theory which, put simply, is the theory that states that order can be found in randomness (early 1960s).

A fractal is a geometric pattern that is repeated at ever smaller scales to produce irregular shapes and surfaces that cannot be represented by classical geometry.

The Julia Set crop formation begins with a circle, spirals away from that center circle with smaller circles that grow in size, until peaking as a large circle, and then spiraling down with shrinking circles. Tiny "moon" circles orbit each of the circles in the set. The shape of the Julia formation mimics the spiral created by the Golden Mean in nature.

A Julia Set can be mapped upwards and downwards to infinity. It is a complex pattern that is visibly awe-inspiring. But is it real?

The story of its discovery is simple. A pilot flew over the field at 5:15 p.m. on his way to Stonehenge. With him was a doctor who had chartered the flight to take pictures of the ancient archaeological site. *Neither of the men saw anything in the field below them as they flew over it at 5:15.* Sometime around 6 p.m., they flew over the same field on their way back to the airport and there it was. An enormous crop formation had seemingly appeared in a span of 45 minutes or less. By 6:15, the police were receiving calls about the formation because of the great number of people stopping on the fast, dangerous road adjacent to the field to look at the formation.

The cynics claim that the formation was already in the field, that it had been created the previous night, and that no one saw it until 6 p.m. the following day.

When challenged on their contention that an entire day went by and no one on the road next to the field saw the massive formation, they say it was because the field slopes down and it is difficult to see from the road into the "bowl" created by the inclined ground without a person getting out of their car. According to their claim, the formation was created clandestinely and undetected in the area near Stonehenge, which is monitored around the clock by security guards. They also claim that the 600-foot crop design was made in a mere few hours, absolutely perfectly, and on the first try.

The Julia Set seen in proximity to Stonehenge (1996).

There are solid responses to these allegations, and I will go through them one at a time.

1. The Julia Set *was clearly visible* from the highway next to the field and a person did not have to leave their car, walk to the edge of the road, and look down into the field to see it. The local police did not have any notice of the formation until minutes after 6:00 p.m. on that day, the first call coming in to them within minutes of the doctor and the pilot seeing it. It is farfetched to believe that an entire day went by without anyone seeing the

enormous formation—including the farmer who owned and worked the fields.

2. The Stonehenge site, which is across the road from the field where the Julia Set appeared, is guarded 24-hours-a-day by a team of at least three, and often, four professional security guards. These guards can see the field from the patrolled, elevated ground on the northern side of the Stonehenge standing stones, but they did not see the pattern until after 6 p.m. on the day it appeared. I personally spoke to all of the guards who were on duty that day and they confirmed that there had been nothing in the field until after 6 p.m. that day.

3. The British Ministry of Defense controls the airspace over Stonehenge and also monitors all aircraft take-offs and landings from the nearby top-secret airfield Boscombe Down. Officials from the Ministry of Defense confirmed to me that the first report of the pattern was made after 6:30 p.m. that day.

4. David Probert, a professional surveying engineer who investigated and surveyed the site at my request, used the very latest infrared locating and layout equipment to measure and evaluate the Julia Set formation. He assured me that it would have taken him approximately two full days to lay out the design as found in the field. It took one full day in the field for us to simply enter each circle position and draw it using his equipment.

5. The pilot and doctor's report supports the reports of many eyewitness who have witnessed formations form in very short periods of time, some form as briefly as 10 to 15 seconds.

6. The central circle of the Julia Set is directly aligned with the circle that is formed by the Stonehenge formation, and this invisible line passing through the crop formation and Stonehenge is aligned with magnetic north, the earth's magnetic pole. The placement of the Julia Set is so specific that if there had even been a slight rotation of the formation while it was being formed, then the line to magnetic north would have been misaligned. It seems unlikely that this meticulous alignment was purely coincidental, and equally unlikely that hoaxers went to the trouble of making and executing the specific calculations necessary to achieve such an alignment.

On a related note, it has been shown that psychics have been able to "sense" the magnetic alignment of the earth and the Julia Set formation simply by looking at photos of the design. These experiments were conducted at the Institute of Resonant Therapy in Capenburg, Germany. The results could not be duplicated with photos of hoaxed formations. These experiments were filmed and personally witnessed by myself and my wife Synthia.

7. The pilot and the doctor are both adamant in their belief that if the Julia

Set had been in the field when they first flew over it, they would have undoubtedly seen it. Both men were looking down from the aircraft at Stonehenge and the fields around it, and the aircraft flew several circuits directly above the field. The Julia Set pattern was enormous: It measured 600 feet across. Not seeing it would be comparable to flying into New York City and not noticing the skyscrapers.

8. Biophysicist William Levengood discovered biophysical changes at the cellular level inside the plants from the Julia Set formation, which he believes could not be caused by hoaxing. An independent analysis at the Springborn Agricultural Laboratories in Massachusetts discovered a fivefold reduction of the pesticide levels within plants from the Julia Set. Both of these results are utterly inconsistent with plants that have been flattened by human feet or wooden boards.

The Julia Set is a conundrum of anomalies and mysteries, and the formation seemed to possess some type of energy information that was used, in several cases, to great environmental benefit.

At the time the Julia Set appeared, Soviet president Mikhail Gorbachev was trying to find ways to reduce the consequences of acid rain on trees and vegetation in the Soviet Union. A friend of Gorbachev's was working with the Institute of Resonant Therapy in Germany. He designed an experiment in which the orgone energy of the Julia Set was quantified, and then generated at specific resonant frequencies on plant life in the Soviet Union.

The people conducting this experiment recorded leaf counts before the orgone application and after, and there was noticeable improvement in the growth and health of the tested plants. This process has since been applied to troubled plant life in other countries with the same positive results.

The conclusion we have drawn from this development is that the geometry of the Julia Set formation contains specific bioenvironmental information that can be read and then used to improve the health of vegetation anywhere in the world.

It is quite possible that authentic crop circles are part of an interconnected network of biological "machines" whose sole purpose is to support the life forms of planet Earth. It is also possible that manmade designs which accidentally contain certain essential ratios and alignments may also create measurable effects. We can see here a potentially important discovery that has come out of this single event.

Chapter 7

Stonehenge:
A Coincidental Discovery

From the *Circles Phenomenon Research International Newsletter*
(Vol. 5, No. 1, Spring/Summer 1996)

In this fascinating article from his now defunct CPRI newsletter, Colin Andrews discusses an odd stone he was "summoned" to find close to Stonehenge, and how, later, a never-published glyph on one of the henge's standing stones seemed to connect to the mysterious rock.

•••

During the early years of crop circle research, Pat Delgado, Terence Meaden, Busty Taylor, and myself were in daily contact and flew weekly over the area of Stonehenge. We were, of course, searching for and photographing the crop circles which were found predominantly in this area. Busty Taylor, the regular pilot of our aircraft, had a near fixation about Stonehenge, always commenting that the simple crop circles which were appearing at that time resembled it and even seemed to compare favorably in size.

To test these observations, I spent the winter of 1987 scaling the existing crop circle patterns to the official floor plan of Stonehenge supplied by English Heritage, the keepers of the site. I discovered that, indeed, there were striking similarities.

The dimensions of most of the single circles fit snugly into the inner horseshoe of the henge and, when crop circles appeared with single and double rings, they fit within the inner and outer edges of the first ring of stones. All of these fits were to an accuracy of just a few centimeters. This very famous archaeological site is the center of crop circle activity, as over 95 percent of the known worldwide formations have been discovered within a 40-mile radius of these formidable monolithic stones.

In 1996, Stonehenge once again took center stage, both with the proximity of the most extraordinary formation (T444: see the *Andrews Catalogue* in this volume, and

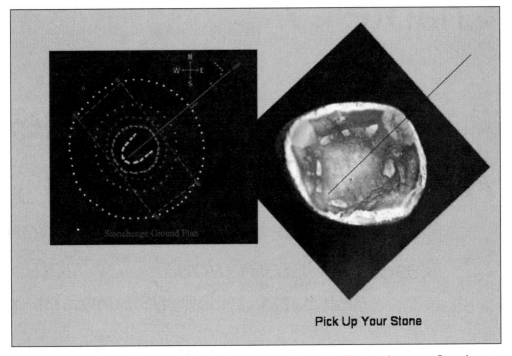

Pick Up Your Stone

A graphic illustration of the stone Colin Andrews was told psychically to pick up near Stonehenge. The underside of the stone (right) shows an image of Stonehenge's standing stones.

Chapter 6, and with the following discovery I made last year.

Actually, the story starts in 1989 when film director Michael Grais (director of *Poltergeist II*) decided to make a movie for television about the long series of unexplained security alarm activations in my home in Andover, England. The film was called *Gateway to the Unknown* and was broadcast throughout the United States with actors dramatizing my situation.

When making the film, Michael arrived with American psychic Sharon Gayle, who was his friend and assistant. While filming an interview with me in a huge "dolphin" formation (see T122 in the *Andrews Catalogue*) at Lockeridge, near Alton Barnes, Sharon suddenly broke into the filming and said, "Colin, they are telling me to ask you to pick up your stone." The filming was stopped, the director looked annoyed but agreed, and

I, in confusion, looked down around my feet at the hundreds of flint stones particular to southern England. I did notice one that seemed slightly different to the rest, a little to my right. I bent down to pick it up and found it was embedded and weathered firmly into the soil. I had to pry it from the ground with both hands. The surface I could see was round and smooth but when I pried it out and brushed the soil off, I saw something quite different. The stone was a beautiful blue found inside broken flint but I could not believe my eyes. I noticed a horseshoe arrangement of white rectangular markings within the blue which looked nearly identical to the rock placement of Stonehenge. I immediately said, "My God! It's Stonehenge!"

I have stared at this stone on many occasions as it sits in my office, and I have studied all aspects of it. The stone has two white spheres on it, one positioned at the center of the open end of the horseshoe. (In Stonehenge this area is positioned to the summer solstice sunrise and locates the famous heel stone. The second sphere was positioned about 210 degrees around the horseshoe.

In July of 1995, I was asked to visit Stonehenge with a group of researchers from the United States who had arranged to tour the crop circle sites and Stonehenge with Joyce Murphy from Beyond Boundaries. My job was to update the group with the latest crop circle discoveries and research progress as the group spent some quality moments inside the henge with the special permission of English Heritage. It was evening, around 11 p.m., and the sun had set. As the group stood around listening to my update, a member accidentally touched the button on their flashlight and cast a beam of light at an angle across one of the stones. Perhaps because I have become so attuned to looking at glyphs over the past years, as the light momentarily struck the rock, I saw a petroglyph. I asked that the light be put back on and there was indeed a glyph worn into the old stone, looking every bit as old as the site itself. I knew that some glyphs had been discovered on the rocks at Stonehenge and asked Stuart Conway, a journalist and photographer from the *Glasgow Herald* in Scotland, to take a photograph so we could compare it to the record.

Immediately on my return to the United States at the end of the summer, I sent the photograph and placement to Professor Gerald Hawkins, author of *Stonehenge Decoded*, who knows every surface of rock personally, not only through his research, but because he has also painted each one. Gerald was adamant that the

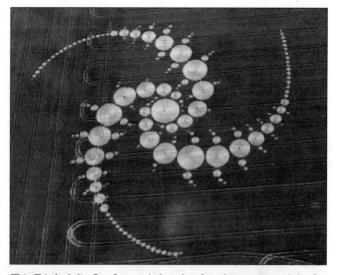

This Triple Julia Set formed shortly after the amazing Julia Set near Stonehenge in 1996. Each circle displayed a different swirl detail. The pattern was over 120 meters across.

glyph had never before been published. I have spent many weeks this summer with English Heritage and they also agree that this is a new discovery, probably only seen this time due to the angle of the light that hit it.

Will you be surprised to hear that the stone the glyph is carved on is at the same placement in the Stonehenge arrangement (210 degrees around the horseshoe from the heel stone) as the second white sphere on my rock?

•••

A final word: On the night of July 14, I went with a group of people to Stonehenge to officially declare the finding with photographs, measurements, and a ceremony. Later that night my car was broken into and, at some point, the film from my camera was removed. This seemed odd. Since there was plenty of additional photographic evidence of the evening, why remove *my* film?

Since this story was published by CPR International, several sources have claimed that the glyph Colin discovered had been previously reported and noted by English Heritage. No official record has yet been provided to support these claims.

Chapter 8

An Interview With Busty Taylor

Busty Taylor is a pilot who regularly flies his light aircraft over the fields of England looking for new crop circles. In 1985, he discovered a set of five crop circles forming a Celtic Cross south of his home, which started him on the long road of crop circle investigation. Taylor has worked with Pat Delgado, Terence Meaden, Colin Andrews, and others. In the 1980s, he was part of the first research team to undertake investigation of the crop circle mystery. In this interview, Busty shares his thoughts concerning the crop circle enigma.

•••

Q In 1985, you saw your first crop circles while flying over a field in your small plane. What were your thoughts when you saw the formation?

A I knew that I had seen this before, but could not remember where. A few days later there was a meeting in New Alresford with Pat Delgado, Omar Fowler, Paul Fuller, and Martin Pain, a local farmer, who pointed out that the crop design I had seen and photographed was a Celtic Cross. That was when I remembered where I had seen the symbol before: in the local churchyards on tombstones.

Q What was the strongest evidence in those early days that convinced you that these strange patterns in the fields were worth further study?

A The plants had no damage that I could see, plus the stalks were bent—not broken—90 degrees at the base. In black-and-white photos, you could see a distinct contrast difference between the design and the other crops. Also, I could not find any human tracks into the formation from any direction.

Q Was there a particular crop formation that convinced you that the trend of hoaxing had begun and that manmade circles would be part of the scene from then on?

A In 1987, I flew over the Cheesefoot Head to take some photos of an authentic ringed circle, and then I flew back to Thruxton. I subsequently drove back to the field I had just flown over and discovered that a small ringed circle had turned up within that last hour. This circle, when viewed from the edge of the field through binoculars, looked very rough compared to the genuine one I had just photographed, and it had irregular edges. I immediately thought it was a fake and, from that point on, it would be important to differentiate between the real and the counterfeit formations.

Q What have you personally seen that convinces you that a real phenomenon exists?

A Over the last 17 years, I have been lucky enough to get into some crop circles very early after their formation, before they have been contaminated by other people. I have seen formations meticulously laid out without any sign of human intervention, and I have seen oil-seed rape stalks with perfect 90-degree bends.

One particularly memorable incident occurred at Headbourne Worthy, where we found a counterclockwise circle with a strange weave inside it. As soon as I saw it, I made a comment into the video camera, remarking on the complexity of the weave on the ground. It was only later when we saw the crop circle from the air that we noticed that the main lay of the circle itself had a clockwise spiral to it. The swirl of the overall pattern was in one direction, but on the ground, the weave was in the opposite, and was an extremely complex plait. To my mind, this was very compelling evidence of some unknown phenomenon.

Q During your research, have you witnessed any specific physical or mental effects on people that have visited crop circles?

A Yes. I have seen people become elated on entering a formation, and I have personally taken a man into the 1989 Winterbourne Stoke Swastika. He claims that his chronic bad back was healed permanently after visiting the crop circle. According to this man, after he left the formation and began driving away from the site towards London, his back got hotter and hotter and then suddenly his back pain stopped for good, and never returned. Interestingly, sometimes the circles seem to stimulate uncommonly authoritative attitudes in people. I have heard people report that a sense of power came over them after they visited a circle, and I have witnessed some people's attitude towards others become very domineering.

Q What do you think the crop circle phenomenon is all about?

A I think it may be a form of communication, as many of the early circles were representations of Celtic symbols that have been used throughout history. Perhaps these symbols were also found in the crops thousands of years ago.

Q In your opinion, what research still needs to be carried out, and how do you think it will advance our knowledge and understanding of the crop circle phenomenon?

A In a nutshell, I think we all need to work together. Crop circle researchers should make a concerted effort to develop a program of structured research that could then be reviewed and collated. At the moment, people are off doing their own thing, and many are carrying out research which somebody else might also be doing without realizing it. If we could organize, we might move much faster with the research and more quickly discover an answer to what this is all about.

Q Have the crop circle counterfeiters taught us anything?

A Yes, they have taught us that man has the ability to replicate what he sees in nature. This might be what happened

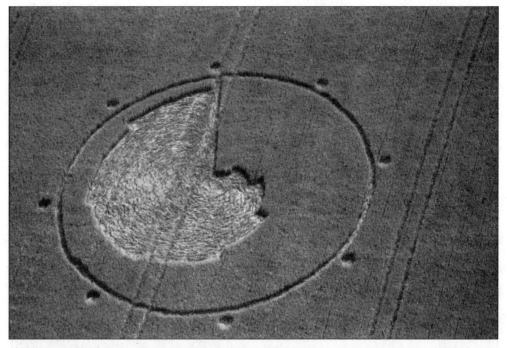

In 1986, an elderly couple driving over Stockbridge Downs, near Stockbridge, Hampshire, England called police after witnessing a large UFO stand on its end over the downs. The sketch they drew closely resembled this crop pattern which appeared at the same spot on the downs in 1995.

thousands of years ago. Man might have duplicated the early crop circle designs and used the patterns in artwork and at archaeological sites. What we now know as a Celtic Cross might very well be a copy of something ancient man saw in the fields. Some circle counterfeiters claim that they have witnessed some strange things during their circle making; I think we should look more deeply into this.

Q Have the crop circles changed your life?

A Yes, my life has changed since my first circle. The circles have spurred me to look into the past of all religions and search for an answer and, in doing so, I consider myself a much wiser person for the experience.

Part IV

Weird Science

Madison Square Garden
Spiraling Views

Looking like a cross between a snowflake and a bunch of magnetic dipoles, this complex pattern appeared on the top of an iron age hill fort called Windmill Hill in Wiltshire, England on July 18, 2002.

From about 500 feet in the air, the spiraling symmetry of crop circles can clearly be seen. You lift the plants up, and underneath them are two overlaid sine waves—out of phase, and breaking away into the center. Peak trough, peak trough, and so forth; a highly complex array of patterning, which is found even in the simple circles. The plants do not always spiral, but when they do, it's like a radial fireworks air burst, straight out from the center to the periphery. These plants are not bent, either. It's as if they're made supple through the phase of formation, and then hardened up again—and then continue to grow.

Chapter 9

Sounds From the Fields

Insects, Birds,
or the Circles Themselves?

Everyone hears only what he understands.

—Jonathan Wolfgang von Goethe

The Sound of the Circles

One day in June 1987 as I was working in my office, I received a phone call from a pilot I knew personally, telling me that he had just seen a crop circle in a field in Kimpton, Hampshire.

Kimpton is a very small hamlet near Andover, about five miles from my home at the time. It is comprised of no more than two dozen houses in a small rural village near a private landing strip in Hampshire, England.

The pilot had seen a crop ring in which the plants were spiraled in a clockwise direction, and he thought I would want to know about it. Because I had a great many hours of personal time owed to me, I decided to leave work and pay a visit to this formation. When I arrived at the farm, I introduced myself to the farmer and together we walked out into the field where the crop ring had appeared. I knew immediately that

it was an authentic manifestation and I requested, and was granted, permission to return the following day with my colleagues for further investigation.

I assembled a team of scientists, engineers and other interested parties—including Dr. Terence Meaden and Pat Delgado—and we went back to the farmer's field the next day and performed our standard investigative routine. We measured for radiation with a Geiger counter. We took a great many physical measurements, we took soil and plant samples. We used a compass to determine the magnetic orientation and alignment of the plants.

Upon conclusion of our research, we all left the field and, because it was nearing the end of the workday, we returned to our respective homes.

Later that day, towards early evening, I was going through my notes at home and

I realized that in order to be completely thorough, I needed to take a few more measurements of the crop circle, some of which I felt could be quite useful.

I decided to return to the field. This time, I decided not to bother the farmer after his day of labor. He had, after all, given me permission to enter his land, and I was certain he would not object to a follow-up visit.

I drove to Kimpton, and I parked my car on the side of the highway out of the line of traffic. I stepped out of the car and I paused for a moment to look at the setting sun. The smell of growing wheat was carried to me on a slight breeze that also bore the gentle smell of heather as it wafted across the fields. I walked slowly towards a small church, and I was quite conscious of how relaxed I was, and I was also aware of how little fear I felt.

I was returning to a field where a crop ring had appeared that afternoon, and which I and my colleagues had already measured and photographed. I was back because something had occurred to me when I was at home and I wanted to take another measurement. This seemed to be a very ordinary activity to me.

Behind the church was a small graveyard that dated back at least to the 15th century. The tombstones stood silent and gray in the gloaming and I was careful not to trod on the graves as I passed through this city of the dead. Respect. Very important.

I reached the back of the cemetery and climbed easily over some low barbed wire, placed there not to keep out humans, but to deter nocturnal marauders, such as foxes and badgers.

As I moved across the field, dusk became dark. It took me a few minutes to reach the crop ring. As I walked, I distinctly heard a dog barking in the distance. Aside from my far-off canine friend, there was silence in the field. I was quite alone.

When I reached the ring, I walked inside its perimeter and stared at the flattened barley plants swirling in a clockwise direction. I took my measurement and then something came over me—an urge, an impulse, a yearning. Call it what you will, but the effect was to prod me to do something I had not planned to do. It was a pure, spontaneous moment, brought on by my fervid desire to understand.

I turned west, where Stonehenge stood silent, I put my hands together, and I prayed.

I did not speak, but in my mind I sent out the plea, "Please, God, give me a clue as to what is happening here and help me understand what this is all about."

At the precise moment that my prayer ended—*the exact second*—I heard an odd crackling sound from approximately seven or eight feet in front of me that sounded a bit like static, but with a more metallic edge to it. It was an unusual, continuous whirring sound at close to ground level and I immediately thought it was being made by some kind of insect. I rejected that straightaway because the sound was too mechanical and much too loud for an insect. As I listened, the sound got louder and louder. I flirted with the idea that it was some kind of rodent, or some other animal, but I also discarded that theory since, again, the mechanical nature of the sound was quite pronounced. As the volume of the sound rose, I could feel the air around me begin to move, and I sensed the hairs on my arms standing up and I could feel air pulsating the cheeks of my face.

At this point, I became quite concerned and, within a very short time, concern had turned to fear. I thought I recognized the sound from my work as an electrical engineer. I had heard similar sounds in laboratories in situations where there was a buildup of high levels of voltage between an anode and a cathode. Just before there is a discharge of electricity, there is a metallic purring sound, and that was similar to what I heard that night in the field.

I say now for the record, and with the utmost sincerity, that the prevailing thought that was running through my mind as I stood there listening to that sound, was that something was going to materialize in front of me, there, in the center of the crop circle. Ultimately, nothing appeared, but the sound continued. I am not ashamed to admit that my fear reached a new level at that point and I began to look for the quickest way out of the field.

This formation discovered by Busty Taylor and Colin Andrews during a reconnaissance flight over Clench Common, Wiltshire on the 10th of August, 2000.

As I prepared to flee, however, the sound suddenly stopped—it was as though a switch had been thrown. And to this day, I believe that the "switch" was my fear. As soon as my trepidation and alarm turned to outright terror, the sound stopped. Did the consciousness that was responsible for the crop circle and its attendant sound respond to my panic and turn off the sound to reassure and comfort me? It did seem that way to me at the time, and I still believe that there was a deliberate response from the intelligence that made the circle. The circles are a gentle, benign presence on earth. I think the presence of the contrary emotion of fear caused some kind of reaction and that the purpose of restoring silence was to bring balance to the situation. The positive energies at the site were being torn apart by my dread and nature responded.

I quickly left the circle, and it would be another year before I would hear that sound again.

•••

I have thought about that first time many times since that night in the field, and the exact moment that my prayer was answered.

It was a straight line for me: I had prayed for an answer; I received one. It was, perhaps, more than I could emotionally handle. I became terribly frightened; the sound of the circle stopped.

Was this all just coincidence? Was it coincidental that the moment my emotions changed from relaxed curiosity to abject terror, the thing that was frightening me ceased?

Two years later, in July 1989, the BBC recorded the same crop circle sound. It was then that I learned that the sound was a 5.2 kilohertz frequency and I now have this sound on tape and I have played it at many lectures and conventions. A BBC TV camera was destroyed during the taping. This event made national headlines in Britain.

Is the sound the sound of the crop circles? I believe it is, and it was Operation White Crow that convinced me of its authenticity—and its importance. (Please see Chapter 15 for more on the sound of the circles.)

Chapter 10

Operation White Crow

If you wish to upset the law that all crows are black, you mustn't seek to show that no crows are; it is enough if you prove one single crow to be white.

—William James

The Devil's Punchbowl

Operation White Crow was the first crop circle surveillance operation, and it took place in the "Devil's Punchbowl" in Cheesefoot Head, Winchester, in Hampshire, in 1989, one year prior to Operation Blackbird.

Operation White Crow is significant to me for several reasons, the most important being the fact that it was the second time I heard the odd "crop circle sound" (see Chapter 9), and also, because of the very strange things that happened to my friend, co-author, and fellow researcher, Pat Delgado.

We had a caravan of vehicles, work stations, and cameras. One evening, some of us who were directly participating in the surveillance operation decided to get away from the main base of operations and walk 100 yards or so away from the bustle.

We all walked off into a single crop circle, the larger of a formation of two circles that had appeared in the field next to the one we were monitoring. There were seven or eight of us, including psychic Rita

Gould, and we all sat down and tried to relax. We did not meditate, or attempt to make contact with the intelligence of the circles—this was not a séance—but we were all in a relaxed state of mind.

Suddenly, we all heard a sound from the east. As we listened, it grew louder and we could sense it getting closer. It was definitely directional, in that we all could tell precisely where it was coming from, and we could follow it as it moved. The sound then rotated around us, floating around the circle three or four times, like an auditory cloud that passed above us in a circle. And again, it was directional: As it moved in its orbit around us, we could follow it with our ears, and if it had been visible, we all felt we would have been able to track it from point to point around the circle. First it was in our left ear, then behind us, then in our right ear.

We were all responsible adults with jobs and families, but we were also all open to the idea of alternate realities and to the notion that strange things were possible. Yet, that said, we were all quite frightened and we huddled together like a bunch of schoolboys. It truly was a scary moment. We were in a pitch black field and we had no idea what this sound was or where it was coming from.

And then the sound stopped moving. We could all still hear it, but it froze and positioned itself in front Pat Delgado and I. At this time, Pat was very involved in researching and trying to understand the phenomenon, as was I. Could the source of the sound somehow sensed this?

We did not know what to expect next, and as we waited for something to happen, suddenly Pat Delgado stood up and began to walk towards the place in the circle from where the sound was now emanating. He walked to the edge of the circle, and he later told me that he knew that the sound was no more than three or four feet in front of him. This was somewhat closer than the sound was to me when I heard it at Kimpton.

And then it got *really* weird.

As Pat stood there at the edge of the circle, he called out: "Colin, come to me," he said. And then, he cupped his left hand and began to "scoop" in the air at the top of the plants closest to the sound and push this *energy* in my direction.

I walked towards him, and when I reached him, he continued his odd cupping and scooping motion across the top of the plants, pushing the air towards me, specifically towards my solar plexus—he aimed it straight at the pit of my stomach. I stood there and went along with this, not knowing how to respond, or what to say. After a bit, Pat stopped and I backed away. I turned around, walked back to the group, and sat down. I was confused and frightened and knew that something strange was occurring. Pat then started to walk toward us. When he reached a point about 25 to 30 feet away from us, he stopped in his tracks,

and his head went back as though he were about to fall backwards.

It was a most extraordinary sight and I truly did not understand what was going on. As I stared at this incredible sight, he then beckoned to me.

Incredibly, his body then leaned back on a 10- to 15-degree angle. He hung there suspended, as though he were leaning against a cushion, or perhaps something more solid.

At this point, Pat was absolutely terrified. I could see fear in his eyes and he started shouting to me. "Colin! Come and hold me up!" I rushed to him and grabbed both his hands and tried to pull him to an upright position. I felt great pressure pulling against me, and it was as though Pat was stuck to glue. I continued to tug at him, and then suddenly he was free. It felt as though a bond had snapped and his body was released from the force that had been holding him. At the precise moment that Pat was pulled free, the crop circle sound stopped.

This was, quite literally, one of the worst things that had ever happened to me or Pat.

Upset and shaken, we returned to the group and sat down, but after only a few moments, Pat said, "Let's get the hell out of here," and we all left the circle.

The following morning, as we were working in the base camp of the operation, a police sergeant drove up. We had obtained all necessary permissions to conduct the operation, so the police knew we were there, and they knew what we were doing.

"Are you aware," the sergeant asked us, pointing off in the direction of the sound from the night before, "that there's a circle with a ring on the top of the hill over there?"

We replied that we were not aware of any new formation and the sergeant offered to drive us there in the police car.

A dumbbell formation appeared mysteriously in full view of surveillance cameras during an operation set up by engineer Mike Curry and BBC production staff at Blackland, Wiltshire on June 28, 1991. Mike Curry returned home from this site to find an identical pattern appeared outside his bedroom window overnight.

We gratefully accepted and we sped off towards the hill he had pointed out.

When we arrived, we were flabbergasted. In the exact direction the sound seemed to travel to when it left us was a fresh crop ring. The plants were still popping up, and still moving, as though a powerful hand had pressed them down, and they were just now springing back up.

I believed then, as I believe now, that the previous night we had inadvertently encroached upon the creation of a crop circle. We had all unwittingly placed ourselves in the middle of a paranormal event. At one point Rita Gould did attempt to make contact with the force behind the sound that we were all hearing, but we do not know for certain that her efforts made any difference.

Pat Delgado was caught in the maelstrom that night, and he pulled me into it with him.

Chapter 11

Hayley's Connection:
Crop Circles and Remote Viewing

A reasonable being should ask himself why—if chemicals can enter into plants, and plants be taken up into animals, and animals be taken into man—why man himself, who is the peak of visible creation, should be denied the privilege of being assimilated into a higher power? The rose has no right to say that there is no life above it and neither has man, who has a vast capacity and unconquerable yearning for eternal life and truth and love.

—**Archbishop Fulton J. Sheen**

ote: This is a somewhat abridged version of an article from the CPRI newsletter that tells of a drawing by my teenage niece, Hayley, that was later seen as a crop circle design in a field near her home. Please refer to the Andrews Catalogue in this volume to see images of the crop formations cited in this article. It was taken from the *Circles Phenomenon Research International Newsletter,* Volume 6, No.1, Spring/Summer 1997.

•••

Remote viewing is a difficult subject to discuss with many people. Once, during a lecture in San Francisco, I spoke of the importance of remote viewing in exploring human potentials. Afterwards, I was approached by a very indignant man who warned me from getting involved in such a load of rubbish. I disagreed and we left it at that. In fact, I have had many events in my life surrounding the crop circles that strongly led me into the study of remote viewing.

Remote viewing is the ability to mentally receive visual and auditory information without being limited by distance or time. Public research into this area began in the early 1970s, with much of it being carried out at Stanford Research Institute at Palo Alto, California. In 1977, physicists Russell Targ and Harold Putoff published their research (*Mind Reach*) in which they described remote viewing as "the ability...to view, by means of mental process, remote geographical or technical targets...."

In another book written by Russell Targ, with Keith Harary (*Mind Race,*

1984), the authors quoted from a congressional committee on science and technology, U.S. House of Representatives, 97th Congress, June 1981:

Recent experiments in remote viewing and other studies in parapsychology suggest there is an interconnectedness of the human mind with other human minds and matter...The implications of these experiments is that the human mind may be able to obtain information independent of geography and time.

This is no surprise to those who are familiar with Rupert Sheldrake and his theories of morphic fields and resonance (*The New Science of Life* and *In the Presence of the Past*). Also along this line is the idea of a "holographic universe" where the universe is seen as an indivisible whole and every piece of the whole has intrinsically within itself access to the whole, much like every cell in our body contains the DNA that has the blueprint of the entire body (Michael Talbot, 1991). Both of these theories are simply new attempts to create a construct within which supernormal events can be explained, as Carl Jung did with his theory of the collective unconscious. In any event, there is strong theoretical support for the process of remote viewing, even stronger experimental support and, to top it off, great governmental interest in this means of obtaining information.

Remote viewing impacts the subject of crop circles in two ways. First, remote viewing can be, and has been used to, obtain information regarding the construction and shape of crop circles. Second, theoretically, the process of remote viewing is reversible. What I mean by that is that if we can use our minds to see things from a distance, we can also use our minds to project things. Additionally, can images be "remote viewed" into our minds from other sources?

Accuracy in remote viewing is attained through rigorous training and practice. A beginning remote viewer is considered to have a "hit," or to have succeeded, if components of the target are seen. They often will not be seen in mirror image to the actual item. For example, Synthia once gave me a target of an overhead fan. What I saw was a propeller with a cone on it. Although not exact, the components were there and, in this case, they were in the correct placement. I was not, however, able to identify what the object was.

It is very interesting that the act of remote viewing can influence the place and people being perceived. This is the case of many people who have had experiences of projecting a mental image of a pattern and then having it appear in the fields. The Celtic Cross of Longstock (1988) was one such incident when I projected the Celtic Cross and asked for it be placed in the field closest to my home. The next day it was there as projected and requested (T8). Another such event occurred in 1992 when Dr. Steven Greer and a group of 18 individuals all agreed on a pattern that they also projected from their minds. Again, it appeared in the fields the next day. In both cases, we projected a meaningful symbol, and it appeared, as if by an interactive force.

On the 18th of June this year (1997), when I arrived at my parents' house in Andover, in the United Kingdom, to start the summer's research, I noticed a beautiful plate next to my parents' fireplace. The dish had a powerful symbol in the center of it. When I asked my parents where they got the dish, my mother replied that my niece Hayley had made it for her. I was very impressed with the professional look of it, especially for a 13-year-old. But what was more impressive was the impact of the

Colin Andrews's niece Hayley holding the dish she painted. The design later appeared as a crop formation.

symbol. I made a mental note to ask Hayley where she obtained the symbol.

On the morning of the 19th of June, in the adjacent field at Longstock where the Celtic Cross had appeared in 1988, the farmer discovered an impressive new crop pattern (T489). He was sure that the pattern was not there the day before as the area was under surveillance by a group of bird watchers and the police during the time of its arrival and for four weeks prior. The interest in the area was due to a very rare and endangered bird that had been nesting nearby. I can vouch for the security myself.

Within moments of parking my car in the road next to the field, I was approached by the police and I could see watchers with binoculars perched in nearby trees. They had seen nothing in the fields for the four weeks they had been bird-watching. This morning, however, there was a majestic and undamaged crop design, with no tracks in or out.

I flew over the formation later that morning and immediately noticed the similarity between this pattern and the symbol on Hayley's dish.

I talked to Hayley later that week and asked where she got the symbol. She told me the symbol came into her mind on the 31st of January and she decided to draw it. Her sketches from January were very close to the 14th of June, T490 formation, including the childlike shakiness of the lines and the unfinished corners. She said she drew it that way because that was the way she saw it. However, when she decided to draw the symbol onto the plate for her Granny, she decided to alter the design, evolving it to contain most of the major components and placements of the formation which appeared on the 19th of June, which was formation T489.

The story does not end here. On the 10th of July I met with a group from America who had come over with researcher/artist Ron Russell. I met them at T489 to give them an update on formations that summer. As I begin to tell them of the

The design drawn by an American woman, appeared days later as a crop circle at Cley Hill, Wiltshire on July 14, 1997.

1997 patterns, a woman in the party waved a sketch in from of me. She had drawn it two weeks earlier in the States. "The pattern kept coming into my head," she said. Her sketch closely resembled Hayley's, and when I showed her a photograph of Hayley's plate, she nearly fell over. It was the same design, only she had placed loops where Hayley had placed inverted Vs. Later, a fresh design appeared which was an even better fit.

So, were the circles the result of my niece imaging a pattern which was then, through an interactive force, projected into the field? Or did my niece and the American woman remote view a future event?

Or perhaps, another possibility: Were the patterns projected into Hayley's and the woman's mind by an interactive force involved in the circle's creation? Is it the same interactive force that responded to my projection in 1988 and Steven Greer's in 1992?

If, as the mystics have always said, our thoughts create the world, perhaps the crop circles are giving us instruction on the creative use of the power of thought. Perhaps it is time we respond and join those using their thoughts to create a better world.

It is possible our best hope for the future lies in our highest ability to imagine.

Chapter 12

The Diatonic Ratios in Crop Circles

by Gerald Hawkins, Ph.D., D.Sc.

Professor Hawkins originally wrote this article about the diatonic ratios found in crop circle dimensions specifically for the CPRI Newsletter, and he has graciously granted us permission to reprint it in *Crop Circles: Signs of Contact.* Although it is somewhat technical in nature, we decided to include it here because of the enormous interest in crop circles by a great many scientists, mathematicians, musicologists, and science-minded lay people. This article was taken from the *Circles Phenomenon Research International Newsletter*, Volume 5, No.2, Fall/Winter 1996/97.

•••

Circular Evidence by Colin Andrews and Pat Delgado provides the only set of accurately measured circle diameters available for rigorous analysis for the early period of the phenomenon, frozen in time, and unbiased by the flood of later activity. Those measured patterns reveal a tell-tale set of numbers: the fractions of the major scale of Western music.

Starting with the tonic, C, each white note on the piano increases in pitch as follows:

C	D	E	F	G	A	B	C'
1	9/8	5/4	4/3	3/2	5/3	15/8	2

The same ratios occur above middle C, but double with each octave. For example, 6:2 gives G', 16:3 gives F", where each mark ' after a note is used to indicate a rise of one octave. There are the perfect diatonic ratios. In well-tempered or equal temperament tuning, the ratio, r, is more complicated:

$$r = 2^{n/12} \text{ (raised to the power of n/12)}$$

where "n" is taken as a number ranging between 0 and 12. The diatonic fractions fall out, or occur, when n is 0, 2, 4, 5, 7, 9, 11, and 12.

I took all the circles where measurements are given in *Circular Evidence*. For satellite patterns, the ratio was the diameter of the large circle to the satellite:

$$Ratio = \frac{Diameter\ of\ Large\ Circle}{Diameter\ of\ Satellite\ Circle}$$

For concentric rings, the ratio was of diameters squared. The measurements at the outside edge of each ring was taken.

Taking intervals of +/- 0.165 as n, 16 of the ratios fell on diatonics as shown in the figure to the right. Each and every white note was hit, and the black notes were not. The statistical probability that this is random is negligible. Noting that in Figure 1 the tonic appears twice (C, C'), there are seven independent targets set in a spread of 35 spaces, making the chance of a single random hit 0.2. The probability that 16 hits or more from 25 shots is real, by the binomial theorem, has a confidence level greater than 99.99 percent.

The Sussex group measured seven formations between 1993 and 1995, and four were diatonic, adding confirmation to the *Circular Evidence* results. This was repeated for the inside edges of the rings, and no significant correlation with the diatonic ratios was found.

Of course we cannot say that the crop circles are "musical." All that can be said is that the crop circles and the eight-note musical scale are based on the same mathematical relationship.

There are two internal checks we can apply. Firstly, we can look at the error distribution. The standard deviation was +/- 0.23, corresponding to +/- 20 centimeters in a 20 meter circle. The deviations were

symmetrical about zero, and showed a tolerable fit to a normal error curve. This confirms that the musical ratios were indeed aimed at, and that the circles were constructed with a tolerance of +/- 1 percent.

Secondly, we can arbitrarily reverse the rules, applying the linear rule to concentric circles, and the square rule to satellites. When this is done, the diatonic ratios disappear statistically. This simple check shows that musical ratios do not easily occur in patterns regardless of assumptions.

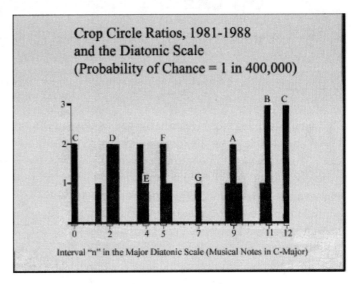

Crop Circle Ratios, 1981-1988 and the Diatonic Scale (Probability of Chance = 1 in 400,000)

Interval "n" in the Major Diatonic Scale (Musical Notes in C-Major)

There is a slight tendency for the measured diameters to cluster at unit values of meters and this raises the question, "Could the hoaxers strike off the ratios 9/8, 5/4, 4/3, and so forth, at random by using a bar of fixed length?" The answer is no. Taking all fractions made from the numbers between one and 16, the non-diatonic ratio 7/4 should occur by chance, but it is avoided in all the data. Yet the diatonic 15/8 was found in the circles, even though it should occur less often than 7/4 by chance. Then again, we would expect the black note ratios, such as 16/9, but none of these black notes were hit.

Known as the "Flower Of Life" design, it was found in a wheat field at Froxfield, Berkshire, England on August 4, 1994. It measured 180 feet across.

It has been argued that a natural phenomenon sometimes makes a design, and so crop patterns can be similarly produced. No. Apart from bird calls and whalesong, the set of diatonic ratios does not occur in nature.

Another possible criticism is the Kepler caveat. He, in 1596, theorized how the solar system orbits were pure geometry, but the measurements of Tycho Brahe proved him wrong. Equally unfortunate, his theory of a universe controlled by musical intervals was destroyed by the facts. With the crop circles, however, the music is not a theory, it is a fact. These diatonic ratios are facts in search of a theory.

Notes

Andrews, Colin and Pat Delgado. *Circular Evidence*. London: Bloomsbury Press, 1990.

Apel. W. *Harvard Dictionary of Music*. Cambridge, Mass: Harvard University Press, 1969.

Part V

Crop Circle Counterfeiting: Liars in the Fields

Madison Square Garden:
A Message From the Environment?

Why might symbols be part of a spiritual nudge?

Why would we need to be given a spiritual nudge? The answers may be found in the news.

- Item: The French government recently joined with the Chinese to begin once again the testing of nuclear devices.

- Item: This same day as in many other parts of the world, weather patterns broke all records.

- Item: Across North America, nearly 900 died in just a few days of unbearably high temperatures of over 115 degrees Fahrenheit...in the shade. The hospitals were full, the morgues were full, and the cattle were falling to the ground, their stomachs exploding.

All this happened on lands that less than 18 months ago experienced record low winter temperatures as areas of the Atlantic Ocean froze.

Our attention should be drawn to the gulf that exists between the actions of nation-states and the environmental needs of mankind. The U.S. Government recently proposed the deregulating of environmental policy.

The effects of the depleted ozone layer continue to become more and more obvious. We have had a loss of surface vegetation and large numbers of deep sea life; in addition to wild swings in global temperatures. Ignoring all this evidence, the United States Congress has recently proposed legislation encouraging the harvesting of trees.

Expanded harvesting will make it easier for the manufacturers of pesticides that are currently restricted by the Environmental Protection Agency to place them on the market for general use.

As we speak, legislation has also been introduced that would limit the ability to declare endangered species habitats off limits to development. According to the authors of this legislation, it will force greater consideration for human needs.

Legislation has also been proposed to revise the 1972 federal Water Pollution Control Act to again allow *voluntary* regulation of water and chemical run-off from the farms and industry.

Just when many of us thought that our political representatives were finally understanding the importance of the environmental

This photograph was sent by Andrews to Hopi Indian elders in The United States seeking their views on what it might mean. They responded by saying "Mother is crying" (meaning Mother Earth). Perhaps by coincidence, it formed as the Gulf War began on August 4, 1990.

situation, we have come full circle, and, indeed, have begun to go backwards.

The unfortunate result of much of these backslides is that the health and safety of the people of the United States of America has been placed in the capable and oh-so trustworthy hands of multinational corporations who have, for the most part, been instrumental in getting us into this mess in the first place. And I do hope my sarcasm is not too subtle.

How much safer do you feel now?

Chapter 13

Crop Circle Hoaxes and the Circus in the Fields

There's a slapstick sort of humor in England that gets a belly laugh out of doing something bloody stupid. And it is bloody stupid. But it gets a laugh. I can't think that American farmers would want this kind of thing to come to their doors.

—Colin Andrews

You can't make a counterfeit without an original to copy. It is the only necessary response to those who insist that because some crop circles are manmade, all crop circles must, therefore, be manmade.

Authentic crop formations were around long before hoaxers butted in and began claiming formations they couldn't possibly have made.

Why has no one studied the profile of a hoaxer?

A detailed study of crop circle counterfeiters has not yet been done and I think it is imperative that such a study be undertaken. It is important to at least make the attempt to understand why people are doing this.

Serious crop circle researchers and students of the phenomena know that we have a hoaxing problem. We know that crop circle counterfeiters create phony crop formations for many reasons, including:

- Skeptics who want to deliberately interfere with the research and put it off track.

- "Earth artists" who see the creation of crop circles as an experiential art form.

- Pranksters having a bit of fun (the early 1990s "ejaculating penis" crop formation in England is a prime example of this type of, ahem, "mischief").

- Enthusiasts who actually believe they are contributing to the field with their efforts.

- Those with an agenda, be it political, social, environmental, or commercial. (Many corporations have of late been hiring "circlemakers" to create crop formations of logos, automobiles, symbols, and other commercial designs.)

Admittedly, the efforts of counterfeiters have become more sophisticated and complex over the past several years, seeming to parallel the sophistication—the *evolution*—of the authentic formations. Yet, it is known that counterfeiters have deliberately laid claim to highly complex authentic formations that they had absolutely nothing to do with. Why would they do such a thing? What could be the reasoning behind claiming responsibility for incredible manifestations in fields around the world, knowing full well they would never be able to duplicate the design if put to the test?

A detailed, comprehensive study of the hoaxing subculture needs to be done. Hoaxing muddies the waters and confuses the public, a populace that may not have much of a grounding, a knowledge base, of this extraordinary miracle taking place on our planet. The crop circle mystery is perplexing enough in and of itself without having these "fibbing bounders" (as researcher Danny Sotham has christened them) tramping all over the place, giddily delighting in tricking people into believing what, in essence, is nothing but a lie.

There has long been suspicion that there is much more to the hoaxing movement than may at first be presumed. Is it possible that the intelligence communities (CIA or M15, for example) in the countries where the phenomena is prevalent have recruited young to middle-aged males to vigorously and repeatedly create fakes? Would they lay claim to real formations, in a concerted attempt to trivialize, minimize, and ultimately discredit all that is genuine?

Disinformation has long been a hoary tactic in the intelligence communities' bag of duplicitous tricks. If, for some reason, world governments and their respective intelligence communities wanted to get the public "off the scent," there might be no better way then to put forth the message that all crop formations are fakes. I have stated that I do not believe that government satellites are responsible for crop circles. However, it is not beyond the realm of possibility that governments may be attempting to completely debunk the phenomena using a trained (and, it must be assumed, paid) team of hoaxers.

War of the Worlds

Why would this be deemed necessary? Some blame Orson Welles' *The War of the Worlds*.

It has long been suspected that world governments are fully apprised of the reality of UFOs and aliens, but that this information has been deliberately kept from the public because of the *War of the Worlds* debacle in 1938.

On Sunday, October 30, 1938, the day before Halloween, Orson Welles dramatized H. G. Wells's classic science fiction novel *War of the Worlds* for his Mercury Theater radio troupe. Welles's broadcast terrified millions of people and caused a national panic. A Princeton University study later determined that a total of 6 million people heard Welles's broadcast. Of those listeners, *1.7 million believed it was a real news bulletin and 1.2 million actually took action because of it.* The New York City police department received *2,000 hysterical emergency calls* from people during the first 15 minutes of the broadcast. The *New York Post*'s headline the following day read, "Radio 'War' Panic Brings Inquiry; U. S. To Scan Broadcast Script. Mars 'Attack' Brings Wave of

A Doug and Dave creation, this one in Chilcomb Down, made in 1991. Looking at these formations, it is easy to conclude that Doug and Dave's crop circle skills did not extend to the more complex patterns they took credit for when they went public with their story.

Hysteria." On their editorial page, the *Post* called Welles's actions "unscrupulous and irresponsible."[1]

In my opinion, it is quite conceivable that a plan has been conceived and executed by intelligence services to employ individuals that will deliberately muddy the crop circles waters by claiming hoaxing, by making particular patterns, and by laying claim to them.

We know that complex designs can be made by people. However, there are complex designs out there that show no evidence of the human hand whatsoever, and yet some of these are also claimed to be made by people. The enigma of the mystery is compounded by the question of why do hoaxers do what they do, and claim to have done things that show no sign of human involvement. I think for the most part, that the manner in which many of the crop circle counterfeiters have conducted themselves is disgraceful.

Counterfeiters fall into two different camps. One group of hoaxers want their artwork to remain mysterious. They claim to be making crop art, but they refuse to identify which specific "works" they are responsible for. They are passionate about maintaining the mystery and anonymity of their formations. They define what they do as experiential art, and they consider themselves invisible observers of the people who experience their art. Supposedly, the act of observing the effects that their artwork has on people is part of the overall artistic experience. This explains their insistence on mystery and anonymity

This appears to be aesthetically noble, and completely respectful of the undeniable beauty and impact crop formations have on people. However, it also serves to make their claims unprovable and it casts doubt on their ceaseless proclamations that they are responsible for this circle, or for that formation. Sophisticated research and equipment and advanced investigative intelligence techniques would be necessary to disprove all their claims and, even more importantly, *prove* their claims, and who would be willing to pay for that? On several occasions during 1999 and 2000, special night vision equipment did observe people making some elaborate patterns, but the large scale claims thus far remain unchallenged.

The second group consists of counterfeiters who have realized that continually hoaxing researchers and the public has become a potentially dangerous game, and that there is an inherent responsibility that comes with such deceptive practices. These are the folks who are more prone to believing that there is an actual phenomena at work out there, and that it is the right thing to do to step forward and admit the ones they've made, and then work with researchers openly. They are the ones who are willing to explain what they do, how they do it, and where they've done it.

I have been in touch with some of these people and many of them understand that there are consequences attached to their actions. Researchers need to know what is real and what is not, because people, governmental agencies, and the media act on such research. Many of these counterfeiters know that I and others provide aerial photographs of crop formations to governments, to civic officials, to the British Royal family, to native Americans and other indigenous peoples, and many others, all of whom are extremely interested in the crop circle phenomenon that is taking place on our planet. (Native Americans in particular are extremely interested in authentic crop circle manifestations, because they believe that these creations may be connected in some way to ancient tribal Hopi prophecy.)

Providing information to these people is an enormous responsibility, and some of the hoaxers now recognize the gravity of their "pranks." And I am just one researcher. All over the world, serious crop circle researchers are providing information of this type to people, governments, and agencies who need to know, and, I'll state it once again emphatically, *hoaxes muddy the waters.*

If, as I sincerely believe, the authentic crop circle formations are a sign from a higher intelligence, and there is a very serious message being communicated to us, it is a grave error in judgement for hoaxers to take this lightly, to mock the serious students of the phenomena, and to deliberately work to deceive. There has been a paradigm shift in consciousness on a global scale regarding the environment over the past several decades and the benign glory of real crop formations has spoken at a primal level to people who know they should be worried about the planet's health.

One of the most fundamental facts about the crop circle phenomenon is that the plants in crop circles *do not die. They are not killed. They continue to grow, and they grow with greater vigor.* The plants in hoaxed circles are badly damaged and, in many cases, are killed. They are crushed to death or broken down.

Hoaxers vex me. They play a game that mocks the work of serious researchers trying to understand a phenomena that could have monumental importance for the fate of the planet and all living things aboard her. The irony in all this is that many counterfeiters themselves—and I have been told this personally—have often come upon the same unusual, paranormal anomalies in crop circles that we have experienced, noted, and recorded. As they go on with their daft business of stomping about with boards and ropes, they have heard the sounds, seen the lights, and felt the energy waves. It seems as though they have somehow become unwitting participants in the gest. Is it possible that by focusing intently on the sacred geometries they use to create a fake crop formation, hoaxers are somehow tapping into a different sensibility, into the higher consciousness many experience when in contact with authentic crop circles? Can the deliberate creation of a fake crop formation—the actual act itself of designing it and making it—be a catalyst for an interaction between the hoaxers and the intelligence behind the true mystery?

Sacred geometry has been used for millennium as a tool for meditation, and as a gateway to achieving a higher state of consciousness. Hoaxers may be closer to the actual phenomenon than they may suspect.

I have used the term "friendly animosity" to describe my relationship with many of the admitted circle makers, but my (mostly) cordial interaction with them has an edge. And in all honesty, the essence of this edge is that I wish they did not exist. I am not wishing that the individuals who comprise the circle makers did not exist. Far from it. Heaven knows I would never wish them harm. I simply wish that all the circle makers who devote their time, their energy, and their resources to deceiving the world would find better ways to spend their time.

Granted, the making of art is often an act of creativity and enlightenment, an inherently positive endeavor: The artist produces a work to mirror a specific circumstance of the human condition. But counterfeiters pervert and debase the artistic process. If a painter creates a stunningly beautiful painting—a work that happens to be an *identical* copy of a Van Gogh, or a Rembrandt, or a Klimt—and then sells it as an original, is this an "inherently positive endeavor"? I think not. And many agree with me.

All that said, though, to reiterate, the circle makers do have a story to tell. Their presence in the fields, and their participation in the phenomena—no matter how tangential or skewed—may ultimately become a study in consciousness. I believe it would do grave harm to allow anger towards the hoaxers to consume those of us who believe that these people are tampering with what might be called a miracle.

Consider this: Imagine if hoaxers simply stopped. One day, they threw away their boards, coiled up their ropes, and simply went away. With confidence and certainty, I will state that, if that happened, crop formations would continue to appear, and every one of them would be a source of wonder. Imagine the state of the research then! Imagine the progress we would make if all we needed to investigate were real crop circles, each one a unique treasure of the fields!

But that is not going to happen, unless all the counterfeiters jointly agree to cease and desist their duplicitous efforts. Because that is unlikely, researchers must factor them into the equation. Thus, we try to discern the fakes from the real ones; we interview hoaxers about their experiences in the fields; and we spend countless hours and untold energy explaining to people interested in crop circles why they should not assume that *every* crop formation is a fake, simply because *some* of them are.

My close friend and my co-author of *Circular Evidence*, Pat Delgado, a man of good heart and intent, was personally devastated by the antics of the crop fakers. The uproar in the media over Doug and Dave, as well as the mindless acceptance of anything claimed by those copycats who followed, caused Pat tremendous grief. When he and I first began investigating the earliest crop circles, we both believed we were working for the good of humanity; that we were trying to help understand something that could be quite extraordinary in the history of man and his interaction with the planet. When Doug and Dave came forward and claimed authorship of a ridiculous number of crop circles (a number so high, in fact, it would have been physically impossible for them to have made them all), we students of the phenomenon were standing in the line of fire; we were suddenly targets for a media not interested in the truth, but only in how much mortification they could rain down upon me and Pat.

Can the mysterious, unknown forces behind authentic crop circles also be manipulating the counterfeiters?

Many counterfeiters, sometimes unknowingly, have duplicated in their manmade creations the same ratios and geometries often found in the real circles. And there are stories told of hoaxers returning to the site and finding additions to the formations that they did not create—and many of the add-ons resulted in their original work now complying with the sacred geometry ratios often found in real formations.

What seems clear to me from all this is the feeling that we must look at the complete picture that is developing; we must try to encompass the entirety of the phenomenon before passing final judgment.

I do not understand hoaxing as a pursuit worthy of good men, but we do need to continue to talk to these deceivers and put all our efforts into figuring out why they *really* do what they do. That is the key to understanding how the hoaxers' involvement in crop circles could be significant. What if we learn that the reason many of the hoaxers take the time to create fake crop circles is because of a subconscious "calling," for want of a better term? As we have repeatedly seen, many hoaxers work with the same geometries as are found in authentic circles. They also lay them in areas where other circles have been found, and sometimes, in alignment with the earth's

ley lines. In fact, there have been occasions when two groups of hoaxers, working independently and unbeknownst to each other, have ended up in adjacent fields, creating similar designs.

Is this mere coincidence? Or is there some force tugging them in the direction of constructing symbolically significant formations? Is it possible that they are all unconsciously receiving their "instructions" from the same force? Are the patterns made by hoaxers part of the overall message?

These are the questions that need to be researched and answered before we decide on how to respond to what I truly believe is some kind of dispatch from a communicator we have yet to meet.

The patterns have been evolving in complexity. Using an alphabetical simile, if the first simple circles were the letter A, and the ultimate, final, still unseen crop formation is the letter Z, I believe that we are currently somewhere around the letters V or W. Each year, we believe that formations cannot get much more complex, and then the following year, the formations that appear outdo the previous ones.

Hidden somewhere in the fractals, and the ratios, and the geometries, is usable information. I believe that the totality of crop formations is a repository of useful information. I think part of this arcane message lies in the alignment of crop circles around the globe. It has something to do with magnetism, of this I am certain. I also think there may be other "brothers" (or perhaps, cousins?) of magnetism that will likewise play a role in our understanding of the ultimate message

Ohm's Law tells us that there are three components to electrical current. Put simply, voltage equals current times resistance. Magnetic fields are created solely by moving electrical charges and, because it is my

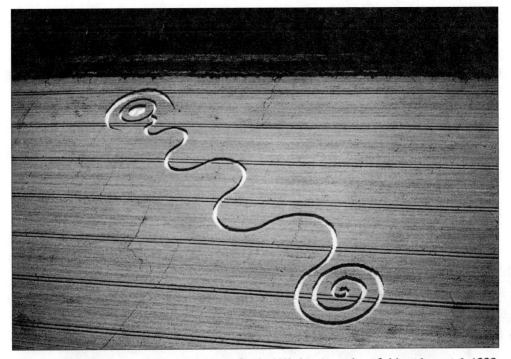

This unusual pattern appeared near Barbury Castle, Wiltshire in a wheat field on August 6, 1999.

contention that the crop circle mystery in a large part involves magnetism in some form, I consider it a possibility that we may not yet understand all the ramifications of the interaction between electricity and magnetism. There may still be yet unknown fields of energy created (or possibly destroyed) when magnetic fields are generated. What happens to the laws of physics when we exceed the speed of light, for instance? I think that when we finally discover *all* the ramifications to the current scientific laws, we will find many brothers and cousins we did not know existed.

Some researchers have suggested that the patterns need to be placed in a particular alignment and that when they are, something wondrous will happen. Human consciousness, this theory posits, is working on fine-tuning this alignment, and that some of the counterfeiters—the ones who truly feel a psychic or spiritual need to make crop circles—may be contributing to the final grid of designs.

This theory attempts to factor in the creations of the hoaxers as part of the overall master plan. I accept this as another hypothesis and will consider the evidence when presented with it, but for me, the most important research would take place if all the fake formations were removed from the equation and we were able to study only the *authentic* manifestations. We seem to be drifting away from this scenario.

(See Chapter 6, "The Stonehenge Julia Set," for more on this critical alignment theory.)

Notes

[1]Stephen Spignesi, *The UFO Book of Lists*, p. 82–83.

Chapter 14

Operation Blackbird

Blackbird fly...into the light of a dark black night...

—Paul McCartney

Operation Blackbird

In July 1990, I coordinated a crop circles surveillance operation called Operation Blackbird. Regardless of the way this event played out, and regardless of how I was treated, my intentions were righteous, and I approached the operation with trust. Was I naive? Many of my critics would respond, "Unquestionably." Nonetheless, I willingly trusted, and hope I was trusted in turn.

Operation Blackbird was an important event in the annals of crop circle history, and it boasted a potpourri of oddities, including a government-sponsored hoax, a secret tape that has never been seen, a genuine crop circle manifestation not revealed to the public, and happenings important enough that the British government issued one of their highest security alerts for the operation. It was eventually revealed that the British Ministry of Defense had ordered a full-scale operation to create a hoax pattern and discredit and humiliate myself and other serious crop circle researchers.

However, there is much more to this story than the embarrassment of one Brit.

•••

The operation was funded 90 percent by Nippon Television of Japan, with the remaining 10 percent funded by BBC Television of Great Britain.

The plan was to set up a bank of specialized cameras in a place where many crop circles had appeared over the years in the hope that we would actually catch a crop circle forming on film.

The location chosen was Bratton Castle, which is an Iron Age hill fort from around the eighth century B.C. on top of highland looking down into the county of Wiltshire, England. It is a gorgeous location, and the land is owned by the Ministry of Defense in Great Britain. We requested, and were granted, permission to conduct the operation. Later we would realize the permission came a bit too readily, but at the time, we were delighted at the willingness with which the Ministry of Defense's office granted us permission.

The scene during Operation Blackbird.

Within a few hours after the operation began, Pat Delgado and I were approached by BBC Television personnel, a representative from Nippon TV, and two uniformed military officers from the British Army.

The operation had already begun to attract attention from the locals, and for good reason. A command and control center had been set up above the field, and there were cameras, wires, antennae, tents, vehicles, and many personnel milling about. The TV representatives and the military officers suggested that we drive off the site in my motorcar to discuss something of importance, and Pat and I readily agreed.

We traveled a short distance to a country lane where we were out of sight of the public and away from the commotion of the site.

The two military officers then told us that they thought we could use some additional equipment and that they were prepared to provide for our use night-viewing, image-intensifying cameras. The specific equipment they offered to us were back-mounted cameras that would be worn in carrying packs on the back and shoulders of the military personnel who would be given the assignment to work with us.

We were told that these recording devices were state-of-the-art and highly efficient, that they would allow us to see a blade of grass from some distance away, at night.

Pat and I, as well as the representatives from the Nippon TV and the BBC, were delighted with the opportunity to use advanced military surveillance equipment for Operation Blackbird, and we all felt that the addition of such gear would guarantee that if a crop circle appeared, we would see it, and we would record it.

The only condition attached to our use of the military cameras was that two British Army officers needed to be assigned to our organizational unit and that they would be the ones to operate the equipment. This made sense, as none of us were trained in the use of such high-tech cameras. We would also be liable for damage to the equipment if something went wrong.

And so, we accepted two military officers and their equipment into the operation and onto the site. At the time, we thought nothing of this condition. However, our views on this were to change radically within a very short time.

Blackbird became operational, and close to $2-million worth of equipment was online and prepared to chronicle whatever might happen. The equipment had all been checked and every camera was functioning perfectly when the operation began.

The plan was to maintain daylight monitoring, and to also keep a crew working throughout the night. If something should occur during the night, I and a number of other people would be awakened at home.

On the second night of the operation, I was at my home in the adjacent county of Hampshire when the phone rang quite late. I was told that something had happened. I was told that an arrangement of crop circles—a fairly complex design—had appeared in the field during the night.

I immediately notified my contact person from Nippon TV, and we mobilized a television crew that had been on standby for just such an eventuality. Because Nippon TV had funded the overwhelming majority of the costs of the operation, they were entitled to the first notification and the first footage of the event. Nippon TV had agreed to participate in Operation Blackbird with the hope that they would record the actual formation of a crop circle and be able to show it on Japanese television.

The TV crew sprang into action, and we all sped to the site, not knowing what we would find when we arrived.

When we arrived, there was great excitement. I was told by personnel there that an event had occurred, and that there was something in the field. I was also told that aerial phenomenon—unusual lights directly over the field—had also been witnessed, and that all of this had been captured on camera.

Operation Blackbird had begun on July 23, 1990, and here it was two days later, on July 25, and a crop formation had appeared!

The formation had first been seen between 3:30 and 3:45 in the morning, not even first light, and it was then that everyone knew that something important had occurred.

After the sun rose and we all saw from a distance what was in the field, I was asked if I would announce the event on live television, which I agreed to do. We had requested helicopters for an accurate aerial view of the formation, but they had not yet arrived. I agreed to announce the discovery even before I had had a chance to enter the site.

The BBC and Nippon TV both had crews there, and they set up the cameras and waited for the proper alignment of their communications satellites for a worldwide broadcast.

Lights, camera, action, as they say, and here is what I said that day:

> *Yes, we have an event here of greatest importance...and we are very much excited, as you can imagine. We do have two major ground markings which have appeared in front of all the surveillance equipment, performing absolutely to form for us. We had a situation at approximately 3:30 A.M. this morning. On the monitor, a number of orange lights taking the form of a triangle....It is a complex situation and we are analyzing it at the moment, but there is undoubtedly something here for science.*

A reporter then said to me, "I'm sure you have the nation agog. Are you quite sure you couldn't have been the victim of some elaborate hoax last night?" To which I replied:

> *No, not indeed. We have high-quality equipment here, and we have indeed secured on high-quality equipment a major event....We do have something here of great, great significance. Yes, we have everything on film, and we do have, as I say, a formed object over the field....We are doing nothing more until we have helicopters over the top, to film in detail what we have, before anyone enters the field.*

What I said was in response to what I had seen from a distance and to what I had been told. My words are now recorded forever in the annals of crop circle history, and I can only say that it was a regrettable milestone in my research career.

Aside from my obvious error in stating unequivocally that this was an authentic event, the essence of my answer, however, still stands as valid and reasonable: We have something here and we are going to investigate it further. I did believe it was an exciting day for science and, in the end, it turned out to be much more than that. A crop formation now existed in the field, unusual lights had been witnessed, and we were continuing to analyze the information.

The lights turned out to be of the most pedestrian nature: British millionaire Richard Branson had flown a hot air balloon over the field during the night and his running lights were interpreted as being something out of the ordinary. One needed to ask, was Branson a part of the hoax? Was Branson asked or paid to fly a silent "aircraft" in pitch darkness over a field where surveillance equipment had been set up on the particular evening when his flight would be noticed? Branson stated emphatically that his was nothing but a curiosity trip and that he had not intended to disrupt an operation, nor annoy the crop circle researchers. So be it.

When the sun finally rose on that ill-fated day, we could see clearly what we had in the field. The helicopter had arrived and had begun flying photographers and cameramen over the site for aerial photographs. I and some of my colleagues entered the field to investigate the crop formation. My television interview had been broadcast, and there was high expectation around the world as to what we would actually find in the fields.

What we discovered was a disgrace to the British government, and to everyone else involved in the perpetration of one of the biggest deceits in crop circle history. Oh yes, there was a crop formation in the field beneath Bratton Castle, but it was not only obviously manmade, but it was quite obviously *poorly* manmade. We had been set up. The crop circle that had been constructed was ragged, and unlike anything we had seen before. There was considerable damage to the crops, noticeable irregularities in the lines and circles, and, gilding the lily in a way only a bureaucracy could conceive of doing, there were items deliberately placed in the middle of the main circle, including a horoscope game board, and a wooden cross.

It appears that the British government, in an outrageous attempt to defuse the crop circle mania and discredit and humiliate myself and my colleagues, had funded a crop circle hoax. Apparently, the money could not have been put to better use in England, a country where the "4,000 holes in Blackburn, Lancashire" that John Lennon sang about in "A Day in the Life" referred to potholes in the streets.

Pat and I were made to be laughingstocks. Most of the reporters left, and many ended up writing stories in which we were the fools. We truly felt that serious study of the crop circle phenomenon had been impeded considerably, if not damaged irreparably. This was a major setback and the media dropped it like a hot potato.

We later learned the specifics of the hoax from a high contact in the British military. Researcher George Wingfield, speaking in Michael Hesemann's book *The Cosmic Connection*, relayed the following information he received from his anonymous military contact:

> *The Bratton hoax was carried out by a specially-trained unit of the army and the order came directly from the Ministry of Defense. The operation was carefully planned, prepared in advance and then carried out in complete darkness, quickly and precisely. My informant was even able to speak with an officer who was involved in the planning of the operation, which had the highest secrecy level.[1]*

This could have been the end of Operation Blackbird, but it was not. I continued my monitoring of the field, although with far fewer media folk than before the hoax.

Ten days after the fake formation had been constructed, a real crop circle appeared in the field below Bratton Castle.

On August 5, 1990, 440 yards from the site of the hoaxed formation, a real circle appeared—and its formation was captured on film.

This second event, which was most definitely an authentic crop formation, was recorded on what has come to be known as the "yellow camera." I was off the site when this occurred, but I was immediately notified of the event and returned within one hour.

"Where's the tape?" I asked the moment I arrived.

I was told by one of the team members that the tape had been placed in a locked box—I was actually shown a sealed case that was supposedly the box where the tape was secured—and I was also informed that it had only been viewed once. I was not allowed to watch the tape nor was I able in any way to confirm that the actual tape from the yellow camera was now in the locked box.

I later learned the truth. The tape from the yellow camera had been immediately removed from the site by person or persons unknown, and it has never been seen since. I was immediately sworn to secrecy and I was instructed—"ordered" is actually a better word—by a person whom I will not name, to give Mr. Michihito Ogawa of Nippon Television a videotape. I was to tell him that the tape was from the yellow camera, and assure him that it contained the footage of the crop circle event. The tape given to Mr. Ogawa was actually video of the site taken days earlier, and it showed nothing but the silent landscape.

Mr. Ogowa returned to NTV headquarters in Japan, where extensive analysis of the tape was performed. Regrettably, they were analyzing a decoy tape. The tape that they owned the rights to was not provided to them, and to this day I have no knowledge of the whereabouts of the tape from the yellow camera—footage that shows the formation of an authentic crop circle in a field in central southern England.

I say now that I firmly believe that I was not being given a choice when I was told to give NTV a dummy tape. I do not know what would have happened if I had refused to do as I was ordered. I suspect that I would have been banned from the site and that Mr. Ogawa would have been given the phony tape anyway. I was in a very difficult position, seeing as how the

British military—with all the power of the government behind them—was issuing the orders at the Operation Blackbird site.

Some years later, a gentleman I know from BBC radio told me that his station was receiving live broadcasts from the Operation Blackbird site, and that after the second event occurred, a rarely issued D Notice was placed on their broadcasts by the British Government. A D Notice is a Ministry of Defense National Security Notice that gives the British Government the right to immediately terminate a radio or television broadcast, ostensibly for reasons of national security. That day, the D Notice was invoked, and broadcasts from Operation Blackbird were suspended for a period of four hours.

And so, I say again: Operation Blackbird was an important event in crop circle history. It was the first known government attempt to deescalate the public interest in a growing phenomenon, and it was carried out by means of a well-orchestrated, well-funded, multilevel hoax.

This speaks volumes about the importance—and the authenticity—of the crop circle phenomenon. Now, if we could only see that tape from the yellow camera....

Postscript

Charles and Diana

Later on in the 1990s, I learned that Prince Charles had discovered crop circles on his property and that, in fact, he had actually had them on his land for many years. I also learned that crop circles were reported on land near the Queen's Balmoral castle.

At some point, I was contacted by a retired military officer who lived about 20 miles from my home. He told me he was acting as an intermediary for Charles and that the prince was very interested in the phenomenon of crop circles. Of course,

Prince Charles could not contact me directly about this, and so I willingly agreed to work with his liaison. At his request, we began to send our newsletter to Prince Charles, and we also sent it to the duke of Edinburgh at Buckingham Palace, who was interested in crop circles as well.

Following a series of telephone calls, it was arranged for me to take Charles and Diana on a tour of the fields near their home where the crop circles were appearing, explain to them what was going on, and fill them in on what we have learned about the phenomenon.

I agreed to complete confidentiality and can swear that I told no one about the meeting but my wife at the time. I did not even tell my parents or my daughter.

The day before our scheduled meeting, however, all hell broke loose.

The British tabloid newspaper *The Star* (now defunct) published a front-page story revealing that I was scheduled to take Charles and Diana on a tour of crop circles, and that the prince was obsessed with the phenomenon. Somehow, someone at the newspaper had gotten hold of this information and they decided to publish it.

As I have said, the only one on my side who knew about this was my wife, who I know for a fact did not say a word. This leaves one of two possibilities: Either someone in the British royal family, or someone involved with them, leaked the news to the media; or my phone was tapped. Personally, I suspect the story was leaked from inside Buckingham Palace.

As soon as the story broke, I received a frantic phone call from my contact canceling the meeting. He told me that everyone involved in Charles and Diana's camp was angry and embarrassed by the media debacle. I assured him I had nothing to do with leaking the story, but I am not sure if he—or Charles and Diana—believed me.

How it got out remains a mystery to this day, although I have my suspicions. Considering that the British intelligence agencies and the British military mounted Operation Blackbird against me and other crop circle researchers, it would not surprise me if they took it upon themselves to tap my phone and then leak the news to the press, leaving the British royalty completely out of the decision. I suspect that the military, for some reason, felt it was harmful for the British royal family to admit an interest in crop circles, and thus, if I am correct, they torpedoed the plan by means of public humiliation of me, and Charles and Diana. I have no evidence of this, but it makes sense to me, considering the efforts to which British intelligence had gone in the past to discredit crop circle researchers and make them a joke in the mind of the public. It worked, because the result of the tabloid story was to again damage my reputation and belittle my work.

Sometime after this unfortunate episode, the same retired military officer contacted me and invited me to his home to discuss the possibility of my preparing a technical report summarizing my work on crop circles. I asked him for whom this report was intended, and he told me Britain's undersecretary of state for the environment, Nicholas Ridley. Ridley was one of the top five people in Prime Minister Margaret Thatcher's cabinet and he briefed Mrs. Thatcher daily on matters relevant to the environment. I agreed to provide the report, and it was forwarded to Mr. Ridley who then, presumably, advised the prime minister on its contents. I do not know specifically what came of my efforts, but I do know that several members of parliament raised the question of crop circles with the prime minister and home office minister. They wanted to know what the British government knew about these formations; what, if any, was their interest in them; and

what, if anything, were they doing about them at the governmental level.

The chief scientific advisor to the British government and to Prime Minister Margaret Thatcher responded that the Home Office and Ministry of Defense had no particular interest in crop circles and that they were not believed to pose a threat to the security of the United Kingdom.

An important point to emphasize regarding this position by the British government is that they went on the record with their statement that the crop circles were not manmade; thereby confirming that there was, indeed, a phenomenon occurring in the fields of England.

However, they did not suggest anything paranormal or extraterrestrial as its cause. Instead, they stated that they were being created by meteorological forces not yet fully understood. They endorsed the theory that crop circles were formed by a plasma vortex—a new kind of whirlwind or tornado in which electrified air, created in the lee of a hill or by thermal variations, traveled across the fields, leaving geometric formations in its wake.

Contradicting this theory, though, was the fact that there were many reports of crop circles appearing in fields around which were no hills for miles, and most reports were of formations appearing at night, which is highly unlikely if the cause were plasma vortices caused by daytime temperature variations.

The facts did not line up with their statement, and so those of us researching crop circles knew that there was no real science behind their official declaration. There have been no official statements from the British governments about crop circles since that time.

Notes

[1]Michael Hesemann, *The Cosmic Connection*, p. 29.

Chapter 15

The Oliver's Castle Video

How many things we held yesterday as articles of faith which today we tell as fables.

—**Michel de Montaigne**

Hidden in Plain Sight?

We probably should have been suspicious from the moment we first met the young man who claimed to have filmed UFOs making crop circles in a field below Oliver's Castle in England.

Why? Partly because the man told us his name was "Weyleigh." My radar, however, did not pick up on the importance of his name at the time.

"Weyleigh" is a homonym—a sound alike word—for the verb "waylay," which is defined, "to lie in wait for and attack from ambush," or "to accost or intercept unexpectedly."

The truth about this man and his phony video were hidden in plain sight, in his very name, and yet none of us saw this until much later.

Like Cameras at the Creation

If it were true, it would have been one of the most important pieces of film in all of human history.

If it were true, it would have, for the first time, captured actual images of UFOs creating a crop circle.

If it were true, it would have made an enormous contribution toward a deeper understanding of the crop circle phenomenon.

If the Oliver's Castle video was authentic, it would have been on the front page of every newspaper in the world.

But alas, it was not real. It was created by John Wabe, a video editor and producer for a film production company called First Cut in Bristol, England. The Oliver's Castle video is a hoax, but as I have repeatedly said, it is an important hoax.

How can a deliberately manufactured piece of video be important in the field of crop circle research? Wouldn't its ultimate impact be to discredit the efforts of those of us who are serious about understanding what is going on, and render all future evidentiary artifacts suspect?

These are valid questions and legitimate concerns, but the key questions that hover over the Oliver's Castle video like the small white UFOs that hover over the Wiltshire field where the snowflake crop formation "appeared" are, "Why would someone go through the trouble—and expense—of putting together such an elaborate hoax?" and, "Who was behind it?"

We will explore those questions in this chapter and suggest some possible answers. It is quite possible that there was much more to the Oliver's Castle video than met the eye.

On August 11, 1996, a snowflake crop formation appeared in the field at Oliver's Castle, near Devizes, England in Wiltshire.

At the time, so the story goes, a man who was using the name of "John Weyleigh" was camping on the hilltop of Oliver's Castle overlooking the field, hoping to record the formation of a crop circle. Crop formations believed to be authentic had appeared in the area prior to this, so Weyleigh came prepared with a video camera and other gear.

According to Weyleigh's story, at approximately 5 a.m. on the morning of August 11, as the first light of the day barely began to creep over the fields, he saw a small sphere of white light pass swiftly across the field directly below his location. He quickly grabbed his video camera and switched it on, but the camera failed to operate because of the excessive moisture in the air. The moisture sensor inside the camera prevented him from capturing the appearance of this initial white sphere, but Weyleigh waited a moment or two, tried the camera again, and that time it worked. He pointed the camera at the field below him and started filming.

Just seconds into the filming, two white spheres flew into the frame from the right and arced across the field in a large spiral, mimicking in its flight path the shape of the Julia Set crop formation that had appeared at Stonehenge the previous June.

As the spheres flew across the field, a small circle of crop suddenly flattened to the ground and, following within seconds, (corroborating what many eyewitnesses of

crop circle manifestations had previously reported), a complete, large, complex "snowflake" crop pattern materialized. Before the sequence ended, a second pair of white glowing spheres entered the frame from the top left corner, and similarly spiraled above the crops. As they flew, the pathways and smaller circles in this elaborate pattern were formed.

The whole filmed sequence is just a few seconds long and my initial reaction upon first viewing it was that it was one of two things: it was either the most incredibly important UFO and crop circle film footage of all time, or it was one of the most elaborate frauds ever perpetrated on the world.

The following facts gave favor to the film's authenticity:

1. It looked convincing. My personal reaction to the footage was that it fulfilled my expectations as to what we would see if someday someone captured on film the sudden appearance of a crop circle. Features of crop circle formation commonly described by witnesses and in the literature can be seen, especially the speed at which the circles formed.

   Also, Weyleigh reported being awakened by an electronic trilling sound, the "crop circle" sound I have personally witnessed three times and recorded twice. There is an old saying that the secret to the best scams is in the details, and Weyleigh including this sound in his report is truly inspired, because he was attesting to something that had previously been reported by one of the world's authorities on crop circles: me, Colin Andrews. He was inculcating honesty and trustworthiness by association.

2. Several researchers were shown the Oliver's Castle video at the Barge Inn near Devizes at 10:50 p.m., on the evening of August 11, a mere 17 hours after it was allegedly recorded. All it showed were the UFOs. John Weyleigh was the only one who claimed to have seen them "live."

3. Before detailed computer analysis of the film was performed, several film experts stated that the image processing required to blend the two series of events—the formation of the circles and the flight of UFOs—would have required a degree of technical sophistication, as well as the use of professional editing equipment.

4. What would the motive be for committing time and money to the creation of an elaborate crop circle hoax video? After the hoax was revealed and a confession obtained, we have since arrived at some conclusions as to why such an operation would be undertaken.

There has long been strong suspicion, along with some anecdotal evidence, that the Oliver's Castle video was part of a government-sponsored disinformation campaign to discredit crop circle research. After all, the British government did successfully pull off Operation Blackbird. It is not that farfetched to conceive of an ongoing disinformation crusade, signed off on at the highest levels of government—on both sides of the Atlantic. Could this have been a government plot?

The following factors disprove the film's authenticity:

1. The identity of the man purporting to have filmed the UFOs and the crop circle—John Weyleigh—was dubious. Many attempts to contact him were unsuccessful and much of the information he provided turned out to be false.

2. One of the first things Weyleigh wanted to talk about was money. He offered me a handwritten royalty contract almost immediately and seemed to be very interested in how he could profit from sales and broadcast of the video.

3. The camera appeared to be already set up for the event, and the crop pattern conveniently formed in the exact center of the frame. The frame did not change during the construction of the crop design, even as the spheres left the field.

Weyleigh did not follow the flight of the balls of light with his camera, nor did he attempt to zoom in on the original pair of balls, both of which are actions that would be expected if the event and the filming of it were truly spontaneous. The framing of the scene suggested that the cameraman already knew about and anticipated the arrival of the second pair of spheres. Of course, this interpretation would be moot if the footage was created out of "whole cloth" in a video editing bay.

4. Weyleigh's comments on the soundtrack of his footage fall short of the level of excitement one would expect of someone witnessing a truly transdimenional event.

5. Many research discoveries publicly attributed to me appear in the sequence, including: Small UFO spheres seen in the vicinity of the fields where crop circles appear;

Army personnel showing an interest in crop circles (Weyleigh claims he was approached by a military officer who asked him if he had seen anything, but this encounter was not seen on the tape); the design of the pattern is a snowflake, and I have repeatedly publicly used the phrase "like a snowflake freezing" to describe specific patterns.

The claim of hearing an electrostatic crackling or trilling sound before the crop formation appeared, a direct reference to the crop circle sound I have personally witnessed three times and recorded twice; my repeated statements about the speed at which witnesses report crop circles forming; and the snippet of footage showing the plants oscillating, opening, and dropping to the ground like a fan, a characteristic I have described many times.

It was uncanny! Here, in a few seconds of video, were all of the elements that were not only typical of authentic crop circle formations, but were also points of information I had spoken and written about countless times during my career. It was as though someone had made notes on elements that I had emphasized over the years, and then said, "Well, let's be sure to add the sound, and make sure you mention the military guy, and let's make it a snowflake, and let's have the formation appear in less than 10 seconds." The presence of all these factors made me suspicious and, it would turn out, for good cause.

6. When my wife Synthia and I first met Mr. "Weyleigh," he was extremely nervous and wanted to leave the moment he obtained my signature on a handwritten contract granting me a 10 percent share of all monies earned by the video. Wouldn't the natural emotions after filming such an extraordinary event be elation and excitement? Why was he so anxious, unless he was afraid he would be found out?

These suspicions started the wheels turning, and immediately I began to speculate on the possible reasons why this man would go through the trouble of making such a video if it was, indeed, a hoax.

The question, why would he do this? kept playing in a loop in my mind.

Why?

I concluded that there were three possible reasons for Weyleigh to make the Oliver's Castle video:

Money: How would Weyleigh make money from the video? Royalties from sales of the video on VHS and DVD, plus broadcast fees charged to television stations that wanted to air the video. After Wayleigh was uncovered as "John Wabe," and it was confirmed that the film was a hoax, he came forward, admitted his involvement—and then signed a deal with Nippon TV to participate in a documentary about the Oliver's Castle video. This led me to believe that he was trying to recoup whatever profits he could from the video after he resigned himself to accepting that there would be no profit from the sale and airing of the original video.

Mischief: Could it be possible that Wabe would invest his time and money to produce a prank? My initial reaction was "not bloody likely." Yet, in a videotaped confession, Wabe claimed he made the video for "fun" and that it would be "a good laugh." He said he had always been interested in crop circles and that he knew that many

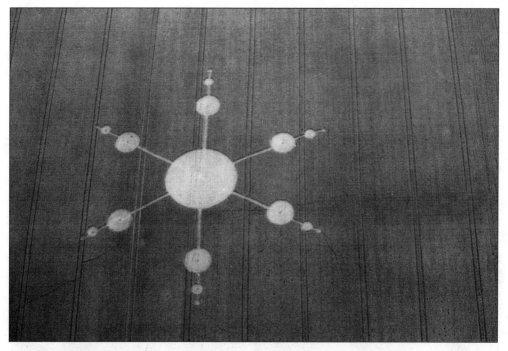

Snowflake formation featured in the hoaxed Oliver's Castle video. It was discovered by the young man who claimed to have filmed UFOs on August 11, 1996.

crop circle followers believed UFOs were making them, so he gave them what they expected.

A disinformation campaign: This theory posits that Wabe was hired by governmental agencies to make a hoaxed video as part of a broader plan to discredit crop circle researchers. This begs the question: Why would they bother? Wouldn't such a video be done better by NASA or NSA, instead of some small British film editing company? Assuming one of the governments were actually involved, they would have had to have known that their ruse would have been uncovered.

After months of speculation, and endless Internet debate, the truth was uncovered: John Weyleigh was actually John Wabe, and he was a video editor for a company called First Cut in Bristol, England. Wabe admitted his involvement in making

the film and in disseminating it to myself. I myself never asked for money from any of the media outlets I granted permission to show the Oliver's Castle footage, so the whole effort paid Mr. "Weyleigh" nothing for his efforts.

Ultimately, the truth is known only to Wabe and his partners, yet fun. His interest in signing a royalty contract almost immediately, however, is persuasive evidence that they may have also been in it for the money.

Postscript

In 2002, John "Weyleigh" Wabe and his partner John Lomas were editors on a wildlife documentary series called *Wildlife*, which was produced by the Scandinature production company. Nice to see he's keeping his editing skills up to snuff, eh?

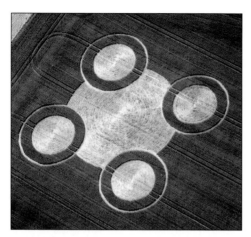

A large Celtic Cross formation that appeared at Headbourne Worthy in 1997.

The Julia Set seen in proximity to Stonehenge (1996).

A spectacular and enormous multiple Julia Set formation comprised of 409 circles in perfect symmetry. This formation appeared in Milk Hill, Wiltshire, England in 2001 in only minutes and showed no sign of human authorship. (Photo by Busty Taylor, used with permission.)

A five-circle Celtic Cross that has been visited by many people. Note the absence of an entry line to the upper left circle.

This pattern appeared at Cley Hill, England in 1997. The drawing seen above the formation was drawn by an American woman who had "remote viewed" the pattern that later appeared in the field, almost identical to her envisioned design. She showed Colin Andrews her drawing during a visit to England in the summer of 1997.

The Triple Julia Set, Windmill Hill, England, 1996. This formation appeared shortly after the original Stonehenge Julia Set.

Simple circles in a pristine field, showing no evidence of human authorship.

This Celtic Cross crop pattern was wished for by Colin Andrews in 1988. It appeared in a field near his home the following morning. This photo was used as the cover of his first book about the phenomenon, *Circular Evidence.*

Colin Andrews investigating the interior of a new crop circle.

Two formations simultaneously manifesting near Avebury. This photo shows the stunning beauty of crop patterns in nature.

A ground-level view of the precise sections found within crop circles.

A crop formation "pointing" to one of England's ancient archaeological sites.

A classic Celtic Cross formation, found in the fields of England.

This huge insectogram appeared within minutes in a pristine field in East Meon, England in 1997. The formation lies dead center on a ley line and, according to researcher Freddie Silva, its coordinates reference 24 ancient burial tumuli, Neolithic sites, and other crop circles.

This petal formation with the "Hamlet" logo is an obvious hoax, and it appeared in a wheat field in Bishops Canning, Wiltshire, in July of 1998. Note the face smoking a cigar in the upper right quadrant of the petal. Hamlet cigars are a popular smoke in England.

This bicycle was created in a wheat field near Cheesefoot Head, Hampshire in July 1994, along the route of the Tour de France, the first year the race ran through Britain.

Inside a crop formation.

The breathtaking beauty of English fields dotted with simple circles.

A large jellyfish formation. This was believed to be a hoax commissioned by the media in July of 1998. Interestingly, at least one visitor to the site reported strange noises on a videotape recorded whilst in the formation.

This formation, the Scorpion, was found at Bishops Canning, Wiltshire, in 1994.

A crop formation next to England's Silbury Hill, one of the oldest manmade mounds on Earth, built c. 2660 B.C.

A circle surrounded by seven rings, embraced by a wide curving border. This pattern manifests diatonic ratios and reflects a "torc" pattern commonly used for Celtic neck bracelets from Iron Age western Europe. Also, the exact center of the center circle lies precisely on the line of an underground aquifer that can not be seen on the ground. (The underground water's effect on the crops can be seen in the band of white passing through the formation.)

A powerful illustration of the clockwise swirl of authentic formations.

A photo taken on August 4, 1987 of a military helicopter above a field in Westbury, in which three simple crop circles had appeared. The helicopter was piloted by Captain D.F. Borrill of 658 Squadron, British Army Air Corps. His assignment was to photograph the three circles. Note the far left circle between the tram lines with no visible means of access. The plants in the righthand circle had originally swirled counterclockwise, but later, a second event occurred in which the plants inexplicably reversed their swirl to clockwise orientation.

A photo of the balls of light often seen in the vicinity of crop circles.

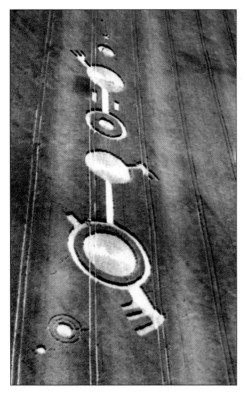

This 600-foot formation appeared in Alton Barnes in 1990. It was the first pattern to use such elements as the key, claw, and straight lines to connect circles.

Another elaborate "key" pictogram. This one appeared in Beckhampton, Wiltshire, on July 27, 1990. The alignment of this formation is perfectly parallel with the border of the field.

A ground view of the Alton Barnes crop circle formation, showing the breadth of space of the fields.

This beautiful, perfectly symmetrical web formation appeared in 1994. In the upper left of this photo is the ancient sacred archaeological site of Avebury.

A close-up of the 1994 Web in its field near Avebury.

An example of a poorly hoaxed formation. Note the irregular lines, the varying widths of the circle borders, and the oval shape of the center circle. The design lacks the precision edges and perfect symmetries found in the authentic formations.

This is one of the most recent manmade designs. It depicts a woman's face, possibly a woman of Native American lineage. Colin Andrews was informed beforehand that this pattern would be made.

Another manmade circle, this one in East Field, Alton Barnes, Wiltshire, in 2002. This manmade creation speaks to Colin's theory that even the counterfeiters are playing a role in the crop circle phenomenon. The tree is a sacred symbol of life, and serves as an organic metaphor of the environment.

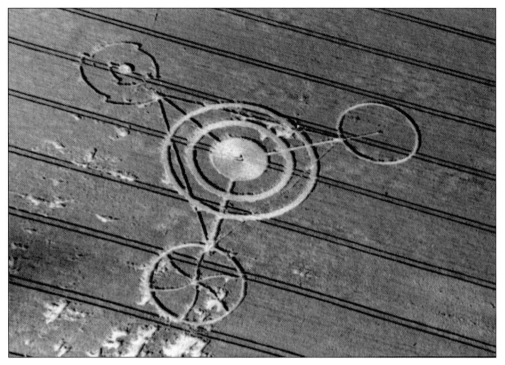

The Barbury Castle Tetrahedron. This geometric formation covered 12,000 square yards and appeared overnight in 1991, near the town of Wroughton, England. During the night, the town and a nearby military base lost all their electrical power and small, brightly colored objects were witnessed flying above the field where the design appeared. A British newspaper later ran a story about the formation with the headline, "Now Explain This One."

Chilcomb Down, near Cheesefoot Head, Wiltshire, 1991. An example of Doug and Dave's work. Note the "double D" signature and the rough, obviously manmade look to the formation.

This car design was commissioned by Mitsubishi and created in a wheat field by Team Satan in August of 1998, in East Field, Alton Barnes, Wiltshire. It took them two full days to make.

A beautiful piece of "earth art" in the fields.

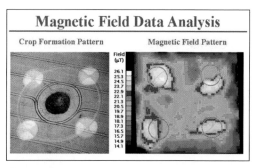

A magnetometer reading showing how the magnetism profile mirrors the design of the crop formation.

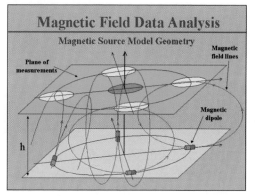

An illustration of the anomalous magnetic fields recorded above and below a crop formation.

Colin Andrews at the site of the extraordinary Stonehenge Julia Set formation. Note the UFO, which was captured with two cameras by two photographers. (Photo by Joan Lundgen, used with permission.)

Colin Andrews (in sunglasses) talks to some of the military personnel assigned to Operation Blackbird.

Chapter 16

Crop Circle Empowerment:
The Cost of Deception
By Synthia Andrews

S ynthia Andrews is Colin Andrews's wife. Synthia originally wrote this piece for Colin's Website *www.cropcircleinfo.com* and updated it for this book.

•••

There is an incredible story to be told about the crop circles of England, and it is not the one on which most people are focused. It is a story of the spiritual potential of humans: the potential we have to interact with the living force of nature through intuition and geometry to create energetically significant, consciousness-shifting tools. Surprisingly, the majority of crop circle enthusiasts overlook this truth in the belief that only a "mysterious force" or "alien intelligence" can be the creator of this phenomenon. It may be that a mysterious force or alien intelligence is indeed involved, but certainly people are as well. It is interesting that the circles are perceived as valuable only if they are made by a non-human source. It is as if we are afraid to be powerful, co-creative, spiritual beings.

Background

In July 1999 my husband, Colin Andrews, announced to BBC News the results of his two-year study into human hoaxing of crop circles. His research indicated that during *the two years of his study*, at least 80 percent of the crop circles he researched (in England) were manmade. This announcement stunned the crop circle community, largely because Colin was one of the original crop circle researchers and has been the subject's primary proponent for the last two decades. He started the first research organization, Circles Phenomenon Research International (CPRI), and has amassed the largest database in the world on the subject. He was in a unique position to evaluate the presently occurring formations against the earlier phenomenon.

The announcement resulted in immediate warfare within the established crop circle research community. Prominent alternative magazines that purported to deal in truth refused to publish his statements. Fellow researchers refuted his report with character assassination rather than with facts. Interestingly, only a handful of people (mostly scientists) paid attention to the rest of his statement—that approximately 20 percent of the circles studied showed no evidence of being manmade, and that many of these demonstrated a unique magnetic signature. Although Colin continues to work with scientists on the magnetic results, as an intuitive energy healer, I find an equally compelling mystery lies with the manmade formations.

Energy healers assist the body's own healing processes by attempting to bring all life systems into harmony through touch, meditation, prayer, and spiritual and organic processes. This can be a compliment to standard medical procedures. The irrefutable evidence of the effects of this placebo effect proves that not all physical ailments need medical intervention to improve.

An energy healer believes that the human body is more than a physical entity. Mind, body, and spirit are unified, coordinated, and animated by interacting energy systems. These systems interface between our internal and external environments. If energy functions are weakened, misaligned, or missing altogether, then disharmony and disease result. Although these systems are largely autonomic, they can be influenced by the individual, a process often facilitated by an energy healer.

To review the historical and experiential record on crop circles:

- The first published report of a mysterious circle appearing in an oat field occurred in 1678. Orange balls of light were witnessed in the sky at the time the circle appeared (*Witchcraft in Hertfordshire* by Lewis Evans and H*ertfordshire Folk Lore* by W.B. Gerish).

- The CPRI database contains first-hand reports from farmers of crop circles occurring as early as the 1920s, in many of the same fields in which they appear today.

- Originally, the formations were simple circles that evolved into ringed circles and circles with satellites.

- The simple formations further evolved during the 1990s into complex patterns.

- The majority of circles have occurred around ancient sacred sites such as Stonehenge, Avebury, and other megalithic complexes. The folklore about these sites includes the same types of experiences reported in relation to crop circles.

- People entering crop circles experience a sense of spiritual awe.

- The phenomenon occurs worldwide.

- Many formations display complex geometries.

- Many formations display diatonic (musical) ratios between component parts.

- There is an association of crop circles with water; sometimes the formations align with watersheds or underground waterways or even cattle troughs. The underground water features are detectable from the air but not from ground level.

- Magnetic distortions have occurred inside formations affecting compasses and electrical equipment. Current research is focusing on magnetometer surveys.

- A high-pitched, two-toned, electromagnetic sound has been heard by multiple witnesses on different occasions and has been recorded on two occasions. A BBC television crew made one recording and the effect of the sound damaged their electronic equipment. A later broadcast of the sound also damaged broadcasting equipment.

- Some people visiting the circles experience physiological effects including heightened awareness, feeling subtle energies, headaches, and a profound sense of peace.

- CPRI research conducted with scientist Masahiro Kahata into brainwave patterns indicates that brainwaves are affected by proximity to crop circles.

- The circles seem to have healing properties. People claim spontaneous healings inside some circles. The use of crop circle photographs as healing tools is practiced at the Institute for Resonance Therapy in Germany and with individual Radionics and energy practitioners.

  The photographs of the crop circles hold a visible record of the patterns and designs and can be very helpful in focusing the intentions of the therapist to heal. In the case of the Institute of Resonant Therapy, computers digitally capture the photograph and, using a proprietary electronic transfer system, applies certain frequencies encoded in the data to the person being healed.

- Scientists have found cellular changes in plants associated with crop circles.

- Unidentified balls of light have been seen and filmed in and around the formations, as well as in and around megalithic sacred sites.

- The patterns are hauntingly familiar and resemble symbols from indigenous cultures. Seeing the patterns for the first time often has an emotional effect on the viewer.

- The formations contain dowsable energy, and energy-sensitive individuals, such as Chi Gung master Nan Lu of the American Taoist Healing Center in New York, apparently can locate the formations by feeling for the energy with their hands.

- The formations usually occur in relation to established lines of earth energy, known as ley lines.

- The phenomenon is interactive. Patterns have appeared in the fields after people have visualized or requested them to appear. Researchers have often noticed that after they consistently observed a feature and then formulated a hypothesis around it, the next formation would break the rule they had just established.

- When Colin Andrews and Pat Delgado made the phenomenon public in 1989 with the publication of *Circular Evidence* (Bloomsbury Press), more and more people were drawn to the fields, some to visit the mysterious markings and others to take up the challenge of making them.

- Most amazingly, as people have consciously begun to make more of the formations, the anomalies and energy effects surrounding the formations continue to occur, even with known hoaxes, regardless of the source of the formation.

It is the anomalies that keep people faithful to the idea of either a supernatural force or aliens as the creator of the circles. The term "supernatural," however, merely refers to a natural force that we do not yet understand. When you have stood in a field and watched balls of light move around a crop pattern, it is hard to believe that the circle was manmade. However, there are substantial reports of these same anomalies occurring in manmade circles. The apparent irreconcilability of these facts is at the foundation of the controversy. It may be time to revise our theories and expand our understanding.

A Theory of Energy

Humans have been making patterns and geometric structures to shift consciousness and move energy for thousands of years. Zuni sand paintings, Tibetan yantras, and Indian mandalas are a few examples of geometric patterns used in this way. The most extravagant examples of energy shifting geometric tools may be Stonehenge in England and the Great Pyramid in Egypt. It is noteworthy that Old English folklore establishes Stonehenge and other stone circles as sites of spontaneous healing, observation points for strange lights, and places where lightning seems to gravitate[1]. The original discoverer of ley lines, Alfred Watkins, author of *The Old Straight*

Track[2] believed that Stonehenge and other megalithic monuments are linked together through energy pathways. The relationship of ancient sacred sites to underground waterways is also well established. Additionally, the Great Pyramid's energy effects, particularly those on physiology, have been the focus of much study[3]. What all of these ancient monuments have in common is that they use sacred geometry to constrain and direct subtle energy for a specific effect.

Paul Devereux writes in his book *Secret of Ancient and Sacred Places*:

> Sacred geometry is the geometry inherent in all nature, whether it be the energy dance of atoms and molecules, the formation of a crystal, the growth of a plant or human skeleton, the motion of weather systems or galaxies. Certain patterns and ratios are used by nature in the formation of the manifest universe: The process of becoming is governed by the implied geometry.
>
> Such geometry is used in magical invocation for the same reasons. The builders of the ancient sacred monuments observed the ways of nature closely and encoded its architecture into their structures so that the holy places would act as microcosms of the whole universe[4].

Can it be that crop circles, in utilizing sacred geometry at energy centers, activate a heretofore unmeasured energy inherent in nature?

John Michell writes in his book *The New View over Atlantis*[5]:

> From the relics of the Stone-age science practiced by the adepts of the ancient world it appears: first, that they recognized the existence of natural forces of whose potential we are now ignorant, and learnt to manipulate them; second, that they gained

thereby certain insights into fundamental questions of philosophy, the nature of the universe and the relationship between life and death.

He continues: "The work of scientists such as Baron C. von Reichenbach and Dr. Wilhelm Reich, further confirms the possibility, indicated in folklore all over the world, that some form of natural energy was known in prehistoric times and that a method was discovered, involving a fusion of the terrestrial spirit with the solar spark, by which this energy could be disposed to human benefit."[6] Is it possible that in making crop circles today, as in ancient times, humans are the "terrestrial spirit" fusing with the "solar spark," thereby activating a powerful force of nature?

I am suggesting that what we think of as causes are really effects. When biologists see cellular changes in plants within formations, the popular conclusion is that a powerful force must have been engaged to create the circle. But what if it is the reverse? What if a powerful force was released as the result of creating the circle?

The evidence shows that ancient sacred sites are aligned to unseen underground waterways and ley lines. It is believed this system was part of a subtle energy matrix the sites were activating and releasing for human use. Researchers have noted the same correlations and similar effects with crop circles, including the same types of dowsing results. It is also interesting that both crop circles and sacred sites are associated with reports of strange lights in the sky and UFO activity. Do they come because they are drawn to the earth energy being activated? Are the objects that have been filmed in crop circles making the circles, exploring them, or utilizing their energy?

Dr. Hans Jennings has demonstrated that sound waves create patterns by vibrating particles into specific geometries. Changing the frequency of the sound changes the geometry of the vibrating particles[7]. Some researchers have speculated that sound waves may have vibrated crops into geometric patterns, thereby creating crop circles. Isn't it equally possible that the creation of a living geometry generates a frequency that produces the observed and recorded sound and activates the energy effects associated with crop circles?

We live in a unique time in history during which the arcane knowledge and mythology of the past are fusing with the science of the present. Nowhere is this more in evidence than in the field of medicine. Modern medicine is open in a way it has never been before to alternative and complementary medicine theories based on subtle energy. Some of these healing modalities, such as Radionics and Reiki, create patterns and symbols that establish precise frequencies and induce specific healing effects. The healing frequencies are used to shift mind and/or matter. Is it possible that the crop circles are working in the same way? Results at the Institute for Resonance Therapy (IRT) in Cappenberg, Germany suggest they do. At IRT, crop circle photographs are used in a complex, repeatable protocol for healing processes. They have been used to revitalize forests and improve farming yields, among others.[8]

Another piece to the puzzle may be seen in the work of nature-energy pioneers such as the founders of Findhorn in Scotland and Perelandra in the United States. Michelle Small Wright, founder of Perelandra, has documented in her books the process of what she calls "co-creative science".[9] In her work she communicates with the intelligence within nature and uses geometrical designs to create energy gardens. As at Findhorn, her gardens exceed the limits imposed by natural laws, as we know them. Forty-pound cabbages grown in the barren rock of northern Scotland would be unbelievable if not seen. Wright describes this ability to transcend natural limits as the spiritual growth of humans joining with nature to become co-creators of the world around us. In fact, we are already co-creators of the world around us, we simply do it without consciousness or intention—look at the chaos of modern times. Perhaps we are being called to return to ancient ways and be co-creative with nature as a matter of choice, not default, and with conscious intent. Perhaps crop circles are a step in this direction.

This theory is already being utilized in California by Mr. Bill Witherspoon, who makes patterns in the landscape with the intention of changing the field of consciousness.[10] Wouldn't it be wonderful if people in all walks of life and places on the earth began to consciously use geometry and natural energy in their gardens, landscapes, homes, offices, and communities? Is this simply a return to the ancient Chinese practice of feng shui?

The Cost of Deception

Why some researchers and hoaxers alike want to obscure the truth of the manmade formations is interesting. Despite the hate mail and raging controversy over Colin's disclosure, most crop circle researchers are already aware that humans are constructing circles. In 1997, Colin first began his in-depth investigation into manmade formations. He hired a detective to track hoaxers and create a profile for distinguishing manmade circles. At this time, farmers were losing patience with the hoards of people trampling their fields whenever a formation appeared. To elicit their cooperation in his study, Colin agreed to provide the farmers with details of any known circle-making activity that occurred on their land. We expected support from the crop circle research community in Colin's efforts to reduce manmade activity, but much to our surprise this generated an angry furor. Some researchers went so far as to ask Colin to stop because "why ruin everyone's fun?"

In August of 1998, Colin and I attended a gathering of several researchers at a seaside restaurant in Southsea, Portsmouth. Photographer Steve Alexander and Karen Douglas were present. During the discussion Karen and Steve began to explain why they believed it was a poor decision on Colin's part to expose the hoaxers. Karen explained her thoughts on the value of hoaxing by describing the experience she had while constructing a circle with Steve for research purposes several years earlier.[11] Karen's description included how beautiful it was to be out in the quiet of the night, joining nature, and in harmony with the landscape as they created a magical formation.

She went on to suggest that exposing people for their role in creating these sacred formations was misguided. I actually agree with Karen's assessment of the value of manmade circles. But why keep the method of creation a secret? If manmade formations are a valuable asset, why not show everyone how creating sacred geometry in nature can create sacred space and be a tool of empowerment?

Other circlemakers describe experiences similar to Karen's. In October of 1996, Colin and I were in Finland at a UFO convention at which Colin was speaking. Present in the audience was Robert Irving, a well-known circle maker. At some point during the proceedings, Irving introduced himself and asked to have a meeting. We agreed to meet in the conference cafeteria. The conversation was so interesting we continued it the next day in downtown Helsinki. At the time, Colin was still resisting his growing alarm at the possibility that many formations were manmade, and

This remarkable 200 foot diameter design was positioned precisely in the center of an old Roman road which could only be seen from hundreds of feet up in an aircraft, making its positioning from the ground almost impossible.

I was personally quite hostile. I must say I ended up with a great deal of respect and genuine liking for Robert Irving.

Irving had been involved in circle making since the early 1990s and was corroborative in much of his detail, confirming site information that Colin knew was privileged information between himself and few other researchers. More interesting, Irving discussed some personal experiences he had while making the circles. He, like many circlemakers, claim unusual experiences in the fields while creating formations.

They speak of lights appearing in the fields while they are working; about designing a pattern, going into the field to make the pattern, and creating an entirely different design—one with symbolic impact, or one that had been previously meditated on by individuals or groups. John Macnish, in his book *Crop Circle Apocalypse*,[12] writes that the first avowed circlemakers, Doug and Dave, felt compelled "by an unknown source" to go out into the fields at night and create patterns.

To illustrate his motivations in making formations, Irving related an event during which he entered a pattern the morning after he and several others had made it. A number of people were in the formation and Irving was enjoying hearing their comments, praises, and impressions. He reported witnessing a woman's swollen ankle significantly reduce in size while she was in the formation.

When I asked him directly why circlemakers didn't acknowledge the artwork they created, he said that for him, if people knew they were manmade, the magic results would stop happening. It seemed his opinion was that the energy effects were induced by the person's belief in the mysterious source of the circles. I disagree. I think the effects are real, palpable, and part of ancient knowledge.

We live in a time when we need to become more conscious, where we need, in Colin's words, "to recognize our place in the natural world" and find the tools of empowerment necessary to change the direction in which we are heading. If crop circles are a part of that, it is time to stop hiding from the truth and pretending people are not a part of the magic and mystery. Aliens, or a mysterious force, may have originated the circles and may still make some or inspire the making of others. Perhaps we are in training. The importance is that we can use geometries and natural forces to change our consciousness and in so doing, the world in which we live.

The cost of deception, of ignoring the human component, is the loss of the opportunity for spiritual growth. We have the choice to either give our power to an outside source, or to embrace our own abilities. Let us accept our spiritual evolution and consciously begin our training in co-creative living.

Notes

[1]Devereux, Paul. *Secrets of Ancient and Sacred Places*. London: Cassell Publications, 1995, p. 24.

[2]Watkins, Alfred. *The Old Straight Track*. London: Garnstone Press republication, 1970.

[3]King, Serge Kahili. *Earth Energies*. Wheaton, Il.: Theosophical Publishing House, 1992, Chapter 5.

[4]Devereux, p. 22.

[5]Michell, John. *The New View Over Atlantis*. San Francisco: Harper & Row, 1986, p. 197.

[6]Mitchell, p. 197.

[7]The Institute for Resonance Therapy Cappenberg, 1994 IRT, Cappenberg, Germany: *IRT-Cappenberg@T-Online.de*.

[8]Jennings, Dr. Hans. *Cymatics* (video) Newmarket, N.H.: MACROmedia, 1986.

[9]Smallwrite, Michelle. *Behaving as If the God in All Life Matters*. Warrenton, Va.: Perelandra, Ltd., Perelandra, Ltd., PO Box 3603, Warrenton, Va. 20188, 1997 update.

[10]*artheals.org/artists/Witherspoon_Bill_177/*

[11]June 26-27, 1995, in West Stowell, Wiltshire.

[12]Macnish, John. *Crop Circle Apocalypse*.Wye Valley, South Wales, U.K.: Circlevision, 1993.

Chapter 17

The "80/20" Statement:
The Politics of Truth

Knowing is not understanding. There is a great difference between knowing and understanding: you can know a lot about something and not really understand it.

—**Charles F. Kettering**

Hate mail. Threats. Red-faced zealots screaming in my face. Contempt. Media ridicule. Professional scorn. Hatred. Insults.

These are some of the tribulations I have had to endure since Wednesday, August 9, 2000, the day I made an announcement on British radio and television that would change my life.

That day, I announced the outcome of a two-year long magnetometer survey of crop circles in England, along with my findings from this investigation into the crop circle hoaxing problem.

People who had a serious interest in the crop circle phenomenon—and I am speaking of those who fervently believed that all crop circles were of paranormal origin—thought their world had come to an end that day.

The furious backlash immediately heaped upon me made that quite clear.

For several years prior to my announcement, I had been aware of a growing number of manmade crop circle formations.

During the mid-1990s, I was shown confidential information by a BBC journalist who had gone undercover for two years, and who had worked closely with Dave Chorley and Doug Bowers—the two most famous crop circle hoaxers—in an attempt to establish the truth behind their claims to be making all the crop circles in England.

I was shown letters mailed by Doug and Dave that contained the hand-drawn patterns of crop circles that they planned to make in Hampshire and Wiltshire, and also provided dates and places for the formations. On the envelopes of some of these letters, they had sketched the planned design and then placed a stamp over it. The envelopes had then been postmarked by the Royal Mail.

These patterns did appear, and they appeared where and when the letters had said they would. On one occasion, Doug and Dave even made a crop design as a birthday surprise for the reporter's young son.

Unbeknown to Doug and Dave, though, they were being filmed by this BBC journalist as they made their circles, and in ensuing weeks, other hoaxers were tracked and their handiwork was also filmed.

This information was devastating to me . Frankly, I did not want to believe the evidence being shown to me, as others now do not want to believe me.

To satisfy my own desire and *need* for the truth, I began my own investigation into human hoaxing of crop circles.

They Laid It Down for All to See

In 1999, I began my investigation into hoaxing.

I was fortunate and grateful to have the project fully funded by well-known philanthropist Laurence Rockefeller as part of an overall crop circle research funding package provided by Mr. Rockefeller himself. Mr. Rockefeller has funded a number of my research projects into the crop circle mystery, beginning in July 1997, when one of his close advisors asked if I would be interested in submitting for funding consideration a proposal for a long-term program of research. My proposal was accepted and, in 1999, I turned my attention to investigating crop circle counterfeiting.

My hoaxing investigation took place in England during 1999 and 2000.

My research included engaging retired police detectives as private investigators; crop circle site inspections; collection of physical evidence; extensive aerial photography; recording of personal experiences; and gathering information from the media.

By this time, several media organizations in London and elsewhere, including NBC, the BBC, Nippon TV, Sky TV, and others, had paid people to create crop formations for television programs. We were fortunate to receive help from many of these media outlets in the form of information as to when crop formations would be made, who would be making them, and where they would be located. We also enlisted the help of undercover researchers who were able to infiltrate the hoaxers and convince them that they could be trusted.

Once we had concrete evidence that a crop circle was manmade, we went in and recorded the ground details of the formation with great specificity. We were then able to look for these same details in aerial photographs taken of all the patterns in England during those two years.

In many of the designs we investigated, we not only found underlying tracks where people had gained access to vital construction points, but also peg holes were found where lay-out stakes had been used and then removed.

When these documented facts were combined with the undercover films of people making crop circles, we were able to reach accurate conclusions as to the number of formations that were hoaxed in England during that period.

This was unassailable evidence, and yet it was still not enough for those cereozealots who insisted on believing that every crop circle was "real."

Based on our research, I concluded that approximately 80 percent of all the crop circles we investigated in England from 1999 through the year 2000 were manmade.

This was one of the most important research findings to date because it cut to the core of what was truly important: *the remaining 20 percent of the crop circles showed no sign of human hands.*

And the Band Begins to Play

It all began the morning of August 6, 2000. I received a telephone call at my U.K. research base in Andover, England from Francesca Kasteliz of the BBC National News in London.

She asked a simple question: Did I have any new crop circle research developments to report?

My answer to that question, and the events that soon followed, set in motion an extraordinary wave of change; something that caused joy, as well as anger—more anger than anything I have ever witnessed in my life—in the crop circle community.

Two days after agreeing to share my latest findings with the BBC, I was standing in a large simple crop circle at Alton Barnes, Wiltshire with an array of television cameras pointed at me.

I had arrived at approximately 7:30 a.m. as the crew were raising the transmitter mast up into the overcast sky, and making their final preparations for a live broadcast.

The TV journalist who would be interviewing me arrived shortly thereafter, and we chatted briefly as we awaited the word that the segment would begin. We were minutes from broadcasting the latest crop circle news live throughout Great Britain.

As is common in England, there was a heavy fog hugging the field in which we stood that morning, and fog also blanketed the hills behind us. The director was hoping the haze would lift in time for the broadcast. There was a complex, manmade crop formation in the field adjacent to ours, and he hoped to show it on camera during the airing of my interview.

Unfortunately, the weather did not cooperate this day, and when we went on the air, the director had to be satisfied with showing only the simple circle in which I stood. I found this truly ironic. Nature had spoken and she had decided that the complex, manmade designs were to be removed from the equation—at least for this broadcast.

During the interview, I stated that most of the complex crop circle designs that we had investigated were judged to have been manmade, but that approximately 20 percent of those that we had researched were not. I then went on to explain that what was significant about our findings was that in that 20 percent, magnetic anomalies had been conclusively recorded and measured and, again, these readings were only found in the simple circles.

As I spoke, the BBC showed elaborate animated computer graphics illustrating how magnetism may play a role in the creation of simple circles.

My interviewer then concluded the interview by saying, "Well, the mystery remains."

Overall, it was a well-produced segment, and I believed that I had succeeded in communicating my findings to the world. At the time, I had no idea what kind of response my words would provoke.

That evening, the first hate mail arrived in the form of venomous e-mails. This was followed in the ensuing days by similar noxious missives in my mailbox. Then the verbal attacks came from researchers and members of the public who had not taken kindly to what I had revealed. I was barred from farmers' fields where I had worked without interference many times; and I was "disinvited" from a well-known U.S. radio program by the host, who denounced me as a "deliberate disinformer." In a letter to me, the host told me that he was certain that I had been lying about my findings. Around the same time, an article began circulating on the Internet in which the author accused me of having been "bought off" by the Rockefeller family. An international magazine refused to publish details of my research and results, instead adding to the anti-Colin-Andrews rhetoric by stating that I was either a funded disinformer in the employ of the Rockefeller family, or that I was being paid by the CIA to deliberately spread disinformation.

I was stunned by the vitriol that was hurled my way, and I learned a great deal about people during this experience. In the minds of many, my statement had crossed the line and instantly transformed me into an enemy. I had evidence to bolster my conclusions, but none of that mattered. I had said something certain people had not wanted to hear, and thus, I was ostracized from the crop circle community.

I tried to ignore a great deal of this unpleasant nonsense, but I was not always successful in avoiding confrontations.

On several occasions, my way into the fields was blocked by angry researchers or rabid believers who not only physically prevented me from doing my work, but also insisted on confronting me personally so that they could express their feelings to me about what I had said.

Grown men stood nose to nose with me, shouting into my face, spouting crazed nonsense with uncontrolled fury. The behavior of some of these fanatics was abominable, and they should be ashamed of themselves.

Thankfully, the situation has improved somewhat.

In recent months, I have been given the opportunity to discuss my findings on television, radio, and in print, and what has also tempered the reaction to my conclusions is the fact that others—independent researchers with whom I have nothing to do with— are arriving at the same conclusions.

That said, though, I must acknowledge that there still exists today an extreme fringe faction of crop circle devotees who not only believe that *all* the patterns around the world are "real," but are hell-bent on the public believing likewise.

One example of this type of blind denial occurred during one of my appearances on the hugely popular U.S. radio program *Coast to Coast* with Art Bell during the summer of 2002.

On this occasion, George Noory was hosting the show, and we had already been on the air for two hours when a caller phoned in to have his say about my work and my "80/20" conclusion.

"Everything you have just said is not true," he proclaimed.

"*What* is not true?" George replied. "I have not heard him say a single thing that I thought was untrue or, for that matter, unreasonable."

The caller "non-answered" George's question by responding, "It's just not true. Ask other researchers like Michael Glickman or Andy Thomas."

I then asked George if I could speak with this caller myself and answer his questions, but as is often the case in these type of situations, the caller hung up when George began to challenge his claims.

The reaction by many in this camp seems to be "Don't tell me something I don't want to hear." It is not simple disagreement. It appears to be an inability to modify their position in the face of new facts.

I believe it is critically important that those who are finding it difficult to accept these new discoveries not allow denial to pummel them into blindness.

Denial and deception—the *other* "D & D"—are synonymous with Doug and Dave in the crop circle field, and the metaphor is apt: Doug and Dave practiced deception and denial for years, and even after they admitted that they were responsible for some circlemaking, they continued to deceive by laying claim to formations they had nothing to do with.

Hearing Troubles

With hindsight, I now know that my 80/20 statement was wildly misunderstood.

It was misinterpreted as me saying that *all* crop circles are manmade, when I had gone to great pains at the time, and have continued to do so ever since, to make it clear that the mysterious, unexplainable 20 percent was a gift to mankind. My statement was also misinterpreted as me saying that 80 percent of crop formations *around the world*, and *spanning all of history*, were manmade. As I said then, and will say yet again, I was referring to the crop circles we investigated *in England*, in the specific *two-year period* during which we conducted our research.

I rocked the boat. I understood why this happened: Mine was the loudest voice out there reporting the results and supporting the research.

It was my face that was seen on TV, and my voice that was heard on the radio. It was my findings that were being written about in books, newspapers, and magazines; and I was the one lecturing around the world about my conclusions.

There is some small measure of satisfaction in the fact that since that notorious BBC interview aired, a number of other crop circle researchers have publicly agreed with my findings.

It staggers me to realize to what extent people will go to hang on to their beliefs, and how hard it is for many to accept change—even when they are presented with evidence of the truth.

I have repeatedly said that to prove just one crop circle real is to establish the presence of a very important phenomenon on Earth.

I committed thousands of dollars, along with a great deal of professional expertise and expensive equipment, towards *proving* that 54 crop circle events in the United Kingdom, out of an event total of 236 countrywide crop formations during those two years, could not be explained.

If we extrapolate, and apply that number's ratio to the formations reported in the rest of the world during 1999 and 2000—236 in 1999, and 175 in 2000—then 82 of the 411 confirmed worldwide crop circle reports would be unexplained.

A few days after the BBC television news program aired, I received an invitation from Professor Andrei Ol'khovatov in Moscow to present my findings at a Geophysicist Congress in Russia, planned to discuss the Tunguska explosion event of 1908.

Magnetometer anomalies had been discovered at the Tunguska site, and the Russian scientists wanted to check their findings against the magnetometer readings I recorded in authentic crop circles.

The Russian scientists wanted to learn more about the real crop circles, especially after hearing that my research had determined that there was, indeed, a baffling mystery in the crop circle phenomenon. They were especially intrigued by findings showing that numerous simple crop designs had strange magnetic anomalies associated with them.

•••

I have often been asked why I made my announcement before conferring with my fellow researchers and allowing a peer review process to confirm my results.

It's a good question.

The answer is that I felt then—and, in fact, I still feel—a strong sense of societal, scientific, and moral responsibility surrounding my work. I carry the unasked-for title of best-known voice on the subject of crop circles and I feel strongly that my role is to *keep everyone informed*. Fellow researchers, scientists, governments, and the public all deserve nothing less than the best data I can provide, and I decided that it was best to go public with my findings as soon as possible.

I have willingly presented my research to government scientists, the British and German governments, indigenous people in many countries, individual seekers of truth, and religious leaders.

It is very important that the truth be told.

What is happening on earth with the "signs" of the crop circles is of great significance to many cultures.

The council of Hopi Elders, for instance, are the caretakers of a prophecy that has been kept secret for hundreds of years. The prophecy is known to concern profound changes in the world that would manifest as changes in human behavior, attitudes, and consciousness, accompanied by visible environmental changes. The Hopis believe they hold a sacred responsibility to reveal the prophecy to the United Nations when they see the signs that signal the beginning of the changes that have been foretold. The Hopis believe that the crop circle phenomenon plays a role in this prophecy, and they have eagerly embraced my research and used it to help them further understand what is going on.[1]

I speak of the Hopis to make the point that there are many people all over

Hopi Elder Thomas Benjaca.

the world carefully monitoring the crop circle enigma and it is to them I feel I owe the greatest responsibility with my work.

Notes

[1] See *www.memorologyllc.com/ CropCircleInfo/Research_Route_5.htm.*

Chapter 18

Half and Half:
Where I Stand Today

I am half scientist and half intuitive.

—Colin Andrews

I have learned a great deal about crop circles since driving along that road near Stonehenge in July 1983, and I have learned perhaps even more about people. I will try to state for the record where I stand today.

What I Know Now
That I Did Not Know Then

About Crop Circles:

- There is a real mystery involved in their creation and in their purpose.

- They frequently appear in ancient places.

- The geometries of crop circles are found in the artifacts of ancient cultures, especially their writings and artwork.

- There are "hot spots" of crop circle activity around the world.

- Absolute proof of a real phenomenon is elusive using current scientific technology.

- The symbols seen in crop circles often bring together a wide range of people.

- The vast majority of crop circles appear in vegetation which we later consume.

- Crop circles attract extraordinary attention when they appear.

- The patterns have evolved over time, and some designs now have identifiable meaning.

- There is frequently a high level of interference with electronic equipment inside the crop circles.

About People:

- A cult-like, pseudoreligious obsession with the crop circle mystery has formed more quickly than I would have ever expected.

- Crop circles are now perceived by some people to hold great spiritual meaning, as well as possible scientific potential, and this has sparked creative thinking and new ideas in many who are studying the phenomenon. The mystery has become a catalyst for the pursuit of knowledge.

- Fear of the unknown has created a faction of organized, vocal skeptics, a group whose voices sometimes seem to be louder than those of the individuals objectively seeking the truth.

- Religious belief systems are challenged by the crop circle enigma. People who are committed to a particular religious philosophy feel ill at ease attributing any profound meaning or significance to the crop circle mystery.

- Some of the first people to respond to my research findings were representatives from intelligence organizations in the United States, Germany, and the United Kingdom. Many of them infiltrated research groups, and some even visited researcher's homes and spoke to their families in an effort to acquire information about the burgeoning crop circle mystery.

- The benign and beautiful subject of crop circles has provided a unique glimpse into human behavior, and I often think that we have learned more in the past 20 years about people, than about crop circles. Sad to say, not all of what we have learned about the behavior of certain members of the human family is encouraging.

•••

Nothing you read anywhere—not even in this book—will fully explain the crop circle mystery; not today or even tomorrow.

The enigma may never be fully explained, but I am certain that we are being given hints as to where it comes from, and where it might be going.

These hints are fascinating, and they fill me with intrigue and excitement. But not having all the answers does not mean that we should stop using our imagination in an attempt to understand. Imagining possible futures and searching for answers is what drives the evolving engine of human potential, and it is what contributes to the growth of our human civilization.

It is quite possible that mankind will never fully understand the intricate workings of the master plan of our existence. But we are regularly being given hints and clues, and I think that many of us have evolved enough to intuitively sense when we are being presented with glimpses of the underlying structure of this master plan.

The crop circle mystery could simply be outside our realm of understanding. The answers may be locked in a dimension somewhere external to the boundaries of our current reality. Some crop researchers have speculated that the crop circle patterns are visible energy discharges between dimensions, and that we can only see half (or less) of the actual anomaly. That may be true, and the theory illustrates the difficulties—knowing what to consider and what to reject—when working with the crop circle riddle.

We are now living in an age of microbiology, genetic engineering, and nanotechnology. We are regularly creating new materials and developing new techniques that allow us to employ the highest levels of technological skills known to man in our pursuit of knowledge. Eyeing some hoped-for human benefit, we are now able to combine genes from the plant kingdom with genes from the animal kingdom. Man can now play God, but as we enter the 21st century acting as God, we should understand that this does not make us God.

One alarming reality of our current biotechnological developments and genetic manipulations is that there is not a single scientist working in this field today who can state with certainty what the effect on other species, the environment, or man himself will be from incorporating these new, genetically contrived creations into nature.

This lack of knowledge, however, has not stopped or prevented the introduction of these products into the biosphere. Today, 65 percent of all soybeans packaged for human consumption in the United States are genetically altered. Only time will tell what the effects are of the incorporation of genetically altered foods and animals into the human gene pool.

Those of you reading this book are seeing through eyes that see what no one of any other era has seen. We have seen man unleash the power of the atom to produce both extraordinary levels of energy, and an extraordinary power to destroy. And we did this before we fully understood the ramifications of such a monumental act, and before we knew what to do with the byproducts of nuclear energy. We now store radioactive materials under mountains, but this does not assure the safety of mankind. Only metal cans and concrete stand between us and deadly harm. And to make matters worse, some nations simply dump their nuclear waste into the sea.

These are frightening realities of our modern age, and another of those realities is that we live in troubling times with more questions than answers.

Curiously, into this amalgam of threats comes the crop circles: What do the crop circles mean to us?

I believe that we need to understand the role that human consciousness plays in the crop circle enigma. Darwin was right: On this planet, only the fittest survive.

But that oversimplifies the paradigm of life on earth by not factoring in the *will* of a species to survive—consciously or unconsciously—and how deliberately applied means of survival affect this equation.

I believe that all species on earth feel the constant threat of extinction. Call it the "high mind"—another term for Jung's collective unconscious—a sensory self that registers and responds to threats on a purely instinctual basis. Animals instinctively use strength and/or flight (depending upon the threatening animal) to maintain their place in the ecology.

Man also uses the ability to dominate both animals and other humans, but there is an additional factor in man's quest for survival. We can use our spiritual awareness, our intelligence, and our emotional identity to apply compassion, love, and empathy to our actions. These emotions are quite powerful and cannot be faked (although many politicians, in their quest for power and wealth, try to fake feelings on a regular basis). When our intentions are sincere and deeply held, the results can be amazing.

In the beginning days of my research into crop circles, I realized that the clues—and sometimes the answers—that I sought were often provided for me if I prayed quietly, with an open heart, and endeavoring to maintain a genuineness and sincerity in my requests.

I have experienced some incredible things. And what was common to all of my most profound revelations was that I had asked not for a final answer, but instead, for true knowledge and spiritual awareness. From those prayers came a glorious event or stunning clue that helped shine a brighter light on this puzzling enigma.

I have heard both male and female voices speaking to me in single, sometimes cryptic sentences. I have had a Celtic Cross crop pattern appear close to my home shortly after I prayed for just such a symbol. I have heard strange sounds inside crop circles that still cannot be explained. And I am not alone in these experiences. Other sincere researchers have reported similar happenings.

Here are two of the most intriguing examples:

- Filmmaker William Gazecki told me that when he arrived in England to start filming his movie *Crop Circles: Quest for Truth*, he asked for a crop circle to appear and one did—right outside his bedroom window that night.

- Inventor and engineer Mike Curry left a surveillance operation at Blackland, Wiltshire after having witnessed a dumbbell crop formation appear in a field fully monitored and protected by cameras and infrared beams to stop intruders. Even with all this surveillance, the crop pattern appeared unbidden, in a small bank of fog and without detection or being seen by the cameras. Mike left the site frustrated and confused, repeatedly asking the question: Could this happen anywhere and at any time? He was still puzzled when he arrived at his home, which is several hundred miles north of the surveillance site. He woke the next day to find the identical crop

design in the field outside his bedroom window.

Also, there have been many occasions when it seems as though the creators of the circles have listened in on conversations between researchers and then acted in response to what was specifically discussed.

One day, while flying over southern England with Busty Taylor, Busty commented to me that he would love to someday find all the previous crop designs wrapped into one stunning new formation. The next day, just such a formation appeared, precisely below where the aircraft had been when Busty had expressed his wish 24 hours earlier.

Pat Delgado and I were once discussing the law of angular momentum, the law of physics that describes the direction and velocity of spin in natural vortices. We were standing in a field at the time and talking about the fact that all the crop circles that had rings around them complied with this law. The next day a new crop circle appeared in the field next to where we had stood. This new formation, for the first time in our research, did not comply with the law of angular momentum.

The examples are numerous, and they have convinced me that some form of intelligence is involved in this mystery, and that this intelligence seems to be aware of our thoughts. I began to hint at this conclusion publicly towards the end of the 1980s.

But I completely agree with those who say that extraordinary claims need to be backed up with extraordinary evidence.

In the case of these crop circle experiences, this is difficult, for how does one scientifically *prove*—after the fact—that any one of the people involved *did* pray, or *did* make the statements they claim to have made? The demand for that evidence and the questions of skeptics are important to public debate, however, and are an important part of understanding the crop circle phenomenon.

Over time, I have established cordial, yet guarded, relationships with some of the people making counterfeit crop circles. Many of them have told me of strange experiences in the fields while making crop circles, and some of these events so closely resembled what I, along with other serious researchers, had witnessed, that sometimes I felt as though I was listening to myself, or one of my colleagues talking.

Some of these circlemakers had seen globes flying above the fields, inexplicable flashes of light, sudden shadows, and many other anomalous happenings.

One of these counterfeiters is a man named Rodney Dickinson, who is from a group in London using the unfortunate name of "Team Satan," (although they also call themselves the Circlemakers). Rodney has taken several of the most impressive photographs of UFOs ever seen. Rodney also has videotaped UFOs and is credited with some of the best UFO footage ever obtained. All of Rodney's photographic evidence of UFOs was shot from inside crop circles.

I have received similar reports from many other hoaxers, and I have concluded that it is possible that they may have something significant to contribute to the picture. Of course, all the work of the serious researchers would be much easier if the hoaxers would simply stop doing what they are doing, but that is unlikely, and it seems as though the phenomenon has begun to use them in its own mystifying way.

If researchers and hoaxers have the same paranormal experiences in and around crop circles, whether the circles are manmade or genuine, we have a very interesting situation. Both sides of this equation witness the paranormal, and yet each interprets these events within the context of their own reality. The researchers are trying to prove that some of the crop circles on earth are "real," while the hoaxers attempt to test these claims with counterfeits. It is while this dance goes on that the major clues manifest themselves and, hopefully, some day, we will all see the complete picture.

I believe that we are all involved in some kind of experiment with consciousness.

None of us now know whose experiment it is, but if it does not belong to an off-planet source, then we should own it ourselves, because it may be important to our future.

Something strange is going on, and I think the hearts and souls of the researchers and hoaxers hold the answers. I believe that our God-given ability to think and act with highly evolved brain functions, manifested in such elevated emotions as love and compassion, links us to the Divine. When we explore the crop circle phenomenon with these qualities in place, an emotional energy is produced that seems to put us "online" with the creators of the crop circles. As all lifeforms live and die by the message codes of their DNA, so, perhaps, is the message of the crop circles similarly encoded, and honesty and an open heart are the keys to a true understanding of this communication.

I do think that this makes sense, and that it helps to explain why these strange things happen at places where crop circle researchers and crop circle counterfeiters regularly meet: *inside the crop circles.*

A fascinating element of the mystery is the glowing orbs that are regularly seen near, and occasionally inside the crop circles. They have been witnessed and filmed many times and I have no doubt that they are real and that they have something to do with the intelligence behind crop circles.

I saw my first ball of light in 1986 while waiting for Dr. Terrence Meaden at a crop formation. The orb moved behind the only small cumulus cloud in that part of the sky and remained there. The moment I locked onto it with my eyes, it suddenly seemed to be aware of me and it began to move in a deliberate manner, almost as if it were toying with me. Also, when I later asked for some kind of clue as to the true nature of the crop circles, the alarming "crop circle sound" began and I became quite afraid. As soon as I became fearful, the noise stopped, as if the source of the sound was aware of my fear and responded to restore an emotional balance for me.

How much of this was created by my own mind? Skeptics will tell you, "all of it."

But could it be that the orbs are not machines built by some alien beings, but are "nature's machines"—visual manifestations of some kind of natural energy that serve to connect one dimension to another?

•••

There seems to be a yin/yang paradigm in the game that is being jointly played out by the researchers and the hoaxers. Is it possible that the players on both sides of the game board are vital to the ultimate understanding of the mystery, and that the answers will be found in a study of human consciousness?

After two decades of research I can not say how the crop circles are made but, perhaps more importantly, I believe I know why.

I believe that human beings are an essential and integral part of what is occurring in the crop fields around the world—in what is manifesting as crop circles. The designs encompass both spiritual and natural elements, some of which can be "read" mathematically. I believe that they are being offered to us at a time when our "living" planet is in trouble, much of which we ourselves have caused.

I think we are being summoned to address these problems, but first we must come to terms with ourselves and ask the questions, "Who are we?" and "What contributions can we make that will benefit all life on earth?" We may never know why we are here. But we do know that we *are* here as a species, and that we need to determine our ultimate fate.

We have limited resources on Earth. Sharing these fragile gifts should be our highest priority as we enter this new and critical millennium.

If we do not recognize our interconnectedness with all of nature, then we will continue our environmental—and spiritual—downslide.

Our future, and the future of all life on earth, will depend upon respecting ourselves, and respecting the living planet.

We all have to share this responsibility.

I believe that all of this ties in with crop circle consciousness.

We are being challenged to learn, and the tools of our instruction are ancient spiritual symbols, mandalas, and other innate, natural patterns.

We are being touched by the angels, and given the chance to learn about ourselves.

Since 1975, there has been a consistent cascade of beautiful crop circles, and there were random reports of formations even earlier.

This coincides with a time of extraordinary and unprecedented changes in our world.

Human survival seems threatened in ways never before seen—profound environmental degradation, war and the threat of war, political upheaval, terrorism of all types, religious conflict, poverty, starvation, natural disasters, and more. And yet now, with the Damoclean sword of extinction hanging over our head, the *signs of contact* appeared.

Who—or what—is making contact with us? It is not yet clear if we have made contact with a paradimensional part of ourselves, or with something or someone else. Scientists at Purdue University, doing research funded by the U.S. Department of Energy, have discovered the possible existence of other dimensions outside the three spatial dimensions of length, width, and height. In a paper published in the November 4, 2002 issue of *Physical Review Letters*, Purdue physics professor Ephraim Fischbach wrote, "A new kind of gravity-like force would be the fingerprint of the fact that we may really live in a world that is more than three spatial dimensions. You wouldn't see this force over large distances, but you could see it over small distances." Some crop circle theorists have long suggested that the crop patterns may be energy signatures from another dimension. If this is the case, and we are, indeed living in more than three dimensions, then it is quite possible that some yet-to-be identified energy, which may be part of human consciousness, is playing a role in the crop circle enigma.

I believe that what is taking place in the fields of our planet is evidence of signs of contact, and that the orbs and other associated phenomenon are further proof that this contact—the source of which may be Professor Fischbach's other dimensions—is transdimensional and important enough to cross the barriers between these states of being.

The crop designs run parallel to other major signs of change on earth.

Is the source a spiritual one? Are we being urged towards a new awakening in our consciousness?

I believe we are being given a wake-up call and that it is our responsibility to acknowledge the message, and take action.

A closing thought: I believe that all good has come from positive thinking. Our forefathers all believed in a wonderful future, and acted to make it so.

A positive thought is a construct of hopeful energy sent out into the world.

Like some of our friends in the indigenous peoples who safeguard and study ancient prophecies that speak of signs of change, we, too, should observe the multiple signs of change occurring around us—in our beliefs, our industries, our politics, and our environment—but especially in our fields.

We should respond to our intuition. We can not afford not to.

Part VI

At the Movies

'A Place To Stay'

Chapter 19

Crop Circle Movies and Documentaries

This chapter looks at a small sampling of the many films and documentaries that look at paranormal phenomena in general, and crop circles specifically. This is but a *tiny* representation of the many resources available to the crop circle enthusiast.

21.1 *Signs* (2002)

- Feature Film
- Writer and Director: M. Night Shyamalan
- Disney/Touchstone
- Rated PG-13
- Starring: Mel Gibson, Joaquin Phoenix, Cherry Jones, Rory Culkin, Abigail Breslin, Patricia Kalember

"Colin, of all the people we knew of, has had the longest career researching the crop circles and has the largest database of information. I've been working with Colin almost exclusively because, of all the people, he's the cream of the crop."

—**Warren Betts, publicity director for the movie *Signs***

Colin standing beside a poster for the movie Signs.

My involvement with the movie *Signs* was to provide visual materials and information about 15 crop circle events to Touchstone/Disney for use during the promotion of the film and afterward. (By the way, I do not know with certainty that the title of the movie was drawn from my work, but I have been describing crop formations as "signs" for more than a decade, and it seems as though this particular element of my message struck a chord with Night Shyamalan and the producers of the film.)

The crop circle events I chose were all very important manifestations about which I was able to provide significant amounts of data, including reports of recorded paranormal activity in the formations. They were all very dramatic, very impressive patterns and I had a number of aerial photographs of each of them.

These photographs were used to promote the movie, and the studio is continuing to use my pictures and information in materials pertaining to the film.

Touchstone/Disney also asked that I make myself available for media questions regarding crop circles, and I willingly agreed to that request. I was, in a sense, the studio's "point man" for specific questions about the phenomenon. Sometimes, questions were passed on to me from the studio; sometimes I dealt with the media people one on one.

My Thoughts About the Film

Signs is an exciting and scary science fiction film that uses crop circles as a plot device to advance its "alien invasion" storyline.

I thought the script was quite clever, and I found interesting the suggestions scattered throughout the story that, for instance, extraterrestrials can read our minds. There is a scene in which the daughter of the farmer played by Mel Gibson says to her father, "ETs can't read our minds, can they?" And the implication is, "Why yes, of course, they can." I also liked that director and writer Night Shyamalan hinted that the concept of synchronicity—the theory of the coincidence of events that seem to be meaningfully related—might

not, in fact, be what we think it is. It did provide food for thought.

This is interesting writing and adds to the forward movement of the story, but I do not think the movie itself does very much to further the serious study of crop circles.

In essence, the crop circle phenomenon, which I believe has already offered a great deal for mankind, and will continue to offer much more, was used solely as a device in a typical Hollywood extravaganza, complete with the standard "razzmatazz" of threatening aliens, frightening scenes, and expensive special effects. There was very little real insight into the phenomena, and, in a sense, the film debased what many of us believe is the true purpose of the manifestations: spiritual enlightenment and higher consciousness. In *Signs*, the crop circles are used as landing signals for an alien invasion: a negative, evil purpose.

But, hey, that's show business, right?

I also felt that the overall sentiment of the film—and I base this not only on the script but on some of the comments made by the actors on the film—was skeptical. Some of the comments I heard gave the impression that almost everybody involved with the movie believed that all of the world's crop formations were hoaxes, and that there were no paranormal events going on in the fields. This was regrettable, in my opinion. Everyone involved in *Signs* had the opportunity to further the discussion of the real phenomena taking place on our planet.

Shyamalan did, to his credit, leave some doors open. He did leave room for the possibility that crop circles were real, and that there might be some benefit to mankind if we try to understand them, but overall, the feeling one comes away with after viewing *Signs* is that crop circles are hoaxes, and that if they were real, they

Colin shaking the hand of William Gazecki, director of Crop Circles: Quest for Truth.

in England, most of it in the form of aerial photography. The original music is reverential and uplifting, and director Gazecki wisely keeps himself out of the picture and allows his experts and the crop circles to speak for themselves.

Hopefully, this will get wide airing on network or cable, and be readily available for rental. It really is an important overview of something quite extraordinary and is also a truly moving and emotional viewing experience.

would likely be used for nefarious purposes. As I said, I found this regrettable.

21.2 *Crop Circles: Quest for Truth* (2002)

- Director: William Gazecki
- OpenAge Media
- Not Rated
- Starring: Colin Andrews, Nancy Talbott, Steve Alexander, Busty Taylor, Michael Glickman, Andy Thomas, and others.

A magnificent look at the phenomena and, in fact, this is the crop circle documentary that absolutely *needed* to be made, and which should be must-viewing for every person involved in government at any level anywhere around the world. Something is happening on our planet, and *Quest for Truth* takes a reasoned, comprehensive look at what might be going on.

The film alternates between one-on-one interviews with researchers, photographers, writers, farmers, and witnesses, and stunning footage of crop formations

21.3 *A Place to Stay* (2002)

- Feature Film
- Director: Marcus Thompson
- Hollywood Daze Motion Pictures
- Not rated
- Starring: Johnny Dallas, Amanda Ray King, Colm O'Maonlai, Miranda Llewellyn Jenkins, Joe Ferrera, Graham Elwell

I was chief consultant on this emotionally powerful film set in Alton Barnes, England, and writer and director Marcus Thompson successfully communicates the lure of crop circles, interwoven with a powerful and dramatic love story. My 1991 documentary *Undeniable Evidence* was apparently the inspiration for Thompson to create *A Place to Stay*, and I was greatly honored to play myself in the movie. The movie is an engaging romance with *X-File*-type elements that will appeal to the conspiracy-minded viewer. The film is slated to debut at the 2003 Sundance Festival and then will be released to theaters.

21.4
Undeniable Evidence (1991)

- Documentary
- Director: Kevin Redpath
- ARK Soundwaves
- Not rated
- Starring: Colin Andrews

This is a comprehensive crop circles documentary written, produced, and starring Colin Andrews. It includes coverage of the scientific research to that point; interviews with farmers and eyewitnesses; a lengthy interpretative narration by me, Colin Andrews; and, of course, stunning images—both on video and in still photographs—of crop formations and the beautiful English countryside. The video is still in print and is available for purchase from many book and video Websites. *Undeniable Evidence* can also often be found in video stores for rental, such as Blockbuster. It is highly recommended.

21.5 *History's Mysteries: Crop Circle Controversy* (2000)

- Documentary
- Host: Arthur Kent
- The History Channel, A & E Networks
- Not rated
- Starring: Colin Andrews, Nancy Talbot, Lucy Pringle, George Bishop, John Lundberg, Douglas Bower, Terry Wilson, farmers.

This brief documentary (40 minutes that ran as an hour on The History Channel) does a decent job of introducing the viewer to the crop circle phenomenon and covering all the myriad elements of the mystery, albeit somewhat perfunctorily. Everything seems to be here: The Barge Inn, the Princess Diana story, historical accounts of crop circles, the various theories and, of course, Doug and Dave. To

the producers' credit, though, the documentary makes the argument that Doug and Dave's story has a great many holes in it, and that it cannot account for the worldwide extent of the phenomenon. (One of the best lines in the piece is "How can a worldwide phenomenon be explained by two guys and a board?") The documentary covers my "80/20" statement (see Chapter 18), and also, unfortunately, tries to make a connection between a single case of crop circles appearing close to a mysterious cattle mutilation (see Chapter 4.11).

One of the highlights of the documentary is an interview with admitted crop circle "artist" John Lundberg who, in the end, seems to support the theory that there is a real phenomenon outside of the work of the hoaxers. All in all, a quality documentary done with the attention to detail one would expect from The History Channel.

21.6 *Ultimate Crop Circles: Signs from Space?* (DVD, 2002)

- Documentary
- Director: Tim Werenko
- Central Park Media
- Not rated
- Starring: Colin Andrews, Peter Robbins

This interactive DVD consists of a lengthy one-on-one interview with me, conducted by UFOlogist Peter Robbins, author of the best-selling book, *Left at East Gate*. The interview is broken into several sections: *Beginnings, Personal Cost, Set Up, Enter the CIA, Pressured, Full Circle, Intelligence*, and *Then and Now*. The DVD also includes an extensive still photograph gallery accompanied by my commentary, along with several video segments, most notably the complete footage of the Oliver's Castle video (see Chapter 16).

Closing Words:

Carrying Out Instructions

What I have learned during my 20 years researching crop circles is that interaction is occurring between a creative intelligence and the human mind. This realization has impacted me greatly.

There is overwhelming evidence of *signs of contact.*

What I see, and what I have faith in, is that it was never intended that we "believe" in crop circles, but, instead, that they serve as a tool for us to learn more about ourselves.

Moody Blues singer and crop circle enthusiast Mike Pinder recently reminded me of words he wrote some time ago, "We are lost in a lost world." Now, more than ever, we need to believe in *something* and, most importantly, we need to believe in ourselves.

Crop circles are the visual manifestation of an experiment with human consciousness. My research and study has proven to me that we, as a species that has a powerful spiritual side to its being, *do* have what it takes to create a new and sustainable future for our planet and ourselves.

Sadly, it is late in the day for this realization, and there are many who still do not see the truth. But we must apply ourselves to the urgent needs of our species and our planet because, frankly, we do no have a single moment to waste.

Our complete disregard for the environment has already taken an enormous toll on all living things, and is easily seen on a planetwide scale. As I write this, a sunken oil tanker sits at the bottom of the ocean off the coast of Spain. If its hull ruptures (and many experts believe it will), the oil it releases into the ocean will be double what was spilled by the Exxon *Valdez.* We cannot go on like this. Clearly, a change in human attitude is called for.

In my view, the number of crop circles that are manmade versus those that are not, has become irrelevant. *All* the signs in the fields play a role in awakening mankind to the ongoing opportunity to reverse our self-destructive course and achieve true spiritual maturity.

To convince the masses of the importance of this quest, however, we must all do our work, and speak our message, with humility, respect, and above all, honesty.

We are all in this together: researchers, the lay public and those who make counterfeit crop circles.

When the whole picture ultimately unfolds, I think it will be seen that we were all just carrying out instructions.

—**Colin Andrews**
December 1, 2002

Appendices

Appendix A

A Crop Circle F.A.Q.

The FAQ—*Frequently Asked Questions*—file is common on the Internet these days, and is found on Websites and newsgroups that regularly have new visitors and sign up new members.

Many sites and newsgroups focus on a single subject (UFOs, the Civil War, Spanish cooking) and present and discuss a great deal of information, resulting in a flood of data that could be daunting to a newcomer.

This FAQ by no means covers the entire range of information and knowledge about the subject of crop circles, but its 15 questions are the ones most commonly asked, and we have attempted to answer them concisely, accurately, and completely.

More information on all the topics covered in these questions can be found elsewhere in this book.

1. What are crop circles?
2. Aren't all crop circles manmade?
3. Where are most crop circles found?
4. What kinds of vegetation are crop circles found in?
5. Is there a particular time of the year that crop circles appear?
6. How can you tell when a crop circle is real?
7. Who are Doug and Dave?
8. Is it true that all crop circles are made by aliens and UFOs?
9. Has anyone ever seen a crop circle form?
10. Have crop circles ever appeared in exactly the same place?
11. How long do crop circles last?
12. How large are crop circles?
13. What happens to the plants inside crop circles? Are they cut or broken? Is it true some plants are burned?
14. Are the plants always swirled in one particular direction?
15. Have "crop" circles ever been reported in snow?

1. What Are Crop Circles?

Crop circles are geometric designs created in fields when cereal crops such as wheat, oats, oil-seed rape (canola), and corn are flattened. Originally, they were simple circular areas in vegetation in which the plants were bent over at right angles and swirled to the ground in a uniform fashion. In the past 13 years, more complex patterns have appeared, which include straight lines, appendages and extensions in various shapes, and repetitive geometric patterns. The word "pictogram" is used to describe these agriglyphs.

2. Aren't All Crop Circles Manmade?

Absolutely not. There is concrete scientific evidence that many crop formations show no sign of human creation. Before 1989 and the publication of my first book, *Circular Evidence* (the first book written about the crop circle phenomenon), very few crop circles were manmade. As the subject of crop circles received increasing publicity over the ensuing years, the number of counterfeits increased dramatically. I believe very strongly, however, that the manmade factor is important and must not be ignored or cavalierly dismissed. All activity in the fields, regardless of its source, should be fully researched. That being said, I again state with certainty that the truth would be revealed much sooner if all hoaxing ceased immediately.

3. Where Are Most Crop Circles Found?

The majority of crop circles, both historically and currently, are in England, with a high concentration of formations in southern central England. Other "hot spots" include Germany, the United States, Canada, and the Netherlands. They have appeared in dozens of countries all over the world (see Chapter 5).

4. What Kinds of Vegetation Are Crop Circles Found in?

Crop circles are found in the whole range of cereal crops, with the vast majority found in barley and wheat. They also appear in oats and many other forms of vegetation, including canola (called oil seed rape in United Kingdom), long grass, corn, tobacco, and rice. There have been a few reports of crop circles in vegetable crops, especially spinach and potatoes. Crop formations have also been found in groves of small trees.

5. Is There a Particular Time of the Year That Crop Circles Appear?

In the northern hemisphere, crop circles appear from late April until early September This coincides with the period of the growing season when the vegetation has grown in excess of three inches in height.

6. How Can You Tell When a Crop Circle Is Real?

These days, identifying genuine formations by physical inspection alone is becoming increasingly difficult, and often requires scientific equipment and testing to confirm authenticity. In the 1980s, crop circles rarely drew visitors, and thus, no damage was done to the site after initial discovery. It is a different situation today. In addition to a site being compromised by tourists tramping through the fields, many formations that are initially thought to be genuine are, in fact, counterfeits. This is due in large part to hoaxers applying to their fakes the characteristics researchers recorded and reported in the early years of the phenomenon.

That being said, there are certain key signature characteristics that can be looked for when trying to identify a real circle. If the following are found in a crop circle, the formation is probably authentic.

- There are no tracks into the circle.
- There are no signs of interference with the soil or the plants at points in the circle where hoaxers would have had to stand to create the formation.
- The plants are not damaged.
- The plants are more vibrant in appearance and the root structure is more extensive than usual.
- The swirl symmetry is even and there is usually two or fewer rotations of the spiral vein of the circle before it strikes the standing wall of the circle's circumference.
- There are magnetic and electrostatic anomalies in the formation, and compass rotation occurs when inside the circle.
- The plants are changed at the cellular level.
- Small quantities of an unknown magnetic material are found in the crop circle's soil and impregnated into the plant tissue.
- A magnetic profile as registered on a magnetometer mimics the actual design of the crop circle.
- The profile of the electrostatic field found in a crop circle shows unusual patterning.

Features that have long been associated with real circles but have, in the last 20 years, been perfected by those making counterfeits include:

- Very precise geometries made without obvious mistakes.
- Well-formed cut-off lines around the circle or pattern.
- The plants involved are bent over evenly during the early stages of growth. In later stages, though, the plants are broken. This "bending but not breaking" feature has not been successfully hoaxed in oil-seed rape (canola) plants.
- Some impressive spiral veins have been reproduced.

It should be kept in mind that all of these features have not been achieved with some evidence of human involvement and this is another way researchers can distinguish counterfeits from the authentic formations.

7. Who Are Doug and Dave?

Doug Bower and Dave Chorley are two elderly British men who came forward in 1990 and laid claim to having created *all* the crop circles in England. These senior citizens lived in the Southampton area in Hampshire, England and their "confession" ended up plastered on the front page of the British tabloid *Today*. Their story quickly made its way around the world and there are still people who credit the two men with creating the crop circle phenomenon. When confronted with evidence proving that they had nothing to do with certain formations, they backed down and modified their claim. At one point, they claimed to have made the Celtic Cross design that appears on the cover of my book, *Circular Evidence*, but could not even duplicate it on paper when asked by myself and Pat Delgado. They then withdrew their claim to that formation.

It is accepted today that Doug and Dave did make some—perhaps many—crop circles. However, it is also accepted by skeptics and believers alike that it is patently impossible for them to have made all that they claimed they did.

Doug and Dave did, however, deal a serious blow to the perception of the crop circle phenomenon in the mind of the general public. And there is suspicion that that is precisely what their intentions were all along. A conspiracy has not been proven, but many believe that powers with money (governmental, military, or otherwise) used Doug and Dave as part of a disinformation campaign. Dave Chorley died of cancer in the mid-1990s. Doug Bower has kept a relatively low profile in recent years.

8. Is It True That All Crop Circles Are Made by Aliens and UFOs?

A There has long been suspicion that crop circles were formed by UFO landing gear, or by energy rays beamed down from an alien spacecraft onto the field. Most serious crop circle researchers allow that an extraterrestrial intelligence may be involved in the phenomenon, but the majority discount the possibility of the formations being created by alien ships.

9. Has Anyone Ever Seen a Crop Circle Form?

A Yes, there have been eyewitnesses to the formation of crop circles. Currently, there are approximately 50 people worldwide who have reported seeing a crop circle form in realtime as they watched.

The first reports came from Argentina in 1959, and again in 1960. There were two witnesses to the 1960 event.

The next credible report came from Australia in 1966, followed by several believable accounts over a number of years from people in the county of Wiltshire, England.

One of the British eyewitnesses was a local journalist named Arthur Shuttlewood

from Warminster, Wiltshire. Shuttlewood was standing in a field near Warminster with several others late one evening when they all heard a strange sound crackling in the long grass. As they watched, the plants swayed back and forth hypnotically like a snake, and when the movement and sound ceased, they all saw that a crop circle had formed.

Also, a bicycle shop owner named Ray Barnes, who lived in a small village near Warminster, watched as a line of plants bent over and swept across the field in an undulating wave. This line of demarcation eventually stopped its forward movement and the plants then rotated and formed a single circle in the crops.

Researcher Nancy Talbott and a colleague witnessed strange lights over a field in the Netherlands in 2001 and, shortly thereafter, a simple dumbbell pattern was discovered in the crops. Talbott's colleague also claims to have witnessed a circle form in the same field during 1999.

In almost every case, eyewitnesses report seeing only simple crop circles forming.

10. Have Crop Circles Ever Appeared in Exactly the Same Place?

A This is a very rare occurrence but it has happened. One such place where crop circles have appeared several times is in the field below Bratton Castle in Wiltshire, England. (For more information about one such event in 1987, check out my first book, *Circular Evidence*.)

11. How Long Do Crop Circles Last?

A Crop circles remain in the fields until the plants are harvested, or until they die naturally at the end of the growing season. The crop circle "season" usually begins when the plants are approximately three inches high, in late April and May in the United Kingdom, along with other countries in the northern hemisphere. Harvest occurs during late August, early September.

12. How Large Are Crop Circles?

The smallest reported crop circle is approximately one foot in diameter, but these are very rare. The average crop circle is about 60 feet in diameter. The more elaborate designs have stretched out across the landscape over distances of three quarters of a mile. Among these, the 1994 formations at Ashbury, Berkshire; and 1996 designs at Etchilhampton, Wiltshire are the most notable. Most major designs that include complex patterns are 200 to 300 feet wide.

13. What Happens to the Plants Inside Crop Circles? Are They Cut or Broken? Is It True Some Plants Are Burned?

The individual plants are bent over at right angles without being broken or cut. I have never witnessed burning of any kind in the hundreds of circles I have inspected, but several reports of burnt plants do exist. Biophysicist William Levengood has reported finding evidence of burning inside some of the plants he has analyzed.

14. Are the Plants Always Swirled in one Particular Direction?

Until 1986, almost all the plants in crop circles were spiraled in a clockwise direction. After circles were discovered with single and double rings around, the plants in the central circles were found to be swirled counterclockwise as well. (See T9 and T10 in the Andrews Catalogue on page 206.) Since 1986, the data reports about the same numbers of clockwise and counterclockwise circles. There are also reports of patterns in which both directions of rotation occur in the same circle.

15. Have "Crop" Circles Ever Been Reported in Snow?

Snow circles have been reported on a few occasions but it is not known if they represent the same phenomenon as crop circles.

The most impressive snow circle was seen and photographed by students at MIT University in Boston, on the 2nd of February in 1993. Many shapes, including circles and rings, were formed in the light snow that covered a very thin layer of ice on the Charles River. The ice was very thin and would not have been able to support even the weight of a small child, so the suspicion that the acres of geometric designs were made by the students was quickly ruled out.

Snow is not that common in southern England, but on those occasions that snow *has* covered the usual areas where crop circles form, no designs have been reported in the snow. However, in January 1983, Mr. F. B. James witnessed something at Winterbourne Monxton near Avebury, Wiltshire that might well be the same phenomena as the crop circles. One morning, Mr. James discovered several perfect, 15-foot diameter circles in young wheat plants that had been heavily covered in frost. The circles were only noticed because the frost had melted inside each circle. Interestingly, swirled crop circles have since been reported in this area since 1987.

Appendix B

A Crop Circle A to Z

Agriglyph. A word coined to describe crop circle patterns and designs. Its genesis was the word "petroglyph," which is a carving or a line drawing on rock. The Greek prefix "petro-" was replaced with "agri-", a variant of "agro-" to indicate that the drawings were being done in fields. The suffix "glyph" means "word."

Alton Barnes. Area in Wiltshire, England, known for its scenic splendor, archaeological sites, crop circle manifestations, and UFO sightings. Alton Barnes is within the 41.5-mile crop circle equilateral triangle in central southern England identified by Colin Andrews.

The Andrews Catalogue. A catalogue of black-and-white silhouettes of hundreds of crop circle designs, both authentic and manmade. Colin Andrews continues to add designs to this massive compilation. The *Catalogue*, complete through the formations of 2002, is reprinted in this volume.

Avebury. Village built inside the world's largest stone circle in Wiltshire, England, one mile north of Silbury Hill, with Stonehenge and other prehistoric archaeological sites nearby. A great deal of crop circle activity occurs in Avebury and surrounding environs.

Balls of Light. Many witnesses to crop circle formation have reported seeing balls of golden light floating and flitting above fields where, shortly thereafter, a crop circle appeared. Sometimes, the balls are reported as being silvery and metallic.

Some witnesses state that the balls move with purpose and that they seemed to be reading their minds. These balls of light are prevalent in the Avebury area of England. They particularly center around one hill where they are seen so often that the hill is known as "Golden Ball Hill." There is no concrete evidence that these balls are responsible for, or in some way connected to, the creation of crop circles. However, there is a great deal of anecdotal evidence (as well as quite a bit of movie footage of the lights) that indicates that they are often seen in the area of crop circles. The association with crop circles is still unknown, but there does indeed seem to be some kind of nexus between the balls and the circles.

Barbury Castle Tetrahedron. A massive, 12,000-square-yard crop formation that appeared in one night on July 16, 1991, in a field near the hill fort of Barbury Castle in Wiltshire, England. The night before its appearance, residents of the nearby village of Wroughton experienced a power blackout and many residents witnessed and reported flying balls of colored light above the field where the formation later manifested. The day after it appeared, a British newspaper ran a photo of the design with the headline, "Now Explain This One." The formation consisted of a triple ring in the middle with a triangle surrounding it as a perimeter, and three varied circular satellites extending out from the three angles of the triangle.

Brain Waves. The brain wave patterns of people participating in crop circle experiments (including Colin Andrews himself) have registered a distinct change when the subjects enter crop circles.

Celtic Cross. A Latin cross is the standard Christian cross, consisting of a vertical bar with a shorter horizontal bar two-thirds up its length. A Celtic cross is a Latin cross with a circle superimposed over its center. A crop formation described as a Celtic cross design consists of a center circle surrounded by four circles at each point of the compass, at the bottom, top, and side of the cross. Colin Andrews wished for a Celtic cross crop design to appear near his home, and a design did manifest shortly thereafter. A photo of this pattern appears on the cover of Colin's first book, *Circular Evidence*.

Cereal Crops. Edible grass crops grown for food. The vast majority of crop circles appear in cereal crops, specifically wheat, oats, corn, oil-seed rape, buckwheat, and barley.

Cerealogy. Also known as "cereology." The study of crop circles. The word was coined to describe the discipline of crop circle research, much the way "UFOlogy" was coined to describe the study of the UFO phenomenon.

Chaos Theory. The theory that within the chaos of seemingly random, unconnected events, order can be found. The "butterfly effect" is the most oft-cited example of chaos theory. In Ian Stewart's *The Mathematics of Chaos*, he explains this effect:

The flapping of a single butterfly's wing today produces a tiny change in the state of the atmosphere. Over a period of time, what the atmosphere actually does diverges from what it would have done. So, in a month's time, a tornado that would have devastated the Indonesian coast doesn't happen. Or maybe one that wasn't going to happen, does.[1]

Chaos theory is relevant to crop circles because when the variations in a specific model are plotted on a graph, what is known as a Koch Curve emerges; a square fractal that is known for its infinite expansion and diminution. Fractals are also found in many crop circle designs.

Cheesefoot Head. A natural amphitheater near Hampshire, England, known for unusual goings-on, including crop circle manifestations, odd sounds, and elusive lights.

CIA. U.S. intelligence agency rumored to be interested in crop circles and the folks who study them. Colin Andrews was approached by a man claiming to be a CIA agent when he lived in England, and much of what Colin was told by this man came to pass. His credibility was shattered, however, by his erratic, especially "non-agent" behavior.

The alleged "agent" was discredited by individuals I consulted who had knowledge of the standard tactics and methods used by the CIA. Most damning was this man's appearance on national television, combined with his unrelenting focus on gaining access to the bank accounts into which all "shared" monies would be deposited. This was obviously the behavior of a con man who tried to use my fame and reputation to capitalize on what he saw as a money-making scheme. He constantly spoke of producing a video showing UFOs making crop circles, but he needed me to sell it to the media. After I severed ties with him, his ruse fell apart.

Circles Phenomenon Research International. The crop circle research organization founded by Colin Andrews. CPR published a newsletter for many years and is considered the preeminent crop circle research group.

Circular Evidence. The first book written about the crop circle phenomenon. It was written by Colin Andrews and Pat Delgado and published in 1989. It quickly became a worldwide best-seller.

Crop Circles. Circular geometries most commonly found in cereal crops. In authentic crop circles, the vegetation is bent over at right angles and spiraled into often complex patterns. Many crop circles around the world are hoaxes. However, there is a percentage of formations that exhibit characteristics that cannot be duplicated by hoaxing and cannot yet be completely explained.

Crop Circles: The Latest Evidence. Colin Andrews's and Pat Delgado's follow-up to *Circular Evidence*, published in 1990.

Crop Rings. Simple rings that appear in fields, usually without the crops in its center being flattened. Sometimes they appear as double or triple rings. The difference between crop rings and crop circles is that the plants inside crop circles are all flattened.

The Cosmic Connection. Book by crop circle authority Michael Hesemann, published in Germany in 1993, and translated in England in 1996. It suggests a strong link between UFOs, extraterrestrials, and the formation of crop circles.

Diatonic Ratios. The diatonic scale consists of the eight notes of the musical scale, without flats or sharps. The diatonic scale comprises the white keys on a piano: C, D, E, F, G, A, B, C. There is a specific interval between each note of the diatonic scale—C to D, G to A, etc.—and this difference is measured by adding or subtracting the vibration of a particular note in kilohertz from the vibration in kilohertz of the note one step above or below. The difference between the two notes is called a diatonic ratio.

What does all this have to do with crop circles? Professor Gerald Hawkins discovered that the differences in diameters of larger and smaller circles in crop formations result in a diatonic ratio (the identical ratio exists for the size differences of multiple circles as for the difference between the intervals of musical notes on the diatonic scale). These ratios have been found in formations all over the world which are considered authentic by the experts and their existence deflates somewhat the "all the circles are hoaxed" theory. If all circles are hoaxed, the argument goes, and countless circles manifest specific diatonic ratios, then there exists an enormous, global conspiracy to include dimensions in counterfeit circles that will produce these esoteric, mathematical ratios.

Dowsing. Searching for and sometimes locating underground water, minerals, underground mines, or buried objects by using a divining rod, which is usually a forked branch or stick made of hazel wood, ash, or rowan, that bends downward when held over a source. A pendulum suspended above the ground or a map is also sometimes used. Steel wire clothes hangers bent at right angles are also commonly used. Many dowsers report strong reactions from crop circles.

Earth Energies. Magnetism, gravity, electrostatic fields, radiation, and other energy forms that are manifest in the biosystem of the earth and often associated with the appearance and location of crop circles.

4:15. The time Colin Andrews's home alarm system triggered for many nights, until he figured out what the numbers meant (see Chapter 2.9).

Fractals. A geometric pattern that is infinitely complex, infinitely repeating, and infinitesimal. A fractal creates shapes and surfaces that cannot be represented by classical geometry. Fractals are used especially in computer modeling of irregular patterns and structures in nature. Many crop circles manifest fractals, especially in "Golden Mean" designs, such as the Julia Set found opposite Stonehenge.

Gaia Theory. The theory that the earth and all its component biological "parts" comprise an enormous living organism (see Chapter 4.1).

Grass Circles. Circles that appear in grass, as opposed to cereal crops.

Grasshopper Warbler. A bird indigenous to England that makes a high-pitched, trilling sound. When Colin Andrews first heard the sound of the crop circles (See Chapters 9 and 10), at least one entomologist claimed that the sound was actually that of the grasshopper warbler, ignoring the fact that the sound's movement, duration, volume, and dynamic variation seemed to clearly preclude the possibility that it was being created by a bird. Not to mention the fact that the grasshopper warbler is a very rare bird and is almost always found in marshes; also the sound Colin recorded in a crop circle is 5.2 kilohertz and the warbler is 6 kilohertz. Another important fact to consider is that the sound has also been recorded as radio waves, which precludes the sound coming from a bird.

Healings. Some people have reported remarkable healings after visiting a crop circle. There have been claims of improvements to severe arthritis, reduction of tremors, the elimination of allergies and their attendant symptoms, and other improvements in health. Proponents believe that there are energy fields in crop circles that have positive effects on the human body. People have also reported improvements in psychological problems and many claim elevated spirits and new vigor after visiting a crop circle. Ironically, the exact opposite effect has also been reported, with some people experiencing headaches, nausea, dizziness, abnormal menopausal bleeding, disorientation, excessive fatigue, and other negative consequences after visiting a crop circle.

Hedgehogs. "Rutting hedgehogs" was a sarcastic explanation for crop circles coined by Gordon Creighton of the *Flying Saucer Review*. Creighton intended it as a put-down of the media for their often ridiculous explanations of the crop circle phenomenon. True to form, many in the media took Creighton seriously and "rutting hedgehogs" ended up being cited by journalists as one hypothetical cause for crop circles.

Hoaxers. One or more people who enter farmers' fields and create crop patterns. Hoaxers produce their designs for one of two reasons: to deliberately deceive or to create "earth art." Hoaxers do not usually admit their work, no matter what their real purpose. Some earth artists take credit for a creation, but most do not. Hoaxers, also known as counterfeiters, use boards and rollers to flatten crops, and many plot out their designs on computers first. Hoaxers usually damage or kill the plants in their designs. Hoaxers sometimes get permission from farmers (and pay them a stipend), many times they do not. Many serious cereologists are in agreement that hoaxers have "muddied the waters" of crop circle research and have skewed the perception of the phenomenon in the eyes of the general public, leading many to believe that all crop circles are manmade. (See Chapter 2.13.)

Hopi Indians. Native American indigenous people who believe that crop circles are part of a series of earth changes that tie into an important prophecy in the guardianship of the Hopi Elders.

Ice Circles. Circles and geometric patterns that appear on ice in designs that are very similar to crop circles found in fields. Often, ice circles materialize on ice that is so thin and fragile that it wouldn't be able to support the weight of a dog, let alone hoaxers with tools to cut the ice.

Institute of Resonance Therapy. German clinic that has experimented with crop circle images in ecosystem revitalization protocols. The ecosystems of today are facing unprecedented challenges to their very existence, and the survival information genetically imprinted in lifeforms does not contain viable strategies to combat the destruction, toxins, and assaults against them. IRT has been working with crop circles as remedies and has had documented success.

Julia Set. A massive crop formation that seemingly appeared in a period of 45 minutes in a field across the road from the Stonehenge site. See Chapter 6 for more information on this fractal-based, spiraling crop formation.

Ley Lines. Invisible lines of "earth energies," especially magnetism, that crisscross the planet in a geodetic grid. Many sacred sites are aligned along ley lines, as are many crop circles. Psychics and sensitives, using faculties similar to those employed in dowsing, can "read" ley lines and are usually proven correct when equipment is used to register magnetic and other readings. Ley lines were originally recognized and reported by Alfred Watkins in 1921 after he noticed that an invisible straight line ran through the hilltops where ancient sacred sites were situated.

M15. British intelligence agency reportedly behind the Operation Blackbird deception, which was implemented to discredit Colin Andrews and Pat Delgado and to defuse public interest in the crop circle phenomenon.

Magnetism. One of the theories for the creation of crop circles. It states that a mysterious shift in the earth's magnetic field produces a current that "electrocutes" plants and forces them to lie flat on the ground.

This theory could explain why electronic equipment being used in some crop circles has malfunctioned or has been destroyed. This theory does not explain the "blown nodes" factor of authentic crop circles. Some plant nodes are as big as 200 times their original size. A corollary to the magnetism theory is that the current produced by shifts in the earth's magnetic field combines with energies from underground aquifers, or even from water in the air, to create the "blown nodes." (See Chapter 4.2.)

Mandelbrot Set. The first fractal crop circle design. The Mandelbrot design was discovered by the French mathematician and chaos theorist Benoit Mandelbrot while working with a mathematical model he was experimenting with. Mandelbrot conducted his experiment at Cambridge University in England, which is very close to where a Mandelbrot crop formation ultimately appeared.

Microwaves. Some crop circle researchers suspect microwave radiation in crop formations as being responsible for feelings of both ill health and well-being experienced by many visitors to crop circle sites. Also, biophysicist William Levengood believes that microwaves may be responsible for the expulsion cavities found in the plants in authentic crop circles.

Military Helicopters. Military helicopters have often been seen flying above new crop formations and also above empty fields that later manifest a crop circle. One of the first public confirmations of military helicopter reconnaissance flights are the photos of helicopters flying over crop circles in Colin Andrews's and Pat Delgado's 1989 book, *Circular Evidence*.

Mowing Devil. A mysterious figure, possibly the devil himself, who appeared one night in 1678 in a ball of fire and cut a farmer's crops into an oval. One of the earliest accounts of a crop circle forming (see Chapter 2.5).

Music. After studying the crop circle photos in *Circular Evidence*, Professor Gerald Hawkins remarked to his wife that he was looking at music. His hunch paid off after further research revealed that the ratios of size differences in crop circles were the same as the ratios of intervals between one note on the western scale and another.

These diatonic ratios have been found in many authentic formations. Hawkins later refined position in his 1996 article "The Diatonic Ratios in Crop Circles," which appeared in the Fall/Winter 1996/97 issue of the *Circles Phenomenon Research* newsletter. "Of course we cannot say that the crop circles are 'musical.' All that can be said is that the crop circles and the eight-note musical scale are based on the same mathematical relationship." (See Chapter 12.)

Nodes. The joint or knuckle of a plant stem. William Levengood believes that in authentic crop circles, the nodes of the plant stems have exploded, as though the minute amounts of water inside them was superheated quickly and blew out the nodes. This effect is not found in plants from hoaxed formations. Sometimes, the nodes are swollen and enlarged, but not ruptured, and the plants continue to grow.

Oil-Seed Rape. A European plant (*Brassica napus*) of the mustard family, which is cultivated as fodder and for its seed that yields a valuable oil. Oil-seed rape, which is also known as canola, is one of the crops in which crop circles appear most frequently.

Oliver's Castle Video. A video purporting to show flying white balls (UFOs) creating a snowflake crop circle pattern in a field below Oliver's Castle near Devizes, in Wiltshire, in England. The pattern appears in only a few seconds, and then the balls fly out of the frame. The video was eventually proven to be a hoax (see Chapter 16).

Operation Blackbird. A crop circle surveillance operation in July 1990, coordinated by Colin Andrews, and funded by the BBC and Japanese television. The purpose of the operation was to film the formation of a crop circle. In actuality, it was the first known government attempt to deescalate the public interest in the growing phenomenon of crop circles, and a plot was concocted to discredit Colin Andrews and devalue his work. Operation Blackbird was carried out by means of a well-orchestrated, well-funded, multilevel hoax perpetrated on Colin Andrews and the global public by the British government (see Chapter 15).

Operation White Crow. One of the first crop circle surveillance operations. It took place in the "Devil's Punchbowl" in Cheesefoot Head, Winchester, in Hampshire, in 1989, one year prior to Operation Blackbird. During this operation, Colin Andrews recorded the unusual trilling sound that was accompanied by physical effects on one of the team members (see Chapter 10).

Petroglyphs. Lines or drawings found on rock, and believed to have been created by prehistoric man. (See *Agriglyphs*.)

Pictogram. Another word for pictograph, used when referring to crop formations. A pictorial representation of numerical data or numerical relationships, or the use of hieroglyphic symbols to communicate a message. The highly complex crop formations are believed to have some type of encoded message and may be an agricultural hieroglyphic.

Plant Analysis. A general term for the series of tests performed on plants taken from crop circles. These tests include radioactivity measurement, spectrographic analysis, magnetometer readings, microscopic study, cellular crystal experiments, weighing, photographing, and more.

Plasma Vortex. An electrically neutral, highly ionized gas composed of ions, electrons, and neutral particles concentrated into a powerful whirlwind believed to be capable of, and responsible in some cases, for creating crop circles (see Chapter 4.6).

Radiation. Radioactive isotopes were at one time discovered in crop circles but for some reason the military lab performing the tests stopped the research and did not issue a conclusive statement. Colin Andrews has carried a Geiger counter into crop circles with him for years and reports he has never registered anything unusual. See Chapter 3 for more on Colin's research into radioactivity in crop circles.

Remote Viewing. The ability to perceive people, objects, places, or events at a location removed from the "viewer" by either space or time. Remote viewing has been used in crop circle experiments with mixed results.

Sacred Geometry. Specific patterns and ratios found in nature embodying the complete range of scale: from the energy signature of atoms and molecules, to the spiraling arm of the Milky Way galaxy. Man has consciously applied sacred geometric ratios in everything from architecture to art, mimicking deliberately what nature achieves spontaneously, striving to create an artificial microcosm of the universe with his science and art (see Chapter 2.8).

Sand Circles. Crop circle–like geometric patterns and designs that appear unbidden in expanses of desert sands. Sand circles are always presumed to be authentic manifestations, because footprints in the sand surrounding the formations are never found, and they are often discovered in exceptionally remote areas.

Secrets in the Fields. Book by crop circle authority Freddy Silva. Subtitled "The Science and Mysticism of Crop Circles."

SETI. The Search for Extraterrestrial Intelligence.

Signs. Blockbuster 2002 Disney/Touchstone movie written and directed by M. Night Shyamalan and starring Mel Gibson. *Signs* used the appearance of crop circles on a former priest's (Gibson) farm as a plot device for an alien invasion movie. Colin Andrews was a consultant on the film and was used by Disney as a media liaison, in addition to providing data and photographs.

Silbury Hill. An enormous artificial mound south of Avebury in Wiltshire, England that was built in 2660 B.C. with chalk and soil. It covers more than five acres and is approximately 130 feet high. We do not know why Silbury was originally built but one theory is that it, like Stonehenge, is a solar observatory. Silbury Hill is positioned on a ley line, and crop circle activity is commonplace around Silbury Hill and Avebury.

Snow Circles. Circles and geometric patterns that appear in fresh snow in designs very similar to the crop circles found in fields.

Sounds. A specific metallic trilling sound has been reported in crop circles. There is also often electrostatic interference with video and recording equipment when this sound is heard. Colin Andrews personally experienced this sound three times and has two tape recordings of it that he often plays for his audiences at his lectures. See Chapter 9 for more details on the sounds in, and of the circles.

Stonehenge. A group of standing stones on Salisbury Plain in southern England that date to c. 2000–1800 B.C. The megaliths are enclosed by a circular ditch and embankment that may date to c. 2800 B.C. The arrangement of the stones suggests that Stonehenge was used as a religious center and also as an astronomical observatory. There remains questions as to who designed, shaped, carried, and set up this enormous site. Many crop circle researchers believe that the stone triptychs were placed to permanently record an authentic crop circle formation and, indeed, hypothetical designs that fill in the missing stones do look like commonly seen crop formations (see Chapter 6).

Stonehenge Decoded. The seminal book on the Stonehenge site, written by renowned astronomer and scientist, Gerald Hawkins (see Chapter 6).

Tramlines. The straight lines that run up and down the length of a field of crops that farmers use for their tractors and for walking through the fields. Tramlines can be usually be seen bifurcating crop formations and many skeptics point to them as being easy access for hoaxers to create a formation without leaving tracks. It is true that tramlines can do just that, but there are countless instances of crop circles appearing in the middle of a section of a field that is not accessible by tramlines. Tramlines run nowhere near some crop circles. A tram line is approximately six feet wide, which is the average tractor axle length. This knowledge is useful in scaling the size of crop formations from the air.

Tree Circles. The phenomenon of tree circles is believed to be related to crop circle formation and may employ some of the same energies. There seem to be two types of tree circles reported. The first is when standing trees bend and move to form a geometric pattern similar to that found in the fields. These formations are only visible from the air and there have been random accounts by pilots of a group of trees in a forest forming a design. The other type of tree circle reported occurs when young, still flexible trees bend to the ground and form a circular pattern, similar to the way plants flatten down to create a design. One notable account was reported by Paul Vigay, editor and publisher of *Enigma*. The following is an edited and abridged version of the account given to Paul:

> [This] happened between the years 1963 and 1969 [in] Grand Lake, New Brunswick, Canada....This area had long been strip mined for coal. In 1960, [a] mining company started to reforest the area...trees were planted on both sides of the road. These trees were growing on crown land, in beautiful, perfectly straight lines.
>
> In about three years...they had grown to be quite tall, and the butts of these trees were about 3 inches in diameter. In the middle of a summer afternoon, I was in a car on my way to the lake....When we came...to this stand of pine trees, the road was blocked with police and army vehicles.
>
> There were...police and army personnel walking around inside the pine trees on both sides of the road.

We were motioned...to move along.

While passing by, I noticed, on both sides of the road, two circles.

The trees were all bent to the ground. The circles were about 10 feet away from the edge of the road, one on either side. They were fairly large, about 12 feet in diameter.

The really odd thing was all the trees laid down flat to the ground [and] the tops of these trees all pointed to the circumferences of the circles....Talk around town was that bears had pushed the trees down....I knew that couldn't be the answer....Months later, the trees were cut as close to the ground as they could.

Fencing was put up to keep the curious out, [but] we could see through the fence....You could see the butts of the trees enough to see they were severely curved at ground level, [which would have been] impossible to do without breaking the trees....[F]or years later nothing grew there. This is not a story; this is the truth. Why would they call the army if it were only bears? Why would they fence it off?

UFOs. Unidentified flying objects. UFOs have been suggested as a possible explanation for the formation of crop circles. One theory is that crop circles are formed by the UFO's landing gear; another suggests that UFOs create the formations from their craft using some form of laser or energy beam. UFO sightings around crop circle sites are commonplace. In Australia, crop circles were originally known as "saucer's nests" because of the belief that UFOs were creating them when they landed. While no video documentation of alien craft creating, or flying above crop circles has surfaced, there is a great deal of video footage showing unidentifiable balls of light flying above fields where crop circles later appear or already exist (see Chapters 4.7 and 16).

Ultimate Crop Circles: Signs From Space? An interactive DVD produced in 2002 by Central Park Media on which Colin Andrews is interviewed at length by author Peter Robbins. The DVD also includes a crop circles photo gallery from Colin Andrews's archive, the Oliver's Castle video, and other features.

Undeniable Evidence. An acclaimed 60-minute videotape documentary about the crop circle phenomenon produced by Ark Soundwaves of Glastonbury, UK in 1991, starring Colin Andrews.

Underground Aquifers. An underground bed or layer of earth, gravel, or porous stone that yields water. A great many of the world's authentic crop circles appear in fields above underground aquifers.

United Nations. In 1992, Colin Andrews addressed the Parapsychology Society/ S.E.A.T. group of United Nations employees on the crop circle phenomenon.

Appendix C

A Crop Circle Who's Who

Alexander, Stephen. Crop circle photographer. He first became interested in crop circles during 1990 when he filmed a strange object in a field where a crop circle already existed. His was one of the first films to successfully capture the small orbs seen near crop circles. He has since become one of the best photographers of crop circles in the world.

Amamiya, Kiyoshi. Crop circle researcher and C.P.R. (Circles Phenomenon Research) International coordinator in Japan. Responsible for much of the research on crop circles in Japan. Co-author of 1983's *Project Garuda*.

Anderson, Paul. Director of the C.P.R. International affiliate in Canada since 1995. He has now formed his own organization Canadian Crop Circle Research Network, researching the crop circle phenomenon all throughout Canada.

Anderson, Paul. *(Great Britain)* Worked with Colin Andrews during both crop circle surveillance projects, Operation White Crow in 1989, and Operation Blackbird in 1990. In recent years, he has carried out field work in Oxfordshire County, England.

Andrews, Colin. The world's leading authority on the crop circle phenomenon. Co-authored (with Pat Delgado) the first book on the subject, the international best-seller *Circular Evidence*, and its sequel, *Crop Circles: The Latest Evidence*. He is the researcher who has worked the longest on the crop circle enigma and is the creator and compiler of the most complete database on the subject.

Andrews, Richard. Renowned expert in the ancient art of dowsing. (No relation to Colin Andrews.) A farmer and lover of the countryside, he became involved with crop circle research in 1988. Richard passed away in 1999 and is sadly missed in the fields.

Andrews, Synthia. Wife of Colin Andrews, writer, researcher, and hugely supportive of his work. Synthia Andrews has worked in the field of therapeutic massage and body work for over 20 years. She is a teacher at the Connecticut Center for massage therapy and leads workshops in the United States and United Kingdom. Her work focuses on the emotional and energetic factors in health and healing. She began incorporating crop circles into her practice in 1992.

Aubrun, Dr. Jean-Noel. Physicist and engineer who has worked with Colin Andrews for many years. A highly respected scientist who has many areas of expertise that have been put to good use in crop circle research. Carried out the preliminary analysis of Colin's groundbreaking crop circle magnetometer survey, which is continuing to reveal significant findings.

Barnes, Ray. Eyewitness to the formation of a 100-foot diameter crop circle at Westbury, Wiltshire, England on July 3, 1982. Owns a bicycle store in Westbury.

Bishop, George. Secretary of the Center for Crop Circle Studies. An open-minded man largely responsible for the annual conferences and keeping the CCCS in existence.

Bowers, Douglas. The "Doug" of the most famous crop circle hoaxers, Doug and Dave. An artist and senior citizen who, with his friend Dave Chorley, claimed to have made all the crop circles in England. In 1990, the British newspaper *Today* promised to pay them 10,000 pounds for their story, but they ultimately had to threaten legal action against the paper to get their money. Doug is now retired and rarely speaks to the media about crop circles.

Boerman, Robert. A key crop circle researcher in the Netherlands. Boerman heard about the mystery in 1997 and was investigating his first circle within days. He discovered a white sticky substance in that first circle, which, after extensive analysis, remains unidentified. Author of *Crop Circles: Gods and Their Secrets.*

Chorley, David. The "Dave" of the most famous crop circle hoaxers, Doug and Dave. Friend of Doug Bowers and also an artist. The two elderly men claimed to have made all the crop circles in England. In 1990, they sold their story to a national newspaper in England. It was always Dave who showed an angry edge towards crop circle researchers when he took part in television interviews about the subject. He passed away in 2000. (See Douglas Bowers.)

Charles, Prince. (See Princess Diana.)

Christopher, Ian. Director of the Mariposa Pacific Research Institute based in California. Produced one of the best documentaries ever made about the crop circle mystery, *Something Wonderful Has Happened...But It Was Not in the News,* which won a number of awards.

Collins, Andrew. British writer often confused with Colin Andrews. Author of several popular books, including the 1988 classic, *The Black Alchemist.* In 1991, Collins concluded that orgone energy, a theoretical universal life force emanating from all organic material first hypothesized by Austrian scientist Wilhelm Reich, could explain many of the crop circle mysteries. His findings were published in a book called *The Circlemakers.*

Corso, Colonel Philip. J. U.S. military officer; writer; served on the National Security Council under President Dwight D. Eisenhower. At a meeting with Colin Andrews at a congress in San Marino, Italy before he died, Corso acknowledged that he was aware of crop circle reports coming in to the White House in 1960. He said the reports were forwarded to the National Security agency (NSA) and that they were considered at that time to be some form of as-yet unexplainable communication.

Curry, Mike. Inventor of a high-mast security system employed by Colin Andrews and the BBC during Operation Blackbird. (See Chapter 15.) Curry personally witnessed the strange crop circle sound during one of the special operations.

Delgado, Pat. Co-author with Colin Andrews of the first book written about crop circles, *Circular Evidence.* An electromechanical design engineer, Delgado was contracted to NASA to assist with tracking the *Mariner* Spacecraft from the Woomera tracking station in Australia.

Diana, Princess. Princess Diana and Prince Charles discovered crop circles on their royal property, and through a retired military officer who acted as an intermediary, sought out Colin Andrews for a tour and an explanation. This excursion was quickly canceled and denied when news of Charles and Diana's interest in crop circles was mysteriously leaked to the media and the story appeared on the front page of British newspapers. Colin Andrews, Diana, Charles, and their aides were the only ones who knew of the plan to visit the crop circles and so it is believed today that someone in the royal entourage tipped off the press, or that Colin Andrews's phone was bugged. See Chapter 15 for more details on this incident.

Dickinson, Rod. Artist based in London, England and crop circle counterfeiter. He has participated in the creation of many impressive crop designs, but ironically he has also personally witnessed and photographed several impressive UFOs.

Gazecki, William. Director and producer of the acclaimed 2002 crop circles documentary, *Crop Circles: Quest for Truth,* the first-ever feature film about the phenomenon. Gazecki was also nominated for a Best Director Academy Award for his 1997 film, *Waco: Rules of Engagement.*

Glickman, Michael. Architect and crop circle researcher, best known for his extreme views on crop circles and for being instrumental in helping the police make the first arrest and prosecution of a man hoaxing a crop circle.

Fisk, Dr. David. Scientific Advisor to British Prime Minister Margaret Thatcher's government during the period when the government was being asked the first questions about crop circles in England.

Haddington, Lord John. Former president of the Centre for Crop Circle Studies and an active member of the House of Lords in the British Government.

Hadley, Robert. Professor of physics and astronomy who analyzed Colin Andrews's field data from the type 367 "Solar System" crop pattern (Andrews type 367) in 1995 and concluded that the design was an outstandingly accurate scaled replica of our solar system.

Haselhoff, Dr. Eltjo. Theoretical physicist and author of the book, *The Deepening Complexity of Crop Circles Scientific Research and Urban Legends.* Haselhoff, who has worked at Los Alamos National Laboratories in the United States, has studied the crop circle phenomenon for 10 years.

Hawkins, Gerald. Internationally renowned astronomer working at Harvard-Smithsonian Observatory in Cambridge, Massachusetts, and author of the groundbreaking book, *Stonehenge Decoded.* Professor Hawkins has done extensive work on analyzing the mathematical ratios found in crop circles. He has stated that his interest in the subject began when he read *Circular Evidence* in 1989.

Hein, Dr. Simeon. Ph.D. in Sociology, and Director of the Boulder, Colorado-based Institute for Resonance. He has carried out extensive ground researching into the electrostatic fields found in crop circles and, with colleague Ron Russell, continues to pursue this promising area of investigation. Author of the book, *Opening Minds: A Journey of Extraordinary Encounters, Crop Circles, and Resonance.*

Hesemann, Michael. Historian, science writer, crop circle researcher, and UFOlogist. Among the subjects he has researched and written books about are UFOs, crop circles and the Fatima Secrets. Native of Duselldorf, Germany.

Irving, Robert. Crop circle counterfeitor. He has admitted to making some of the crop circle patterns which later became known as "Thought Bubbles." Instead of a board and rope, Irving prefers to use a lightweight green plastic garden roller to push the plants down.

Jones, Ron. One of the original members of the Center for Crop Circle Studies; has been involved with crop circle research since the late 1980s. Was present and witnessed the first crop circle sound heard during Operation White Crow in the summer of 1989. See Chapter 10.

Kahata, Masahiro. Leading electronics engineer from Japan, now living in the United States, Kahata has extensively investigated why some visitors to crop circles claim healings and why electronic equipment regularly fails inside circles. He is the inventor of IBVA brainwave monitoring equipment, which is used in many hospitals for monitoring patient brainwave activity. He has also looked closely at the science and art of dowsing crop circles by using his equipment.

Keel, Shelly. C.P.R. International (U.K.) researcher who took part in Operation White Crow and Operation Blackbird with Colin Andrews. She was with three other researchers, including one scientist, during a double "missing time" episode when leaving a new crop formation near Silbury Hill on May 23, 1994. Keel experienced first-hand a series of strange happenings following her missing time ordeal.

Kikuchi, Professor. Plasma scientist from Japan who became involved with researching crop circles in Japan and England during 1989.

King, Jon. British UFOlogist and writer; claimed to have knowledge of the importance of Barbury Castle, Wiltshire, England to extraterrestrial contact and UFO sightings many years before one of the most famous crop patterns to date. The

Barbury Castle Tetrahedron appeared there in 1991.

Laumen, Frank. Well-known crop circle researcher in Germany, he has taken most of the impressive photographs of the formations in that country.

Levengood, William. Renowned Michigan biophysicist, who began investigating plants taken from crop circles in 1990 when Colin Andrews and Pat Delgado sent the first samples to him from England. Levengood believes that pinhead-sized holes in the plants, called "expulsion cavities," are caused by moisture inside the stems being heated rapidly and turning to steam.

He believes this is created by microwave energy that happens in microseconds. Other of his published findings relate to elongated nodes, and also his discovery that the seeds from plants in crop circles often grow up to five times faster than control seeds, and that the seedlings can tolerate lack of water and light for a considerable time without apparent harm. In "Anatomical Anomalies in Crop Formation Plants," which appeared in the 1994 issue of the journal *Physiologia Plantarum* (92:356), Levengood summed up his conclusions:

Crop formations consist of geometrically organized regions ranging from two to 80 meters diameter, in which the plants (primarily grain crops) are flattened in a horizontal position. Plants from crop formations display anatomical alterations which cannot be accounted for by assuming the formations are hoaxes. Near the soil surface the curved stems often form complex swirls with "vortex" type patterns. In the present paper, evidence is presented which indicates that structural and cellular alterations take place in plants exposed within the confines of the "circle" type formations, differences which were determined to be statistically significant when compared with control plants taken outside the formation. These transformations were manifested at the macroscopic level as abnormal nodal swelling, gross malformations during embryogenesis, and charred epidermal tissue. Significant changes in seed germination and development were found, and at the microscopic level differences were observed in cell wall pit structures. Affected plants also have characteristics suggesting the involvement of transient high temperatures.

Lodge, Oliver. Spiritualist and scientist who some believe may be trying to communicate from the beyond through crop circles (see Chapter 4.8).

Lucas, Roy. Farmhand working on a farm near Avebury, England who witnessed several strange columns of whirling mist in two fields on the farm shortly before 11 crop circles were found on the land.

Lundburg, John. London crop circle counterfeiter who prefers to be called a "land artist," one of a team calling themselves "Team Satan." The team claim responsibility for many crop circle patterns but refuse to work with researchers in order to identify them.

Lutz, Dr. Franz. Medical doctor, and son of a psychic healer of great repute. Former head of the Institute of Resonant Therapy in Germany, he has worked with crop patterns in the process of healing of plants and animals through resonance. European government scientists have shown a great deal of interest in Lutz's work. Dr. Lutz has worked with Colin Andrews since 1996.

Macnish, John. Television producer and journalist who worked for the British Broadcasting Corporation (BBC) for many years; later formed his own film company called *Circlevision* and began undercover work to try and discover who was making some of the crop circles. Macnish was commissioned by the BBC to work with Director David Morganstern, Colin Andrews, and Pat Delgado on the crop circle surveillance project, Operation Blackbird in 1990.

Maki, Masao. Well-known, highly respected Japanese crop circle and metaphysics researcher; author of several crop circle books published in Japan.

Meaden, Terence. Meteorologist and head of The Tornado and Storm Research Organization in England. In 1980, he became the first scientist to research crop circles. In 1989, he published *The Circles' Effect and Its Mysteries*, the second book ever written about crop circles. Meaden theorized that a new kind of weather phenomena called a "plasma vortex" was causing crop circles. In his essay "Crop Circles: The Real and the Hoaxed," which appeared in the 1992 issue of the journal *Weather* (47:368), Dr. Meaden summed up his conclusions:

We believe that the formation of real crop circles is a rare phenomenon resulting from the motion of a spinning mass of air which Professor Tokio Kikuchi has modelled by computer simulation and calls a nanoburst. This disturbance could involve the breakdown of an up-spinning vortex of the eddy or whirlwind type. On this theoretical model such a process leads to plain circles and ringed circles—types which are known from pre-hoax times in Britain and other countries, and are the only species which credible eyewitnesses have seen forming. All other so-called crop circles reported in the media news in recent years are likely to be the result of intelligent hoaxing, while the so-called paranormal events to which Deardorff alludes are nothing but the consequence of poor observation and/or exaggeration by susceptible mystics and vulnerable pseudoscientists. In the absence of hoaxing, the subject would still be unknown to the general public because the average number of real-circle reports per annum is small (indeed in some years it may be zero).

Mitchell, Sir David. A Member of the British Parliament for northeast Hampshire, England. In 1990, he visited a crop circle in England with Colin Andrews and was later helpful in initiating and maintaining dialogue about the phenomenon with various British government departments.

Morganstern, David. Director of the BBC television program *Daytime Live*. Andrews and Delgado made many appearances on this national program during the early 1990s. It was during one of these programs that a man who first claimed to be a crop circle eyewitness, and then later a CIA operative, made himself known to Andrews and Delgado. Morganstern was present when the strange crop circle sound was recorded during an interview in a crop circle.

Müller, Andreas. Leading crop circle researcher in Germany; his main contribution to the mystery has been in compiling a worldwide database on the subject.

Noyce, Ralph. Former head of the UFO desk in the Defense Staff 8 department at the Ministry of Defense in the United Kingdom. Noyce made his interest in the crop circles known publicly and actively researched them after he retired from the Ministry of Defense. He died in May of 1998.

Pope, Nick. Former Higher Executive Officer in Department 2a of the Air Secretariat in the U.K. Ministry of Defense, the department which deals with UFO and crop circle reports. Pope told Colin Andrews that he believes there is a real crop circle phenomenon and that, like the 5 percent of UFO reports made to his department that are believed to be extraterrestrial, similar numbers can probably be applied to the real circles. Andrews had several meetings with Pope during his time in office.

Presley, Reg. Lead singer in the 1960s pop group The Troggs, and a close friend of Colin Andrews. Colin and Reg lived a few hundred yards from each other in the town of Andover, Hampshire, England. Reg has become very interested in the crop circle mystery and has visited many sites with Andrews. He is the author of a book about the paranormal, which includes crop circles, called *Wild Things They Don't Tell Us* (the title of which is, of course, a tribute to his enormous hit, "Wild Thing.") (See Chapter 15.)

Pringle, Lucy. Well-known crop circle researcher who has specialized in the effects of crop circles on humans. Author of the book, *Crop Circles: The Greatest Mystery of Modern Times.*

Probert, David. A chartered surveyor hired by Colin Andrews to professionally survey the field in which the Julia Set crop formation appeared and come up with an estimate as to how long it would take to make the complicated design. Probert ultimately calculated that it would have taken him two full days to accurately lay out the pattern. Also, while driving home alone in his car one day in 1990 after investigating a series of crop circles at Blackland, Wiltshire, Probert heard a strange voice in his car that said, "Stay out of the crop circles." A number of other people studying crop circles have also heard single sentences from strange voices. (See Chapter 6 for the complete story of the Julia Set formation.)

Ramadan, Mohammad. President of the special interest group at the United Nations who invited Colin Andrews to make a special presentation about his research to staff, delegates, and the public at the United Nations in 1992.

Ramsby, Quinn. Colin Andrews brother-in-law, and owner of the audio-video production company Memorology. Memorology produced Colin's highly acclaimed crop circles CD *Cosmic Artist*. *Cosmic Artist* showcases 280 of the best crop circle photographs taken by Colin since 1983. It also includes the only public record of Police and Ministry of Defense photographs of the crop circle mystery. Maps and captions also accompany a fully automated slide show on the CD.

Robbins, Peter. Internationally-known, highly respected UFO researcher and sales executive with Central Park Media in New York. CPM produced the first in-depth crop circle interview (starring Colin Andrews) recorded on DVD for public sale. Robbins is co-author to the best-selling book, *Left at East Gate*.

Roy, Archie. Professor Emeritus of Astronomy at the University of Glasgow in Scotland and one of the first scientists to research the crop circle mystery. His main field is astrodynamics and he worked with Colin Andrews on crop circle research during the 1980s. Roy is a fellow of the Royal Society of Edinburg, the Royal Astronomical Society, and the British Interplanetary Society. He is currently director of the NATO Advanced Study Institute. He is the former president of the Center for Crop Circle Studies, of which he was a founding member.

Russell, Ron. Internationally renowned "Space Artist" whose work is displayed at the Smithsonian Air and Space Museum, the Jet Propulsion Lab, and elsewhere. He is director of Midwest Research, an organization established to study crop circles in the United States.

Schnabel, Jim. Author of *Round in Circles*, a book that purports to prove that almost all crop circles in existence are hoaxes.

Shyamalan, M. Night. Director and writer of the blockbuster 2002 movie *Signs*, which used crop circles as a plot device. Shyamalan also wrote and directed the movies *The Sixth Sense* and *Unbreakable*.

Silva, Freddy. Crop circle researcher who spent several years walking the fields of southern England researching the mystery with Colin Andrews. After attending one of Andrews' lectures in the United States, he became hooked and began to investigate them himself. He recently published his first book, *Secrets in the Fields*.

Sorensen, Peter. Videographer and director who, since the mid-1990s, has made a major contribution to the archival video record of crop circles in England. The crop circle footage in the highly acclaimed video, *Something Important Has Happened—But You Did Not See It On The News,* was shot by Sorenson. In 2000, he became convinced that many of the complex crop designs in England were manmade and deliberately established working relationships with several of the crop counterfeitors involved.

Spignesi, Stephen J. *New York Times* best-selling author; Colin Andrews's co-author for *Crop Circles: Signs of Contact*; author of more than 30 books.

Talbott, Nancy. Worked as a road manager for several rock groups and became interested in crop circles after watching a program on television. She has had several paranormal experiences and has become the public voice for biophysicist William Levengood. Levengood was the second scientist to study plants from crop circles. Talbott now works with B.L.T., a study group established to carry out scientific research on crop circles. She has appeared in several crop circle documentaries. Her discourse in *Crop Circles: Quest for Truth* is extraordinarily complete, understandable, and persuasive.

Taylor, Busty. A pilot and driving instructor who regularly flies his light aircraft over the fields of England looking for new crop circles. In 1985, he discovered a set of five crop circles forming a Celtic Cross south of his home. When he later drove to the spot, he found a strange white sticky substance in the circles which is still, to this day, unidentified. (See Robert Boerman.) Taylor has worked with Pat Delgado, Terence Meaden, and Colin Andrews and, in the 1980s, was part of the first research team to undertake investigation of the crop circle mystery.

Thomas, Andy. Boy Scout leader who spends all his free time researching crop circles. Thomas has made a valuable contribution to the study of crop circles with his work for the Center for Crop Circle Studies' "West Sussex" group of cereologists. Author of *Vital Signs: A Complete Guide to the Crop Circle Mystery and Why It Is Not a Hoax.*

Thompson, Marcus. Owner of Hollywood Daze Motion Pictures and director of the British movie *A Place To Stay*, which was filmed in the crop circles of Wiltshire, England during 2001 and shown at the Cannes Film Festival in 2002. Thompson engaged Colin Andrews to provide data and serve as the film's chief consultant for the crop circle scenes.

Tuersley, Don. Crop circle enthusiast who often accompanied the C.P.R. team into the fields during the 1980s. Tuersley was one of the first to pay close attention to tracks that were being found on occasion in some fields and circles. He suspected human hoaxing of crop circles well before many other researchers.

Vigay, Paul. Computer programmer and crop circle researcher; has one of the best crop circle sites on the Internet and one of the most extensive online databases. He is also the editor and publisher of *Enigma, the New Sciences Research Journal.*

Wabe, John "Weyleigh." British man who claimed to have captured on film images of UFOs flying very low over a field near Devizes, Wiltshire creating a "snowflake" crop circle design. According to his story, he was camping out on an ancient hill fort known as Oliver's Castle and was doing a "crop watch," hoping to see a circle form. He began filming after seeing strange lights above the field, and he later came to Colin Andrews with his film. Andrews was, at first, intrigued, but then, suspicious. Andrews hired private detectives to investigate the man and his claims and also subjected Weyleigh's footage to professional analysis. It was ultimately learned that Weyleigh's real name was John Wabe, that he was a video editor, and that his film was a fraud. There are still many who believe that the Oliver's Castle video could not have been hoaxed and that it does, indeed, show UFOs creating a crop formation, even though Wabe later confessed to the hoax.

White, John. Writer, editor, and authority on higher consciousness and enlightenment. He is the founder and director of the annual UFO Experience convention; founder of the Noetics Society with astronaut Edgar Mitchell; veteran, civic leader, and devoted patriot; and literary agent for both authors of this book. Colin Andrews met his wife Synthia, as well as many of his key contacts at one of White's UFO conferences in 1991.

Williams, Matthew. The first person to be arrested and charged with trespassing after making a crop circle design in England. Williams has proven to those researchers that are willing to listen that he is capable of making very impressive crop patterns with a small team of workers.

Wingfield, George. Respected crop circle researcher who has been working in the field since 1987. Wingfield has done valuable research on the existence and cause of crop circles, and he also looked into the British and American governments' involvement in the phenomenon.

Withers, James. Crop circle researcher known for his superior observation skills. Withers has spent hundreds of hours over many days and nights looking for clues to the crop circle phenomenon in the fields and in the skies. Withers was a highly valued participant at the Operation White Crow and Operation Blackbird crop circle surveillance operations. Along with Shelly Keel, Withers constructed a crop circle for one of the major scenes in the British movie, *A Place To Stay.* A few days after the crop circle was built, a huge formation now known as "The Galaxy" appeared nearby at Milk Hill.

Appendix D

Crop Circle Websites

home.clara.net/lucypringle
Lucy Pringle's fantastic site. Loaded with stunning photographs. A must-see.

www.busty-taylor.com/cropper/98busty2.htm
Well organized site about crop circles.

www.circlemakers.org
The Website of one of the most organized group of hoaxers, three men who go by the name of "Team Satan," and who Danny Sotham describes as "fibbing bounders." The Circlemakers regularly claim "authorship" of complex crop patterns, including some of the designs to which many experts assign the most credibility. As Freddy Silva says in *Secrets in the Fields*:

> According to the images posted on their Website, one would think they created...the original 'Julia Set,' which, of course, they would have had to make in broad daylight beside Stonehenge while invisible. But then again it's far more convenient to claim a bank robbery than do the deed yourself, just as it is common practice for multiple terrorists to claim responsibility for the same bomb.

The unpleasant violent imagery notwithstanding, Silva's point is well-taken.

www.coasttocoastam.com
The Website that replaced the Art Bell show's site. George Noory's *Coast to Coast* radio show covers a wide range of paranormal topics, including crop circles. Colin Andrews has appeared on Noory's show several times.

www.CosmicArtistCD.com
Website of Colin Andrew's *Cosmic Artist* CD-ROM, which compiles hundreds of Colin's original crop circle photographs, location maps, and detailed explanatory captions.

www.cropcircleanswers.com
Ed and Kris Sherwood's excellent site. Scientific research into the crop circle phenomenon.

www.cropcircleconnector.com
Excellent crop circle site.

www.cropcircleinfo.com
Circles Phenomenon Research International (CPR), Colin Andrews's Website.

www.cropcircleradius.com
Good site for crop circle links.

www.cropcircleresearch.com
A well-organized, comprehensive Website about crop circles. Excellent crop circle search engine.

www.stephenspignesi.com.
Website of Colin Andrews's co-author on *Crop Circles: Signs of Contact*.

www.swirlednews.com
A well-organized, comprehensive Website about crop circles.

Appendix E

The Andrews Catalog

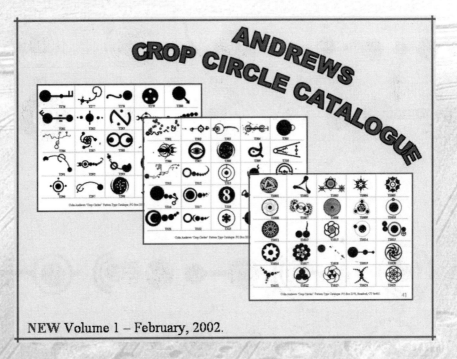

NEW Volume 1 – February, 2002.

I established the Andrews Crop Circle Catalogue system in 1983. Each crop pattern is assigned a specific "T" number. I have included designs for all the crop formations I have come upon during my research over the years, be they authentic or manmade. The designs are not all drawn to scale, although many are. Some patterns have appeared many times in various countries.

A companion pamphlet to the *Andrews Catalogue* is available. This stand-alone publication provides the location, month, and year of appearance of every design shown. For more details, contact either of the authors through their Websites (See Appendix D) or through the publisher.

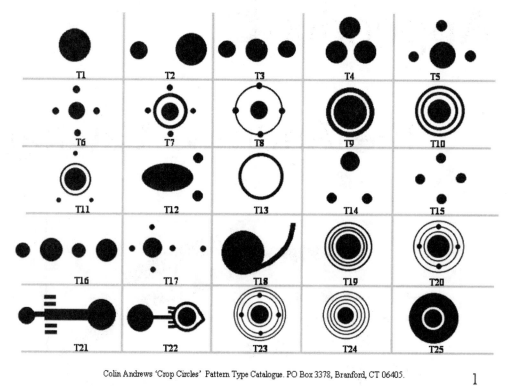

Colin Andrews 'Crop Circles' Pattern Type Catalogue. PO Box 3378, Branford, CT 06405.

1

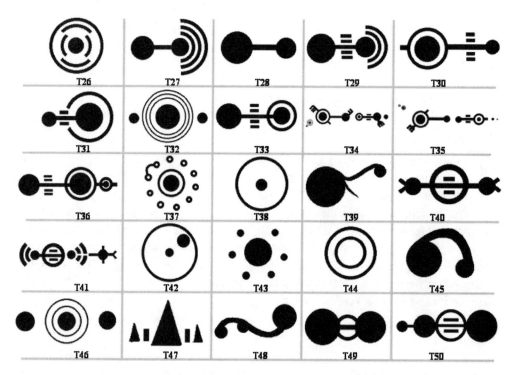

Colin Andrews 'Crop Circles' Pattern Type Catalogue. PO Box 3378, Branford, CT 06405.

2

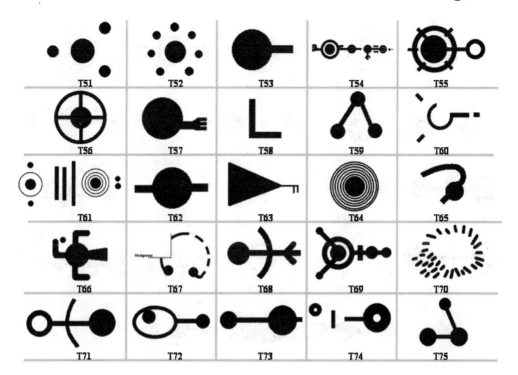

Colin Andrews 'Crop Circles' Pattern Type Catalogue. PO Box 3378, Branford, CT 06405.

3

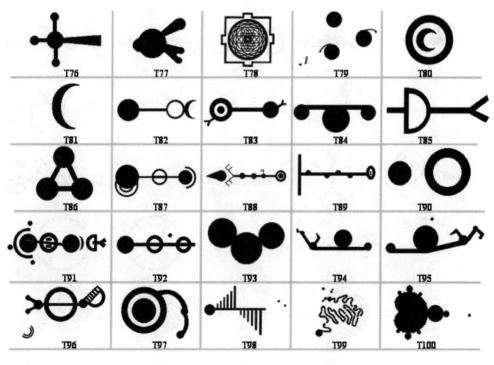

Colin Andrews 'Crop Circles' Pattern Type Catalogue. PO Box 3378, Branford, CT 06405.

4

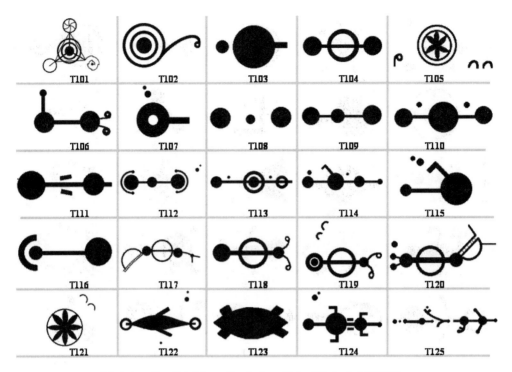

Colin Andrews 'Crop Circles' Pattern Type Catalogue. PO Box 3378, Branford, CT 06405.

5

Colin Andrews 'Crop Circles' Pattern Type Catalogue. PO Box 3378, Branford, CT 06405.

6

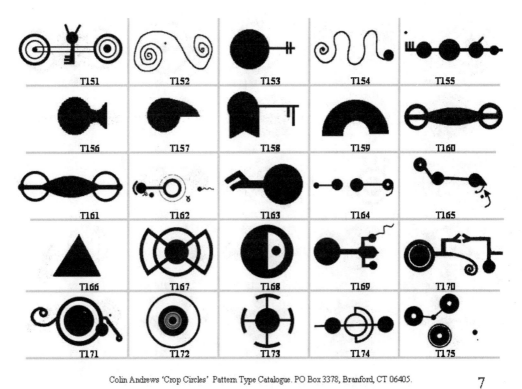

Labels: T151, T152, T153, T154, T155, T156, T157, T158, T159, T160, T161, T162, T163, T164, T165, T166, T167, T168, T169, T170, T171, T172, T173, T174, T175

Colin Andrews 'Crop Circles' Pattern Type Catalogue. PO Box 3378, Branford, CT 06405.

7

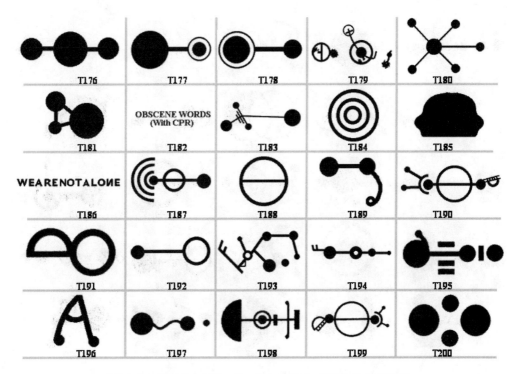

Labels: T176, T177, T178, T179, T180, T181, T182 (OBSCENE WORDS (With CPR)), T183, T184, T185, T186 (WEARENOTALONE), T187, T188, T189, T190, T191, T192, T193, T194, T195, T196, T197, T198, T199, T200

Colin Andrews 'Crop Circles' Pattern Type Catalogue. PO Box 3378, Branford, CT 06405.

8

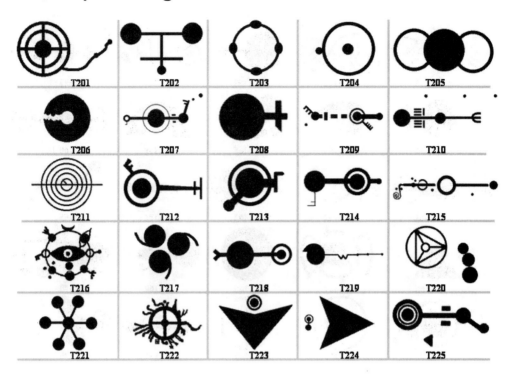

T201 T202 T203 T204 T205
T206 T207 T208 T209 T210
T211 T212 T213 T214 T215
T216 T217 T218 T219 T220
T221 T222 T223 T224 T225

Colin Andrews 'Crop Circles' Pattern Type Catalogue. PO Box 3378, Branford, CT 06405.

9

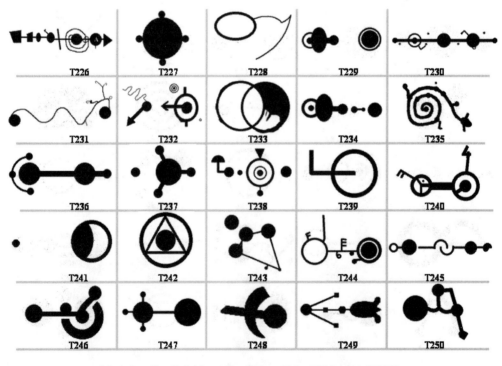

T226 T227 T228 T229 T230
T231 T232 T233 T234 T235
T236 T237 T238 T239 T240
T241 T242 T243 T244 T245
T246 T247 T248 T249 T250

Colin Andrews 'Crop Circles' Pattern Type Catalogue. PO Box 3378, Branford, CT 06405.

10

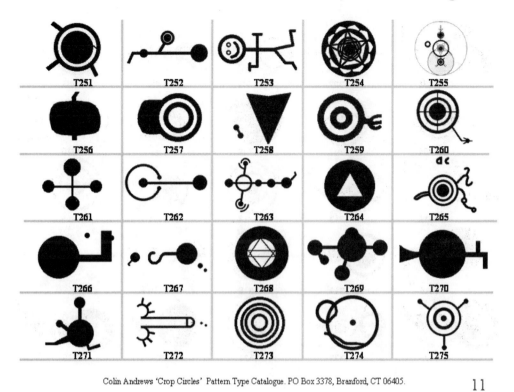

Colin Andrews 'Crop Circles' Pattern Type Catalogue. PO Box 3378, Branford, CT 06405.

11

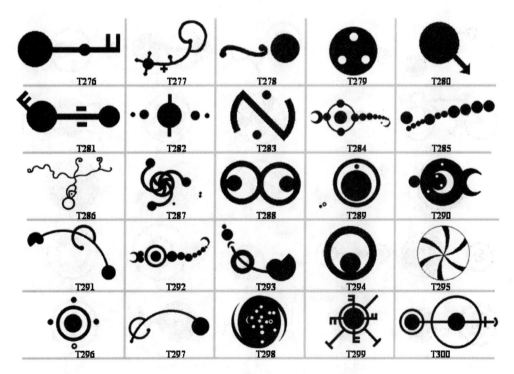

Colin Andrews 'Crop Circles' Pattern Type Catalogue. PO Box 3378, Branford, CT 06405.

12

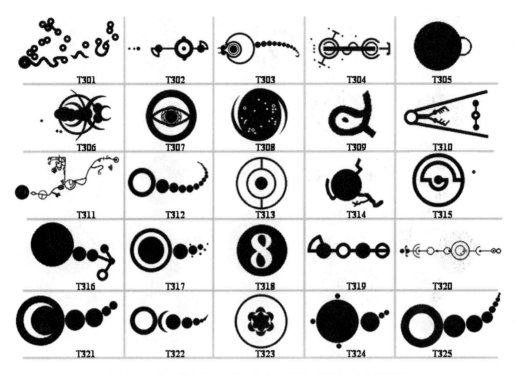

Colin Andrews 'Crop Circles' Pattern Type Catalogue. PO Box 3378, Branford, CT 06405.

13

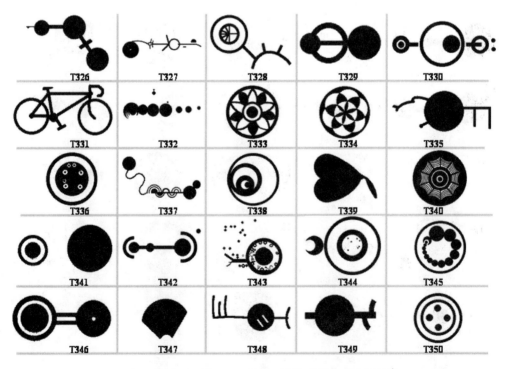

Colin Andrews 'Crop Circles' Pattern Type Catalogue. PO Box 3378, Branford, CT 06405.

14

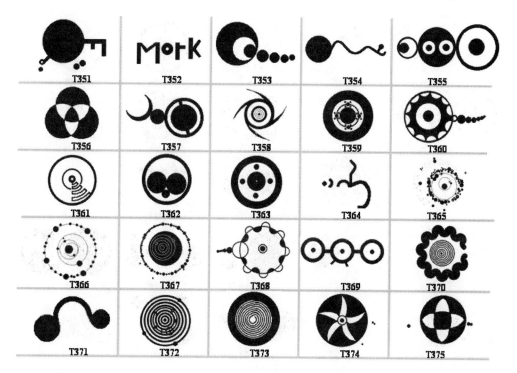

T351 T352 T353 T354 T355
T356 T357 T358 T359 T360
T361 T362 T363 T364 T365
T366 T367 T368 T369 T370
T371 T372 T373 T374 T375

Colin Andrews 'Crop Circles' Pattern Type Catalogue. PO Box 3378, Branford, CT 06405.

15

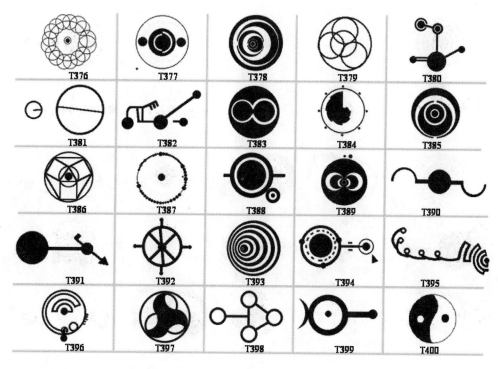

T376 T377 T378 T379 T380
T381 T382 T383 T384 T385
T386 T387 T388 T389 T390
T391 T392 T393 T394 T395
T396 T397 T398 T399 T400

Colin Andrews 'Crop Circles' Pattern Type Catalogue. PO Box 3378, Branford, CT 06405.

16

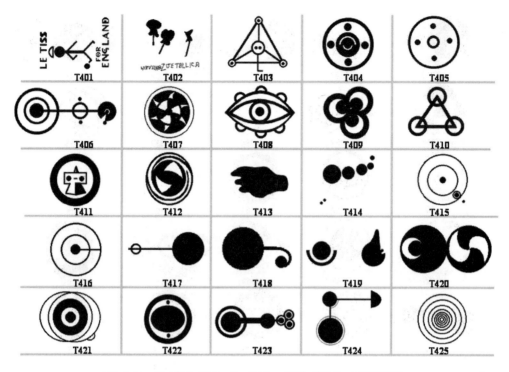

Colin Andrews 'Crop Circles' Pattern Type Catalogue. PO Box 3378, Branford, CT 06405.

17

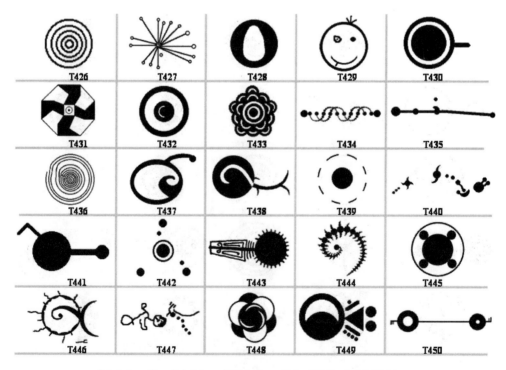

Colin Andrews 'Crop Circles' Pattern Type Catalogue. PO Box 3378, Branford, CT 06405.

18

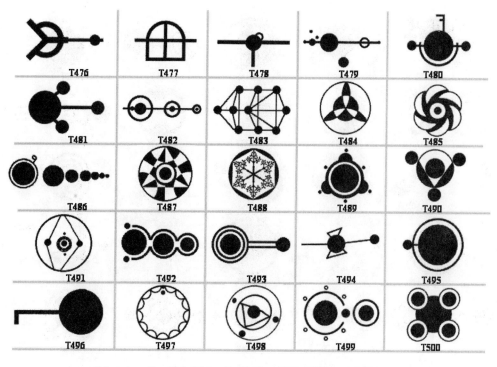

T451
T452
T453
T454
T455 Pattern details to follow Near Martok, Somerset.

T456
T457
T458 Info to follow Near Dunstable
T459
T460

T461
T462
T463
T464
T465

T466
T467
T468
T469
T470

T471
T472
T473
T474
T475

Colin Andrews 'Crop Circles' Pattern Type Catalogue. PO Box 3378, Branford, CT 06405.

19

T476
T477
T478
T479
T480

T481
T482
T483
T484
T485

T486
T487
T488
T489
T490

T491
T492
T493
T494
T495

T496
T497
T498
T499
T500

Colin Andrews 'Crop Circles' Pattern Type Catalogue. PO Box 3378, Branford, CT 06405.

20

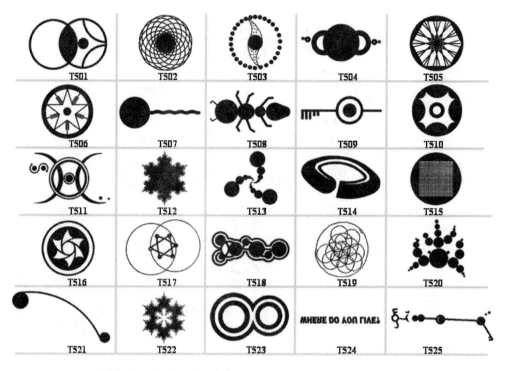

T501	T502	T503	T504	T505
T506	T507	T508	T509	T510
T511	T512	T513	T514	T515
T516	T517	T518	T519	T520
T521	T522	T523	T524	T525

Colin Andrews 'Crop Circles' Pattern Type Catalogue. PO Box 3378, Branford, CT 06405.

T526	T527	T528	T529	T530
T531	T532	T533	T534	T535
T536	T537	T538	T539	T540
T541	T542	T543	T544	T545
T546	T547	T548	T549	T550

Colin Andrews 'Crop Circles' Pattern Type Catalogue. PO Box 3378, Branford, CT 06405.

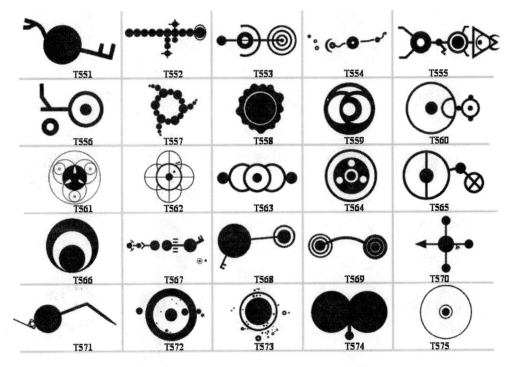

T551 T552 T553 T554 T555
T556 T557 T558 T559 T560
T561 T562 T563 T564 T565
T566 T567 T568 T569 T570
T571 T572 T573 T574 T575

Colin Andrews 'Crop Circles' Pattern Type Catalogue. PO Box 3378, Branford, CT 06405.

23

T576 T577 T578 T579 T580
T581 T582 T583 T584 T585
T586 T587 T588 T589 T590
T591 T592 T593 T594 T595
T596 T597 T598 T599 T600

Colin Andrews 'Crop Circles' Pattern Type Catalogue. PO Box 3378, Branford, CT 06405.

24

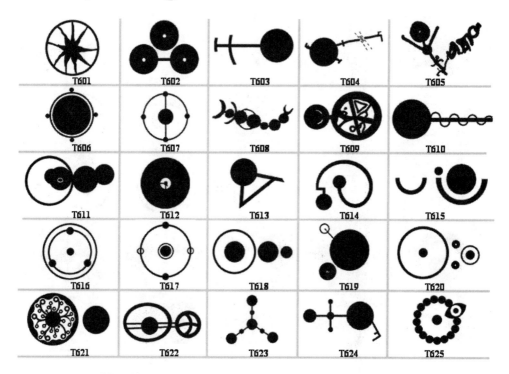

Colin Andrews 'Crop Circles' Pattern Type Catalogue. PO Box 3378, Branford, CT 06405.

25

Colin Andrews 'Crop Circles' Pattern Type Catalogue. PO Box 3378, Branford, CT 06405.

26

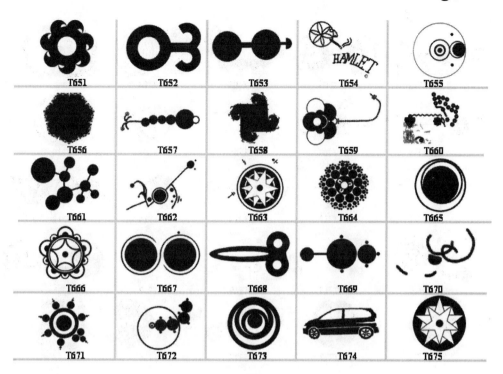

T651 T652 T653 T654 T655
T656 T657 T658 T659 T660
T661 T662 T663 T664 T665
T666 T667 T668 T669 T670
T671 T672 T673 T674 T675

Colin Andrews 'Crop Circles' Pattern Type Catalogue. PO Box 3378, Branford, CT 06405.

27

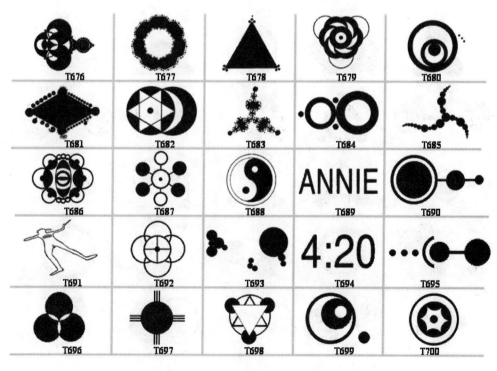

T676 T677 T678 T679 T680
T681 T682 T683 T684 T685
T686 T687 T688 T689 T690
T691 T692 T693 T694 T695
T696 T697 T698 T699 T700

Colin Andrews 'Crop Circles' Pattern Type Catalogue. PO Box 3378, Branford, CT 06405.

28

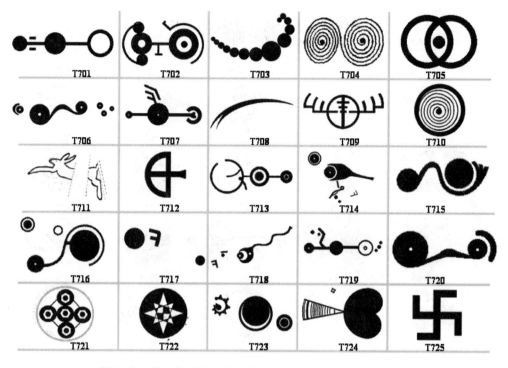

Colin Andrews 'Crop Circles' Pattern Type Catalogue. PO Box 3378, Branford, CT 06405.

29

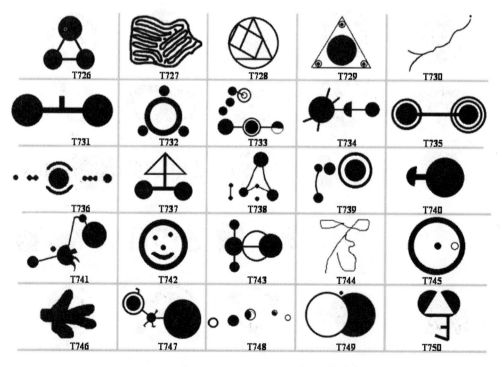

Colin Andrews 'Crop Circles' Pattern Type Catalogue. PO Box 3378, Branford, CT 06405.

30

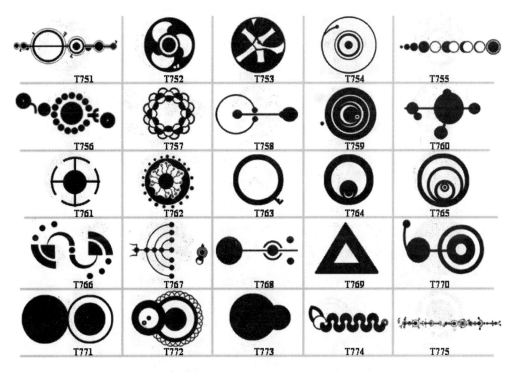

T751 T752 T753 T754 T755
T756 T757 T758 T759 T760
T761 T762 T763 T764 T765
T766 T767 T768 T769 T770
T771 T772 T773 T774 T775

Colin Andrews 'Crop Circles' Pattern Type Catalogue. PO Box 3378, Branford, CT 06405.

31

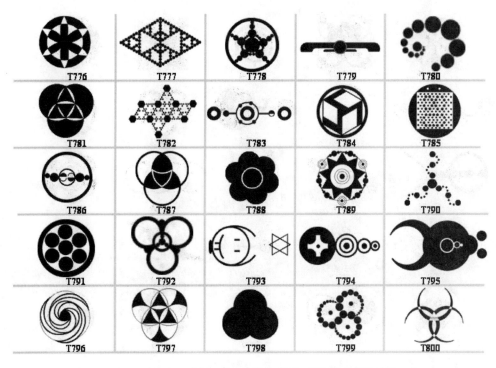

T776 T777 T778 T779 T780
T781 T782 T783 T784 T785
T786 T787 T788 T789 T790
T791 T792 T793 T794 T795
T796 T797 T798 T799 T800

Colin Andrews 'Crop Circles' Pattern Type Catalogue. PO Box 3378, Branford, CT 06405.

32

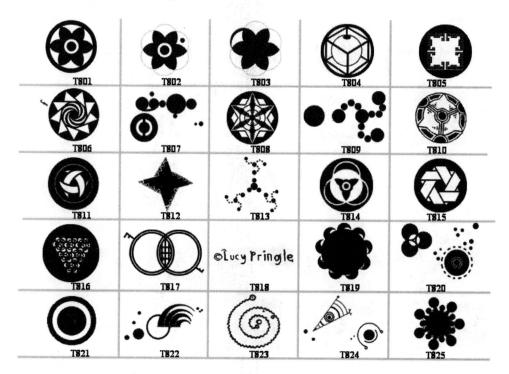

Colin Andrews 'Crop Circles' Pattern Type Catalogue. PO Box 3378, Branford, CT 06405.

33

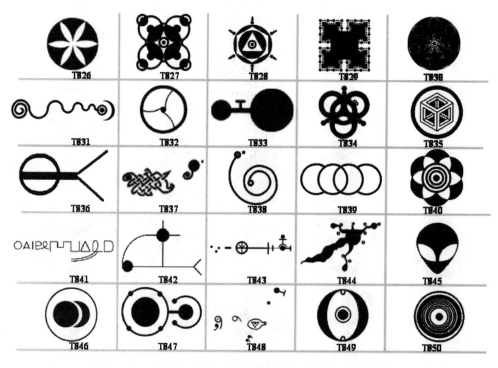

Colin Andrews 'Crop Circles' Pattern Type Catalogue. PO Box 3378, Branford, CT 06405.

34

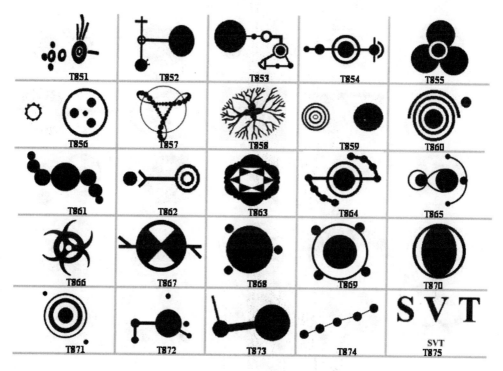

Colin Andrews 'Crop Circles' Pattern Type Catalogue. PO Box 3378, Branford, CT 06405.

35

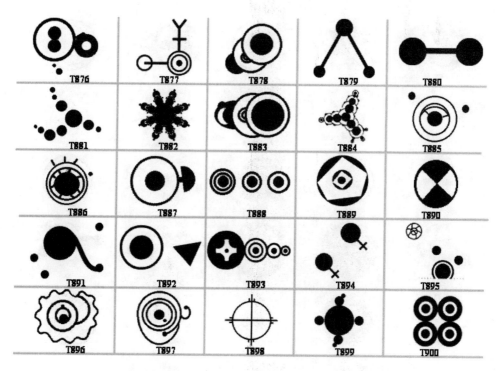

Colin Andrews 'Crop Circles' Pattern Type Catalogue. PO Box 3378, Branford, CT 06405.

36

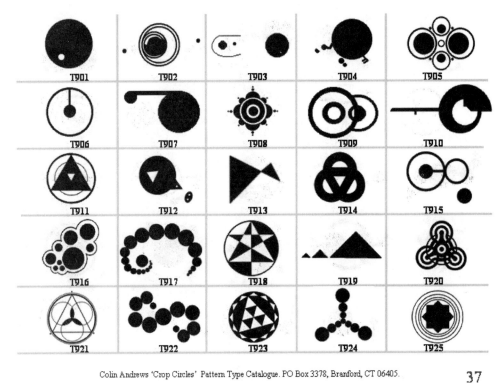

Colin Andrews 'Crop Circles' Pattern Type Catalogue. PO Box 3378, Branford, CT 06405.

37

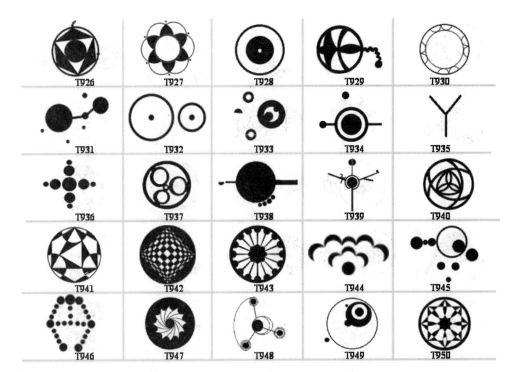

Colin Andrews 'Crop Circles' Pattern Type Catalogue. PO Box 3378, Branford, CT 06405.

38

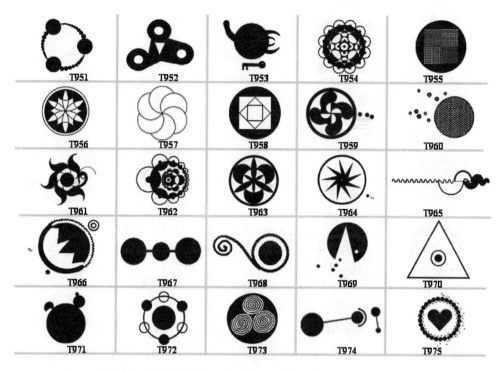

Colin Andrews 'Crop Circles' Pattern Type Catalogue. PO Box 3378, Branford, CT 06405.

39

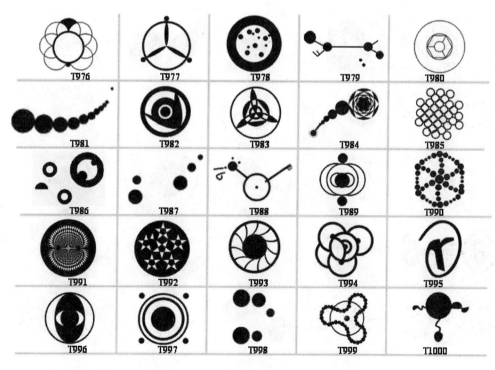

Colin Andrews 'Crop Circles' Pattern Type Catalogue. PO Box 3378, Branford, CT 06405.

40

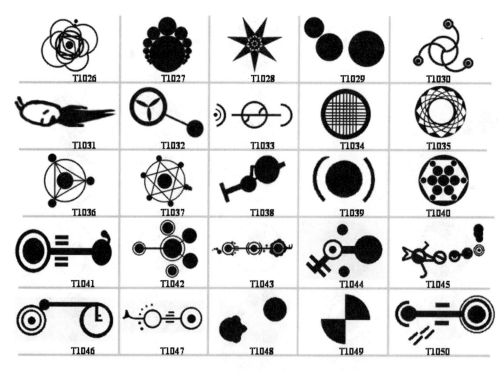

Colin Andrews 'Crop Circles' Pattern Type Catalogue. PO Box 3378, Branford, CT 06405.

41

Colin Andrews 'Crop Circles' Pattern Type Catalogue. PO Box 3378, Branford, CT 06405.

42

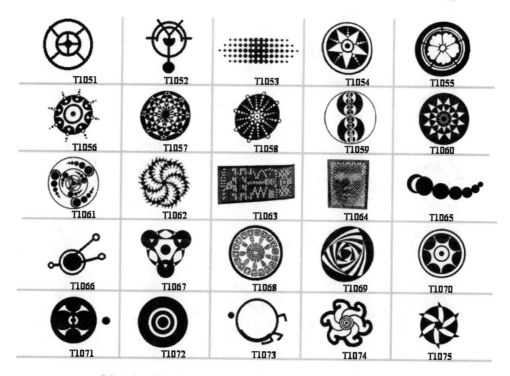

T1051　　T1052　　T1053　　T1054　　T1055

T1056　　T1057　　T1058　　T1059　　T1060

T1061　　T1062　　T1063　　T1064　　T1065

T1066　　T1067　　T1068　　T1069　　T1070

T1071　　T1072　　T1073　　T1074　　T1075

Colin Andrews 'Crop Circles' Pattern Type Catalogue. PO Box 3378, Branford, CT 06405.

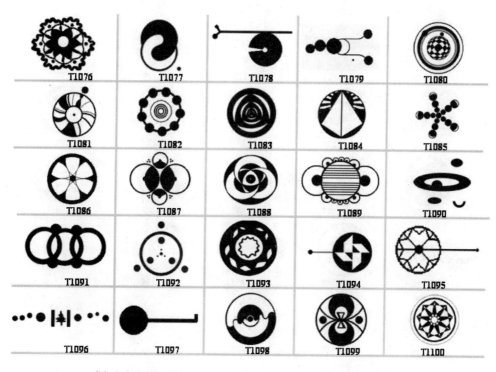

T1076　　T1077　　T1078　　T1079　　T1080

T1081　　T1082　　T1083　　T1084　　T1085

T1086　　T1087　　T1088　　T1089　　T1090

T1091　　T1092　　T1093　　T1094　　T1095

T1096　　T1097　　T1098　　T1099　　T1100

Colin Andrews 'Crop Circles' Pattern Type Catalogue. PO Box 3378, Branford, CT 06405.

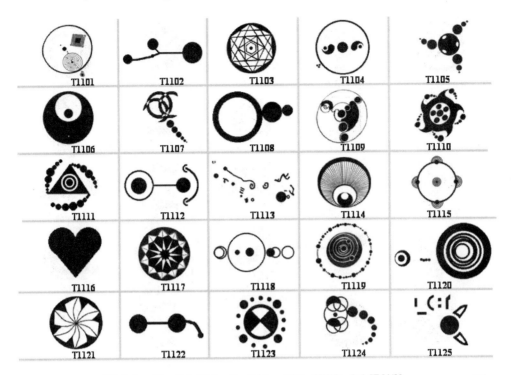

T1101 T1102 T1103 T1104 T1105
T1106 T1107 T1108 T1109 T1110
T1111 T1112 T1113 T1114 T1115
T1116 T1117 T1118 T1119 T1120
T1121 T1122 T1123 T1124 T1125

Colin Andrews 'Crop Circles' Pattern Type Catalogue. PO Box 3378, Branford, CT 06405.

45

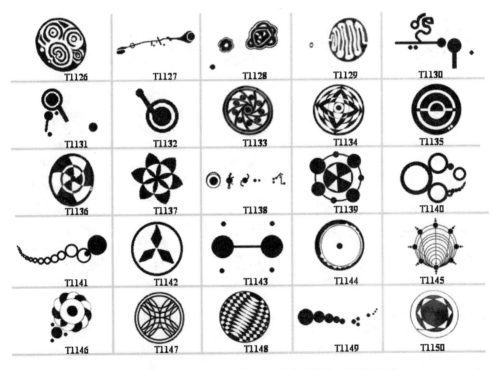

T1126 T1127 T1128 T1129 T1130
T1131 T1132 T1133 T1134 T1135
T1136 T1137 T1138 T1139 T1140
T1141 T1142 T1143 T1144 T1145
T1146 T1147 T1148 T1149 T1150

Colin Andrews 'Crop Circles' Pattern Type Catalogue. PO Box 3378, Branford, CT 06405.

46

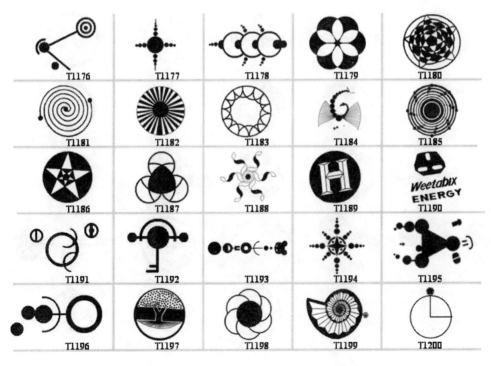

T1151 T1152 T1153 T1154 T1155
T1156 T1157 T1158 T1159 T1160
T1161 T1162 T1163 T1164 T1165
T1166 T1167 T1168 T1169 T1170
T1171 T1172 T1173 T1174 T1175

MAYDAY

T1176 T1177 T1178 T1179 T1180
T1181 T1182 T1183 T1184 T1185
T1186 T1187 T1188 T1189 T1190
T1191 T1192 T1193 T1194 T1195
T1196 T1197 T1198 T1199 T1200

Weetabix ENERGY

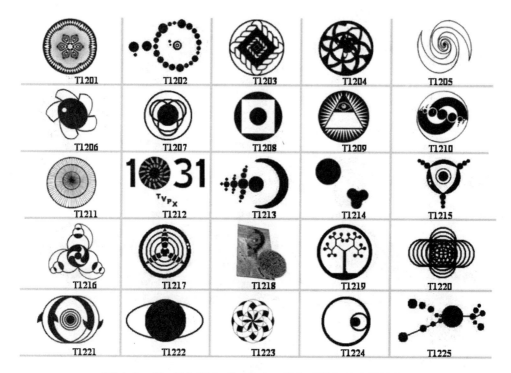

T1201 T1202 T1203 T1204 T1205
T1206 T1207 T1208 T1209 T1210
T1211 T1212 T1213 T1214 T1215
T1216 T1217 T1218 T1219 T1220
T1221 T1222 T1223 T1224 T1225

Colin Andrews 'Crop Circles' Pattern Type Catalogue. PO Box 3378, Branford, CT 06405.

49

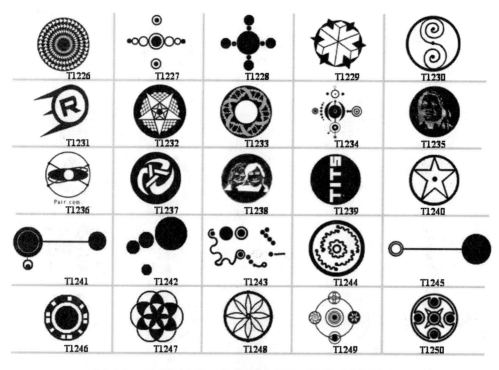

T1226 T1227 T1228 T1229 T1230
T1231 T1232 T1233 T1234 T1235
T1236 T1237 T1238 T1239 T1240
T1241 T1242 T1243 T1244 T1245
T1246 T1247 T1248 T1249 T1250

Colin Andrews 'Crop Circles' Pattern Type Catalogue. PO Box 3378, Branford, CT 06405.

50

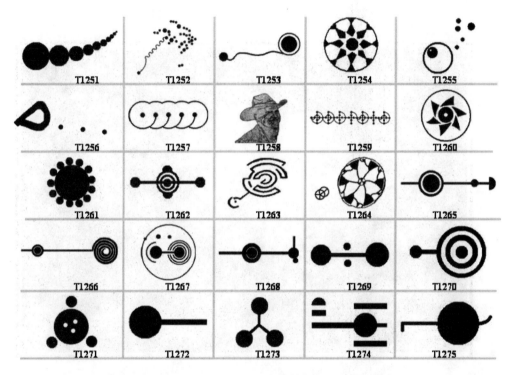

T1251 T1252 T1253 T1254 T1255
T1256 T1257 T1258 T1259 T1260
T1261 T1262 T1263 T1264 T1265
T1266 T1267 T1268 T1269 T1270
T1271 T1272 T1273 T1274 T1275

Colin Andrews 'Crop Circles' Pattern Type Catalogue. PO Box 3378, Branford, CT 06405.

51

Index

Index

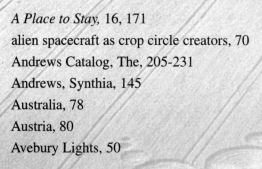

About the Authors

Colin Andrews, a former engineer with the British Government, is universally considered the world's leading authority on the crop circle phenomenon. Beginning his study of crop circles in 1983, his first book, *Circular Evidence,* was a worldwide bestseller. He was a scientific consultant for *Signs*, the blockbuster movie starring Mel Gibson. Colin travels all over the world investigating crop formations, and lectures regularly on the subject. His Website, *CropCircleInfo.com* is an exhaustive resource.

Stephen J. Spignesi is a *New York Times* best-selling author of more than 30 books about American and world history, biography, film, TV, popular culture, crime, and the paranormal.